BEFORE HOLY ROOD

More of Southampton's lost streets

BEFORE HOLY ROOD

More of Southampton's lost streets

Dave Marden

DB PUBLISHING

First published 2025 by DB Publishing, an imprint of JMD Media Ltd,

Nottingham, United Kingdom.

ISBN 9781780916668

Printed in the UK

Contents

Acknowledgements 13
Introduction 15

Part One – Orchard Lane **21**
Orchard Lane 22
Morse's Court 50
Challis Court 53

Part Two – West of Orchard Lane **57**
Upper Back of the Walls 59
Eastgate Street 65
Durkin's Passage 67
Southampton Place 68
Upper Canal Walk 69
Brick Court 103
Bell Street 105
Greens Court 115
Frost's Court 118
Mount Street 120
Mount Court 132
Cross Street 135
Hawkin's Court 139
Nelson's Place 139
Barry's Court 142
Cross Court 143

Union Street	148
Deacon's Court	160
Union Place	162
Union Cut	168
College Street	169
Winchester Terrace	170
Part Three – East of Orchard Lane	**197**
Lime Street	199
Young's Court	214
Bee Hive Buildings	215
Campbell's Court	216
Spring Court	217
Cozen's Court	219
King Street	220
Little Russell Street	229
Petty's Court	235
Coomb's Court	237
Russell Court	238
Miller's Court	241
Queen Street	242
Wheeler's Court	250
Bell's Court	252
Rose's Court	256
Russell Street	257
Eldon Square	257
Eldon Street	274
Chandos Street	277
Threefield Lane	294
Sawmill/Humby's Court	313

Acknowledgements

It has been my pleasure to compile records of the long-lost streets of the area that is now covered by the Holy Rood estate. Hopefully, I have drawn the street maps accurately and the names of occupants are as listed in the directories and census returns, which in the earlier years were not always correct in their spellings by those who collected the information. Unless otherwise indicated, the images in this book have been sourced from Southampton City Archives and I offer my sincere thanks to the staff for permission to use them without which this book would not have been possible. I am also grateful for others who have contacted me with their memories of the past. Other images have arrived from various sources and, despite my best efforts, it has not been possible to trace the origin of some. If I have inadvertently infringed anyone's copyright or ownership, I sincerely apologise.

Dave Marden
2025

The huddled buildings of the area as they were in 1908 bounded by East Street, Back of the Walls, Bernard Street and Threefield Lane

Introduction

The green spaces and trees around today's Holy Rood housing estate are a far cry from what once stood there. The estate was built between the late 1950s and early 1960s with a number of mostly low-rise flats replacing an area of ageing slums that were already in a sorrowful state before being further decimated by wartime bombing.

Street names like Orchard Lane and Threefield Lane suggest the area was, at one time, green and pleasant, but the neighbourhood that is now Holy Rood housing estate, with its neat blocks and open spaces, was once a very dark and dismal place with crumbling Victorian terraces lining its streets where common lodging houses offered the most basic accommodation while, tucked behind them, were pitiful courts where the poorest of the poor lived an existence of deprivation and squalor that is quite unimaginable today. It was second only to the incomprehensible filth and degradation that existed in the old town hovels that tumbled down to what is now West Quay Shopping Centre. This area, to the east of the old walls, came under three parishes – those of All Saints, St Mary's and St James – and could, I suppose, be described as overspill from the crowding inside the old town from medieval times when the neighbourhood became known as Newtown.

Southampton's transition from a genteel provincial spa to an industrial town had accelerated with the coming of the railways and docks in the mid-1800s as workers poured into its streets, migrating from the surrounding countryside and beyond. In 1820 Southampton's population was a mere 20,000 but by 1860 it had trebled to 60,000 and, by the turn of the century, it exceeded 100,000. To accommodate the growing masses, streets of terraces, mainly a mixture of cottages, tenements, and courts, were built. For the most part they were adequate in providing shelter and basic amenities for workers and their families but for many, unscrupulous landlords provided the cheapest possible accommodation. Some were literally thrown up in days, sometimes no more than walls of lath and plaster covered in wooden boards to shield against the elements. Such structures were frequently erected back-to-back and crammed into the smallest available spaces, often surrounded by taller buildings with the only access through narrow passages or alleyways. These became the most appalling slums – with inhabitants to match. By the mid-1800s, parts of Holy Rood had become known as "The Rookery" where overcrowding and poverty was rife. In particular, this was centred around King Street and Queen Street, but worst of all was a section of Cross Street (since renamed Lime Street) that stood between Orchard Lane and King Street.

The courts were odd collections of houses squeezed in between or behind the main buildings of the various streets. Deprived of daylight and air, they were often dark and damp hovels where only the poorest of the poor would seek shelter. Those in employment could at least escape the misery during the day but the sick and infirm would endure the torment continuously. These abodes had few facilities, which were, in the main, set outside in the courtyard where there existed a single tap for water supply, an ash pit for the dumping waste, and a single WC for use by all occupants.

A Detailed Report of Dilapidated and Unhealthy Buildings was the title of a document cataloguing the poor condition of Southampton's housing written by the town's Medical Officer of Health, A. Wellesley Harris, and published in December 1893.

It recorded the appalling living conditions some of its townsfolk were enduring, paying particular attention to the large numbers of cramped and hidden courts, festering behind and between the principal streets, which themselves were quite awful. The report exposed the obnoxious conditions around the town where dirt, damp, leaking sewage, infectious diseases and lack of clean water were highlighted. It was noted that many of the buildings were, in fact, owned by the corporation who were unwilling or unable to bring them to an acceptable standard due to the cost and the inability to provide alternative accommodation.

In that twilight world of deprivation, violence and hunger, those without employment had no fallback other than crime, and severe punishment by the judiciary had minimal effect. Today it is difficult to imagine a society with no state benefits or health service to support the needy, where you worked from childhood until you died. For most there was no retirement, except for the better-off professional classes, leaders of industry, property owners or those who served the military and navy, which afforded them a pension. Life must have been arduous enough for the able-bodied but for others and paupers there was parish relief to ward off starvation, or the only alternative was the workhouse. At least there they could find shelter, food, albeit of minimal nutrition, and a degree of medical help.

While the Victorian powerhouse surged on and created great wealth for its investors, the town's workforce lived lives of deprivation, housed in filthy and overcrowded accommodation where disease and lawlessness went hand in hand. Not that Southampton was so different to many other industrial towns, especially seaports, but the situation grew until a worsening national situation had seen the Housing of the Working Classes Act passed in 1890 and Southampton Corporation had needed to address the problem locally.

One particular aspect of the report referred to 'Common Lodging Houses', whereby it seems the object of many landlords and owners was to cram as many occupants into as many rooms as possible. In some cases the rooms themselves were subdivided by wooden partitions to create even more accommodation with little regard to the type and sex of those using them. Often, bedding consisted of no more than mattresses on floors, the whole being exacerbated by the generally poor conditions of the buildings themselves and the spread of illness and disease.

In 1894, the year following the slum report saw bylaws issued in a bid to regulate and improve such conditions by compelling landlords and owners to register their properties and to adhere to several basic regulations. In particular, these referred to limiting numbers of occupants and cleanliness. Windows were to be opened each morning unless the weather was inclement or the room occupied by a sick person. Bedding should be cleaned and changed regularly and not used by different persons within an eight-hour period. As to the occupants themselves, there was to be no sharing of rooms by any female with a male over the age of ten. This effectively ruled out their use as brothels.

The conclusion of the 1893 report was that improvements, though badly needed, would prove difficult, mainly due to rehousing the already overcrowded tenants while buildings were demolished or upgraded but, despite its hard-hitting condemnation, much of the old Holy Rood survived for several more decades, albeit with some basic improvements. The worst of the decrepit buildings were removed, while plumbing and fresh water was extended into individual buildings. What remained was mostly cleared away in the 1930s when some new tenement flats were built around Lime Street, King Street and Queen Street. These in turn lasted only until the 1970s. Looking around the present-day Orchard Lane area with its agreeable blocks of low-rise flats, it is hard to visualise what had gone before.

Through the pages of this book we shall visit the main thoroughfares that were predominately businesses and lodging houses, then venture through the dark alleyways and passages that led to the murky and foreboding habitations of the courts and places that riddled the neighbourhood. By the time photographers had arrived on the scene to record what was left in the 1930s many of the courts had long since vanished but a few images captured the pitiful dereliction before it finally disappeared.

In many cases, identifying some of the courts has been difficult, as many did not appear on the maps or, if they did, they were not recognised. Even worse, some changed their names over the generations so often the only clue to their existence was a brief reference in a directory or a surprise appearance in a census. If tracking down their locations was difficult, trying to identify those who lived there was even worse as the authorities appear to have overlooked, or turned a blind eye to, their existence. Perhaps the occupants just weren't forthcoming with their personal details. As to the names of the courts, their origins are often obscure. They may be the name of the builder, a permanent resident or just someone who had premises at the entrance. That said, I am confident that in the great majority of the researches, I have successfully identified some rather inconspicuous outlines on various Victorian, Edwardian and pre-World War Two maps.

We shall visit the neighbourhood in three parts. Firstly, through Orchard Lane and then to the streets west and east of it. In my researches, I recently discovered that I am distantly related to the seafaring Crocker family who settled in Southampton. Henry Crocker is the fourth great grandfather of a cousin on my mother's side of my family. He and his family hailed from Portsea Island where he was a sailor in the Royal Navy. Born in 1790, he and his clan moved to Southampton around 1857 and remained for several generations. They feature in several of the Holy Rood streets and I trust you will forgive my indulgence in highlighting them, as their lives seemed so typical of others in that neighbourhood.

PART ONE – ORCHARD LANE

Challis and Morse's Courts

Our exploration of the Holy Rood area begins with Orchard Lane, which ran from East Street down to Bernard Street, then continued south as Orchard Place down to the Town Quay. It was the commercial hub of the district with its businesses, shops and pubs. The many boarding houses added to the mix as rich and poor thronged its busy pavements. Orchard Lane survives today but it is much altered and totally unrecognisable as it once was. These days it is difficult to imagine an orchard in this locality but it was the main thoroughfare of the area once was known as Newtown; the main road was called Newtown Street and that may possibly have been its previous name when the population spilled eastwards outside the old town walls. Like many streets in the area there were several courts leading off it and these will be visited in turn.

A busy early 1900s Orchard Lane with East Street in the distance. The ladder in the centre of the picture is at the entrance to Bell Street (Dave Marden collection)

ORCHARD LANE
East Side, Nos. 1–20

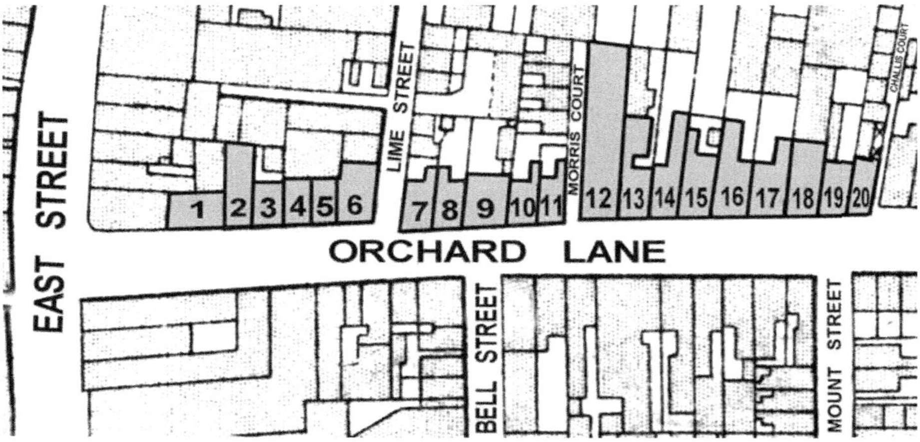

The east side of Orchard Lane from East Street to Challis Court showing Nos. 1–20

Throughout the Victorian era there were six premises on its east side between East Street and Lime Street (which was known as Cross Street until the late 1890s), all of which were destroyed by bombing in World War Two. No. 1 was often listed in East Street until the turn of the century when it was variously a second-hand furniture shop, a fishmongers and then a fruiterers run by Vincent Gargaro. In the 1870s and 1880s No. 2 was occupied by the Voller family who were potato merchants, then into the 20th century it became Frederick Eyers' cycle shop which expanded into motor engineering from the 1930s.

The *Bird In Hand* pub at No. 3 dated back to the 1850s when run by mariner George Hayles. It was owned by the Old Shirley Brewery and later in the hands of Mew Langton's Newport Brewery. A good many publicans followed until it closed in 1908 with Edward Pettit being one of the final licensees. It then became Bailey's house furnishers up until World War Two. Bailey's also took over several of the neighbouring premises from the early 1900s. French polisher and upholsterer Henry Jones occupied No. 4 back in the early 1850s before it became a clothes dealers, then briefly a greengrocers, a marine stores and a pub named the *Alma Inn* from 1869 run by James Brown but that venture was short-lived as the building had become a grocers shop by 1871 and afterwards, a confectioners by the mid-1870s. In the 1880s it was a second-hand clothes shop until Baileys took over.

No. 5 was a greengrocers shop from the 1840s, run by Matthew Reynolds until the Young family of carpenters moved in from the mid-1850s. William Young ran the business until the early 1860s when coach builder George Dugay was resident until he opened an eating house there in 1874 but this was another short-lived enterprise, as was Batini's hairdressers in 1876 before Mary Adams had set up shop there as a furniture dealer by 1881, lasting until the early 1900s when Bailey's expanded their business from Nos. 3 and 4.

On the corner of Lime Street, tin man Richard Cooke occupied No. 6 in 1851 but by the end of the decade it had become a confectioners run by baker William Card. The Card family ran the business until 1869, after which it was a carpenters shop until rag and scrap dealer John Samuel Harman opened up there in the early 1800s. At the turn of the century, Harry Hiscock opened up an eating house until Bailey's furniture enterprise had swallowed it up.

On the opposite corner of Lime Street stood No. 7, a marine store run by Samuel Jewell from 1847 and later, his son Edward was a coach painter there until James Smith arrived around 1857 and ran his business as a clothing outfitter until the mid-1860s. It then had a variety of uses until the early 1900s it had become a fried fish shop, for many years run by Walter Sparks and from the mid-1920s by Sidney E. Godwin, who moved along into Lime Street in the late 1930s where his chip shop became a favourite for many generations.

Looking down Orchard Lane in the 1930s with Godwin's original fish and chip shop on the corner of Lime Street under the Guinness advertisement

The view north up Orchard Lane towards East Street showing Nos. 7 to 11. The former Golden Fleece pub is in the centre of this 1935 photograph

No. 8 was home to various labourers and the occasional trader until the address was taken up in 1874 by the Tout family who ran it as a general store along with a bit of shoe making. By the turn of the century Herbert

Barnard was running the shop, which had a variety of proprietors from World War One until it was lost in the second conflict. No. 9 began as a grocers shop run by bricklayer Charles Ingram and his wife Jane back in the mid-1840s but a decade later it had become a pub named the *Golden Fleece* with Mark Taylor as a beer retailer. As such it survived under many stewardships until 1907 when Jane Dowden was in charge. Having closed in that year, William Dowden ran his furniture business from there until it briefly became Mrs M. Smith's refreshment rooms in the 1930s and, like the adjacent buildings, was lost in the war.

Upholsterer J. Harvie was an early occupant of No. 10 in the 1840s before it was home to a shoe maker and a school master until seaman Charles Gould moved in around 1857. He stayed for a decade until straw bonnet maker Mrs A. Bowyer took up residence. She remained until the mid-1870s when the address became that of several wardrobe dealers, after which it was briefly a hairdressers before Mrs M. Smith extended her refreshment rooms from No. 9 in the 1930s. Throughout most of its time, No. 11 was a grocers shop, originally in the hands of Mrs Young in the 1840s before it was taken over by Mrs Mary Brown who became a permanent inhabitant until retirement in 1881. For a while in the mid-1880s it was a hairdressers, then an ice cream vendor's before reopening as a greengrocers run by Joseph D'Alesio in the early 1900s. He remained until it reverted to a hairdressers before finally being Simon Hamer's tailors shop around 1930.

The entrance to Morse's or Morris Court stood between Nos. 11 and 12, the latter being a workman's mission hall back in the 1860s until the late 1880s, then afterwards housing several businesses including the South of England Ice Wafer Company in 1907 followed by wholesale confectioners Bricknell and Co. James Freemantle and Son ran a garage there in the 1920s and then after World War Two it became Edwin Jones drapery warehouse until the area was redeveloped in the 1950s.

No. 13 began as the *Great Western Tavern* in the 1850s run by sawyer

George Dawkins. This Scrase's Brewery pub changed its name to the *Royal Mail* in the mid-1870s but seems to have been listed under both names for a while in the late 1880s. As such it survived until closure in 1916 with Julius Clark as landlord. Hop bitter dealer Thomas Biggs took over until it became a registered lodging house in the 1930s before Simon Hamer moved his tailoring business there from No. 11.

Mrs Biggs outside No. 13 Orchard Lane in the early 1900s (Dave Marden collection)

Schoolmaster William Henry Bower lived at No. 14 from 1839 until 1843 when boot maker John Goffe was in residence there, and by 1857 it had been the abode of spirit merchant and brewer George Deegee. Soon afterwards it became a beer house until the 1860s, at one time run by horse dealer William Prince. Stevedore Richard Denton was a tenant in the 1860s and 1870s and by 1891 it was the address of a registered lodging house run by Mary Ansell through to 1912. It then remained as such under several landladies until the 1930s.

Gentleman and brewer George Deegee joined forces with fellow brewer Henry Nutley around 1845 when they founded the George Brewery that stood between Orchard Lane and King Street. An outlet from the brewery was the *George and Henry* pub at No. 15, a hostelry that lasted under several landlords with the Martin family running the business through the 1860s and 1870s. It was later under Crowley's Alton Brewery when closed in 1903 but an appeal saw it reopen and survive until closure in the 1930s. In its final days it became a second-hand furniture store run by a Mrs M. Hunt until it was demolished in the 1950s.

Carpenter Henry Hayden and his family were early residents at No. 16 from 1834 through to the mid-1870s; during that time he had become a builder and a pawnbroker. By the 1880s William James Axton had set up his iron merchants business there, which lasted until the area was redeveloped in the 1950s. The Noyes family were also early tenants at No. 17 from the 1830s and 1840s. John had been a carpenter but his wife Mary appears to have been widowed by 1839 and was on parish relief in 1851. Robert M. Morley was briefly a boot maker there before John Thomas Collier opened his grocery shop and bakery from around 1861. He was still there at the turn of the century and it remained as a grocers shop under various other traders.

Edith Annie Andrews, born in 1881 at the Southampton Workhouse, was the illegitimate daughter of Emily Andrews (see David Crocker at Mount Street) and an unknown father. At the age of ten, she was living with her widowed grandmother at No. 36 Mount Street. I can find no trace of her in the 1901 census but by 1911 she was running a grocery shop at No. 17 Orchard Lane in partnership with Florence Mary Rose Smith. The business must have been successful, as both had become property owners by 1939 when they were living together at No. 231 Foundry Lane. Edith never married but by the time of her death in 1963 she had amassed a small fortune of over £18,000. Florence had died in 1948 leaving Edith over £6,000. Mrs Julia Connolly took over the shop in 1920 but had changed its use to dining rooms by 1931, an enterprise that lasted until the mid-1930s. By the time of the redevelopment of the area in the 1950s it had become Conways second-hand shop.

No. 16 Orchard Lane in 1941 where Axton's ironmongery stood for around 70 years

Julia Connolly's shop at No. 17 Orchard Lane in the 1920s (Dave Marden collection)

John Springett had established his boot-and-shoe-making business at No. 18 by 1836 and remained until about 1850 when musician John Strugnell moved in. Brewer Henry Nutley ran the Phoenix Brewery that stood between Orchard Lane and King Street, a little to the south of the aforementioned George Brewery. Nutley had established the *Phoenix Inn* at No. 18 by the mid-1850s and was listed as an innkeeper and spirit store merchant there until 1881 when fellow brewer George Watson took over the business. The inn closed in the 1890s and became the Phoenix Lodging House, at one time catering for women guests only, and was run by a succession of landlords until iron merchant William James Axton occupied the premises from the 1930s and remained until the final days.

The east side of Orchard Lane showing Nos. 18–26 prior to demolition in the 1950s. The lodging house at No. 18, nearest the camera, was formerly the Phoenix Inn (Dave Marden collection)

A closer look at Nos. 18–21 Orchard Lane shortly before demolition in the 1950s showing the entrance to Challis Court next to No. 20, which was Bertram Dunford's fish and chip shop. No. 21 was once the Arno Tavern

No. 19 was once the abode of builder and undertaker John Draper in the 1840s. He remained there for a decade. Brewer and spirit merchant Henry Nutley moved in during the 1860s and used it as a store but by 1881 general dealers of the Harman family dealt there mainly as a marine store until the 1930s when William James Axton extended the business from next door. John William Martin was a hairdresser at No. 20 way back in the 1830s and wielded his scissors until at least the 1860s. He and his wife Elizabeth also had a sideline as ginger beer makers. William Ford had taken over the hairdressing business by 1865 but Elizabeth Martin stayed on until at least 1871. William and Eliza Nash had set up their cab business there by 1881, with Eliza running a general store. By 1907, Eliza was a contractor for mail carts but that enterprise had finished by 1911 when the premises became a fried fish shop and remained as such under several owners with Bertram Dunford being the last when the building was demolished in the 1950s.

ORCHARD LANE
East Side, Nos. 21–41

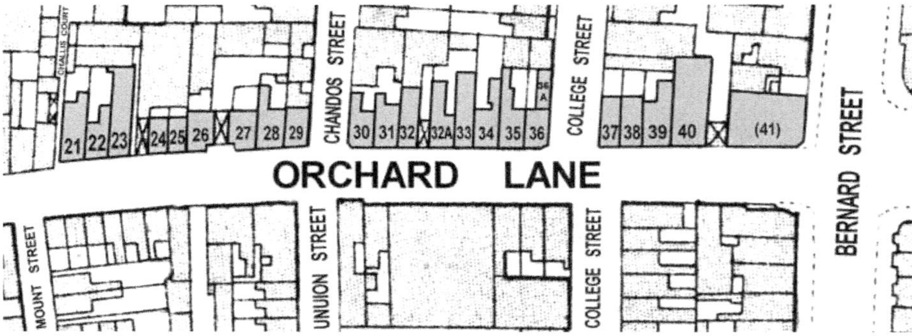

The southern section of Orchard Lane showing Nos. 21–41. The Arno Tavern was at No. 21, the Burton Tavern was at No. 26, the White Lion at No. 30, the Dorset Arms at No. 35 and the Globe Brewery at No. 40. The Globe Hotel on the corner of Bernard Street was sometimes listed as No. 41

Next to No. 20 was at the entrance to Challis Court, and No. 21 had an interesting history. Initially, as a greengrocers shop run by Levi Collis, it became a pork butchers shop with John Sharman who doubled its use as the *Arno Tavern* from the 1850s. In 1907 landlord Arthur Woodford had taken over but in 1915 he was fined for selling alcohol out of hours. The pub, belonging to Scrase's Star Brewery, was refused a licence in 1921 but reprieved the following year before finally closing for good in 1924 when advertised with vacant possession. It then had several uses as a surplus store, dining rooms, wardrobe dealers, and finally Poswall Brothers drapery in the 1950s.

Ann Jones was dressmaking at No. 22 in 1851 and had adapted her skills to making shirts a decade later. Her tenancy was followed in the 1880s by painter and glazier Edwin Walker, shipping clerk William Churchill and lastly William H. Allen as the final occupant. Carpenter and furniture William Chiddel rented No. 23 in the 1830s and 1840s when chair maker George Goodman took that address. George was also making umbrellas until John Pim set up a marine store there in 1861. John and his wife Henrietta ran the business until Ernest Hepworth took it over in 1907 and was the final resident in the 1950s.

Wire worker Richard Copperthwaite lived at No. 24 from the late 1840s until at least 1871, during which time he opened a grocery shop there around 1863. It continued as a general shop under Thomas Fielder until the late 1880s when labourer and firewood dealer William Freeman moved in but by the turn of the century, Henry and Charlotte Neal had reopened the shop again which lasted until World War Two when Mrs Lily Sherin was running the store. After the war, wardrobe dealer Mrs Henrietta Smith moved there from No. 21 and remained until the 1950s demolition. After a succession of tenants through the 1840s to 1860s that included hairdresser Alfred Biles and coal and potato dealer Mrs Lywood, No. 25 was taken over by Thomas Fielder in 1881 who expanded his general shop from next door at No. 24. By the early 1900s, carman William Watts and his family were there until World War Two.

Charles Thorn was selling beer at No. 26 from 1851 and several others continued the trade until Isaac White became landlord about 1857. Under his tenure, it became known as the *Burton Ale House* in the late 1860s. His wife Emma succeeded him around 1870 until 1874. By the mid-1880s its name had changed to the *Burton Tavern* which, after a long list of licensees, closed in the 1950s when the street came down. No. 27 was a marine store run by John Murphy in the 1840s until taken over by the delightfully named Silvanus Pearcy in 1850. He was there until around 1870 when the multi-talented George H. Bulpit spent a few years there operating at various times as a potato merchant, fish dealer, pork butcher and general dealer. Several occupants later it became a marine store again in the early 1900s run by Ernest Hepworth, previously at No. 23, who kept the business going until the 1950s.

Orchard Lane Nos. 25–29 in the 1950s with the Burton Tavern at No. 26 and Helliwells fruit shop on the corner of Chandos Street

The history of No. 28 stretched back to 1836 when carpenter and builder John Foot arrived. He and his wife Mary held the keys until the mid-1850s when P&O ships fireman John Carey and his wife Margaret lived there until Mrs Mary Perrin ran a greengrocers there in the mid-1860s. The late 1860s saw basket maker James Tong in residence until the 1870s when the Lander family opened a confectioners which soon became a newsagents and tobacconist run by Richard and Jane Barnes through the 1880s. Watchmaker George Harris was the occupier in the early 1900s through to 1935 after which Albert John Smith saw out the street's remaining years.

On the corner of Chandos Street, No. 29 was the premises of tea dealer Robert Musslewhite from at least 1836 who had turned to being a greengrocer by 1843. His wife Elizabeth and family ran the business from 1857 until 1871 when grocer Charles Gunning set up shop until the late 1880s. In the early 1900s Archibald Anderson was behind the counter until the outbreak of World War Two when fruit salesmen Helliwell and Co. saw out the final years.

Helliwell and Co.'s greengrocers shop at No. 29 Orchard Lane on the corner of Chandos Street

On the other corner of Chandos Street was No. 30, where Richard Ingram and his family were brewing and selling beer in 1841. In those early days their beer house was known as the *White Lion.* The Ingrams gave way to Stephen Haysom and his wife Augusta in the mid-1850s and they held the licence until about 1871. Many landlords later, the pub changed its name to the *British Lion* around 1890 but that lasted only until closure in 1903. It then became Robert Harrison's grocery shop until 1920 when Albert Edward Croucher ran the business and Mrs May Fowles was its final shopkeeper in 1940 when that part of the street from Nos. 30 to 36A was bombed in the war.

Wheelwright Charles Cummins practised his trade at No. 31 from 1836 until 1865 after which it became a general shop, a hardware store, and then a fried fish shop from 1901 run by Myles Coppel and his wife Teresa. Several other proprietors came and went before Frederick Lawrence became its final fryer in 1940. No. 32 had a very mixed history, dating back to chair maker Joseph Moors in 1834, stone mason Henry Dew in the latter 1840s, watch and clock maker William C.

Beswick through the 1860s and 1870s. By the 20th century it had become a shop run by George Auger with Edward Jones being the final tenant in 1940.

No. 32A first appeared in the census returns of 1891 and 1901 and was then included in the subsequent street directories. A covered passage had separated the two parts of No. 32. The 'new' address was taken up for a decade by carpenter and joiner Richard W. Adams. Boot maker Arthur Watson followed him in 1907 and remained there until the 1920s when it was variously a shop and then dining rooms before becoming a victim of the war. No. 33 was always an industrial premises from back in the 1830s when builder John Brinton was there. He plied his trade until 1850, which saw blacksmith John Read hammer his anvil until the 1870s when fellow smith and wheelwright Joseph S. Strange took over until the late 1880s. French polisher Alfred White had taken residence by 1891 and his wife Charlotte ran a furniture business there from 1911 until the building was destroyed in 1940.

Water Thomas Bartholomew was an early tenant at No. 34 in 1847, followed later by a greenhouse builder by the name of Clare. Clock and watch maker William J. Foster was in residence in the 1850s before painter Ephraim Meadows and his wife Ellen appeared through the 1860s. Basket maker James Tong(s) had moved there from No. 28 by 1871 and weaved his canes until at least 1884. That address seems to have disappeared from the registers until it became a lodging house in the 1920s, at first run by a Mrs Hall in 1925, followed by James Pearle through the 1930s until the war.

Accountant John Clarke lived at No. 35 through the 1840s until printer Charles T. Parsons took up residence in 1849. He was there for almost a decade before handing over the keys to watch maker William Beswick who moved to No. 32 in the early 1860s. It then became a tobacconist shop under James Gookey, and later Daniel Gray, before George T. Coulbert opened the *Dorset Arms* there about 1869. Belonging to

Welsh's Hyde Brewery, the pub was in the hands of Thomas and Sarah Jannaway for 20 years from 1871. George Harper was the final licensee when the pub closed in 1909 and afterwards it became a lodging house named the *Soixante Hotel* run by Albert Robert Newman through to 1916. No. 35 then disappeared from the registers and may have been renumbered to 34 when Mrs Hall took over.

Charles Myrin was an accountant and law stationer residing at No. 36 from the late 1840s until the mid-1850s. He was succeeded there by a cook, a dyer and a tailor before boot maker Frederick Monk arrived in the late 1860s. Monk was in occupation until Joseph and Eliza Mills took over in the early 1880s. Their son Frederick stepped up from 1916 and continued the family boot business until the building was lost in the war. There was a small premises at the rear of No. 36 that sometimes appeared in College Street but was usually listed as 36A Orchard Lane. In early days, back in 1841, Mark Bailey was a baker there and by the mid-1850s it was a grocers run by James Bungay. By 1861 it had become Henry Breacher's butchers shop which lasted until the early 1870s. Basket maker James Lyne was there from 1884 until Edward James Joslin opened his shop there in 1911. By the 1920s it was a Toc H Hostel before the mid-1930s when it became dining rooms with Mrs E. Black serving the final dishes in 1940.

On the corner of College Street at No. 37 in 1851 (in those days known as Winchester Terrace) stood the bakers shop of Edwin Howell where he baked his wares for a decade until fellow baker Alfred Evans succeeded him. Evans was there until 1871 followed by several other bakers over the next decade. The use of the shop seems to have been in limbo through the early 1900s until Antonio Pagbette set up his confectioners there. The Italian theme continued with Allesandro Rimoldi in charge in the 1920s but in the 1930s it became a grocers shop with Francis Blake behind the counter until demolition came in the 1950s.

Carpenter Richard Brixey and his family were at No. 38 in the 1850s until boot and shoe maker James Gandy arrived in 1857 and created his footwear for many years until 1884 when printer Edward Beckingham appeared in the rent book. In the early 1900s the address had become a hairdressers with L. Rossi wielding the scissors in 1907 before moving next door to No. 39 in 1912. Harry Abbot took over the business in that year, snipping away until the mid-1930s after which a couple of others saw out the remaining years before the war.

Master tailor Samuel Stubbington was sewing away at No. 39 in the 1850s until James Gandy extended his boot making from next door at No. 38. It was then occupied by a fruiterer, a rope maker and a cab proprietor before Mr Rossi moved in from next door. It remained a hairdressers under Joseph Pittaccio and his family until wartime ended the business. Although Nos. 38 to 40 fell victims to bombing, it seems they were patched up after the war and reoccupied until demolition in the 1950s.

The Globe Brewery appeared at No. 40 in the 1865 register, being run by R. Farnden and his wife who also were in charge of the *Globe Inn* on the corner of Bernard Street, often listed as No. 41 Orchard Lane. By the late 1860s Richard H. Perkins was in charge and, keeping it in the family, the brewing was continued by Frederick Perkins and Sons from the early 1900s until Brickwoods took over in 1925. However, brewing lasted only until around 1930 when the premises were taken over by the Ocean Trading Company who were initially wireless makers but diverged into fancy goods until closure around 1950.

The store at No. 40 that was once the Globe Brewery attached to the Globe Hotel on the right. The brewery operated until around 1930 when Ocean Trading moved in and lasted until the postwar years when it was demolished

The *Globe Inn* stood on the corner of Bernard Street. In fact, it still does although these days it has long ceased to be a pub and is now private accommodation. It was shown on the 1846 map, although the adjoining Globe Brewery seems to have evolved later. In many early directories it is listed as being No. 41 Orchard Lane but in later years was always No. 78 Bernard Street. It is recorded as being run by Thomas Purchase from 1853 and appears to have changed to the *Globe Hotel* around 1870 but all photographs display it as just the *Globe*. Its colourful past saw at least two landlords fined for allowing drunkenness in 1916 and 1920. Early owners were Barlow's Victoria Brewery who gave way to Perkins Globe Brewery who ran the brewery next door at No. 40. Brickwoods Brewery acquired both premises in 1925 and were absorbed into Whitbread in 1971 until its closure in 1988. After a brief revival as *Harry's Bar* in 1991 it was soon closed again and afterwards restored as apartments, which still stand.

Looking down Orchard Lane with the Globe pub/hotel on the corner of Bernard Street, at times listed as 41 Orchard Lane (Dave Marden collection)

ORCHARD LANE
West Side, Nos. 42–61

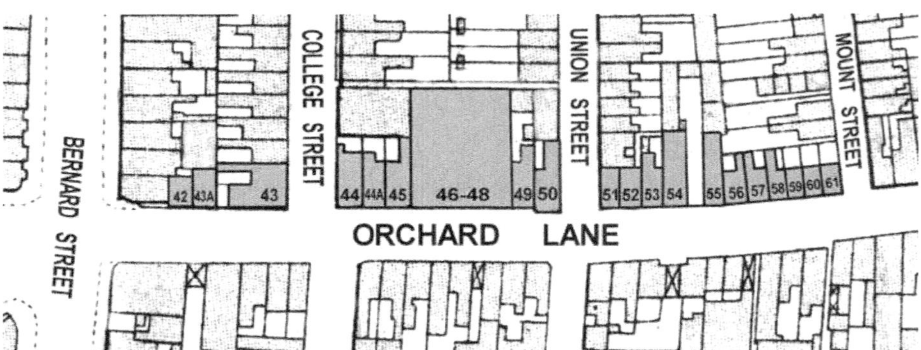

Nos. 42–61 were between Bernard Street and Mount Street on the west side of Orchard Lane. No. 43 was the Napoleon Tavern, No. 44 the Centre Hotel, No. 50 the Harlequin Inn and No. 53 was the Balaclava Tavern

The west side of Orchard Lane began at No. 42 near the corner of Bernard Street, which in 1851 was the home of Royal Navy gunner Alexander J. Gordon. He was followed by dress and mantle maker Mrs E. Beckett and dock labourer Thomas Pettit before the Myers family set up a tailoring establishment there in the 1860s. It was afterwards mainly a boot makers under several occupiers until the 1930s. No. 43A was a premises between Nos. 42 and 43; at one time it was Phillips Printing Office in the 1860s before the Myers family extended their drapery from No. 42 in the later 1860s. Boot maker Benjamin Cross was there in the 1870s and 1880s before several other tenancies until caterer Jack Moore was resident in the 1930s and it 'disappeared', perhaps becoming part of the adjacent pub at No. 43.

The *Napoleon Tavern* was at No. 43 standing on the corner of College Street (also listed as No. 15 College Street in some directories). Charles Judd was selling beer there in the 1850s before it became a Scrase's Brewery pub. Judd was there for a decade and was followed by the usual succession of licensees, including Samuel Cruse who was landlord from the early 1900s until the mid-1920s, and Albert Cass and his wife who ran the bar for a decade from around 1930. Finally under Strongs of Romsey, it closed in 1956 and was then demolished.

On the opposite corner of College Street we find No. 44, which back in the 1830s was home to builder James Beavis, who also became a beer retailer there by 1851. Beavis had moved on by the mid-1850s when Ann Carter was running the bar. From 1861 it carried the name *Victoria and Albert* with Edward Slade in charge and after several changes of landlord it became the *Centre Hotel* by the mid-1870s, although it also appeared as the *Australia Arms* in the 1881 census. By the 1890s it had become a restaurant under William Tryard and then a boarding house in the early 1900s. Through World War One it was the *National Sailors Society Hotel and Convalescent Home*. From the 1920s it was occupied by meat importers Swift and Co. who were there until the street came down in the 1950s. No. 44A was a general residence until Albert Robert

Newman had established his lodging house there by the outbreak of World War One but Swift and Co. had extended their meat business from next door by the mid-1920s.

In the 1840s, No. 45 was home to shoe maker James King, and laundress Elizabeth Stewart. Slater and greengrocer Henry Noice had taken over the premises in the 1850s but by the mid-1860s it had become the hairdressers and tobacconist shop of Albert Biles whose family maintained the business there until wartime bombs destroyed the building in 1940. The *Eagle Tavern* was briefly the name of Nos. 46 and 47 under bar owner Jonathan Wiseman in 1851. About that time, Wiseman was also listed as proprietor of an Orchard Lane beer shop known as either the *Casino* or *Grecian Saloon*, also known as the *Casino Dancing Rooms*. Perhaps they were the same place?

The beer house enterprise was short-lived and No. 46 next became a butchers, a grocers, and then Richard Williams' greengrocers in 1863. Williams was a merchant seaman who had lived there since 1861 and the family shop survived until the mid-1870s when lead oils and varnish makers John C. Munday and Co. established their paint works through Nos. 46 to 48. Following Jonathan Wiseman's tenure, No. 47 was a butcher's shop, grocers, hairdressers, and a tailors shop before Richard Williams extended his greengrocery there from next door in the 1860s before Munday and Co. moved in. John Charles Munday had established his oil and paint company as Heath and Munday at No. 48 as far back as 1849 and the business continued to grow as he expanded into Nos. 46 and 47 in the 1870s, remaining there until it was destroyed by World War Two bombing.

Dairywoman Mrs Hiscock had set up her shop at No. 49 in the 1850s before it was taken over by William Surridge in 1861. It was afterwards a grocers run by Mrs Frances Kirby, then later an undertakers with the Camfield family in the 1870s. General dealer John Richard Cozens had arrived by 1881 and moved into the fishmongers trade. Noah Bowers and Sons continued the business through the early 1900s until John Charles Munday, whose ever-expanding paint company, arrived in 1916 and then encompassed Nos. 46 to 49.

Turner and broker William Camfield occupied No. 50, on the corner of Union Street, from the 1850s (see also No. 49) and he and his wife Maria ran a furniture and undertaker business there until the late 1860s. By 1871 it had become the *Harlequin Inn* run by George Wilkes who was also a coach builder. Under various other keepers the inn continued until closure around 1901 with Sarah Moody in charge. The premises was then used as a greengrocers and furniture shop until hairdresser Arthur B. Clark donned his scissors there from 1914. It remained as a hairdressers until demolition came with Walter Biles being the final stylist.

Inside the works of paint, lead oil and varnish makers Munday and Co. at Nos. 46–49 Orchard Lane (Dave Marden collection)

On the opposite corner of Union Street was No. 51 occupied by shopkeeper Edwin Taylor in 1834, after which it was a bakery from the 1840s when run by John Henry Osbaldiston, followed by Henry Rippington through to the 1860s when his wife Mary Ann worked the ovens. There was then a long succession of bakers including Henry and Florence Rayner in the early 1900s, ending with A.H. Crabb in 1920. It was afterwards briefly a general shop before reverting to a bakery under Walter Smith in the 1930s. After the war, Frank Smith had his greengrocery there until demolition in the 1950s.

No. 52 was the home of school master Charles Welch through the 1840s before cow keeper William Coburn lived there in the early 1850s. Later that decade, hairdresser and tobacconist Alfred Biles had set up shop there and stayed until the mid-1860s when he moved to No. 45. The premises was then a fishmongers for the remainder of its existence through to the 1950s with George Bulpitt at the slab from 1867 until 1891 while the Holmes family were there from 1912 until the final days.

Master mariner Thomas Perkins resided at No. 53 from the 1830s to 1850s when William Keeping was listed as a beer retailer, who also ran a pistol gallery there in 1853. By the middle of the decade it had become the *Balaclava Tavern* owned by Panton's Wareham Brewery with James Bridges as host. Bridges gave way to Charles Holley around 1865 when the pub was extended next door into No. 54. The wonderfully named William Earwaker was the final bar keeper there in 1887. It appears Scrace's Star Brewery purchased the *Balaclava*, along with several other Panton's pubs in 1892, but it never reopened and the buildings were then occupied by coal and firewood dealer William Smith whose family went into the haulage contracting business from 1939 and remained there until the 1950s. No. 55 was a store in the early days when fish and potato dealer George Bulpitt used it in the 1850s while occupying No. 45. Nothing more is recorded until the Smith family extended their business there from next door around the turn of the century.

Boot maker John Plowman had a long association with No. 56 from the 1830s until 1869 when Robert Stubbing carried on the trade until 1887. Tinsmith Joseph Spratt held the keys through the early 1900s until the outbreak of the Great War, after which it had a variety of uses until destroyed in the second conflict. Tailor William Urry lived at No. 57, another abode dating back to the 1830s. He was there until the mid-1840s but through the 1860s the premises was a greengrocers run by the Snook family who, at times, had several other fruit and vegetable stores around the town. It later became an upholsterers, a sweet shop, coal merchants and an undertakers before ending as the Tisi Brothers knife grinding and cutlery business from 1911 until World War Two when that part of the street was destroyed by bombing.

No. 58 was another tailors shop with Henry James Harding at the sewing machine through the 1840s. Builder John Atwood had moved in by 1849 before Mary Ingrams opened her grocery shop in 1859. She was there until the mid-1860s but by the 1870s it had become a second-hand clothes dealers. Bird fancier and naturalist William Smith moved in around 1887 and stayed until 1931 when Yee Gong set up his Chinese laundry there which lasted until the wartime bombing.

No. 59 was always a general residence from the 1840s until the wartime destruction. It had a succession of tenants until Frank Kimber arrived around 1925 and lived there until its final days. Mrs Elizabeth Scource worked as a general servant during her time at No. 60 in the 1840s and by the 1850s it had become the boot makers shop of Robert Morley who stayed until 1871 when fellow cobbler John Donkin took up the business and remained until the turn of the century. Then followed several mostly short-term tenants until the end came in 1940. Likewise, No. 61 on the corner of Mount Street, had a wide variety of tenants including shipwright Charles Aldridge in the 1840s, painter Herbert Martin in the 1850s, cab proprietor William Nash in the 1870s, sugar boiler Charles Mudie in 1884 and fish seller Isabella Taylor in 1901. The final resident in the 1930s was Henry Gregory.

ORCHARD LANE
West Side, Nos. 62–80

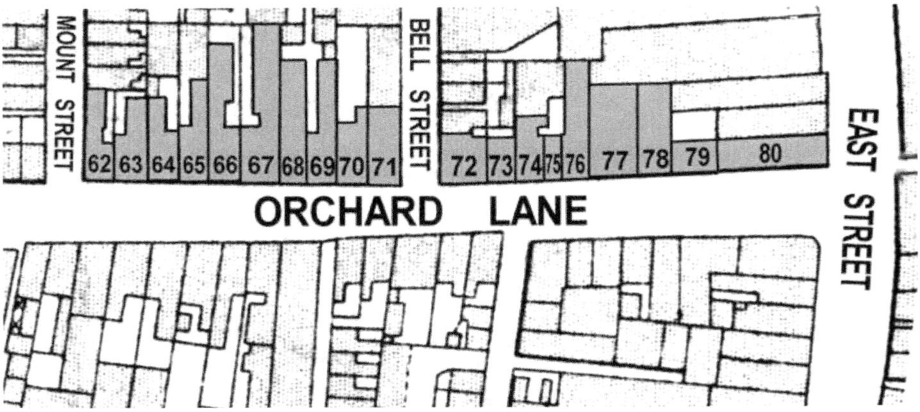

Nos. 62–80 on the west side of Orchard Lane contained several more pubs with the Coach and Horses at No. 63, No. 65 being the Diamond Jubilee, the Black Horse next door at No. 66, the Bell Inn at No. 71 and the Elephant and Castle at No. 72

No. 62, on the corner of Mount Street, was always a shop, beginning with Mary Ingram's grocery store in 1851. Two years later it was a bakery under George Guppy and several others before Joseph Oliver arrived in 1871 and remained there until the turn of the century. Then, in the early 1900s it became a fishmongers with William Donald Douglas and his wife maintaining the business from 1920 until the building was lost to wartime bombing in 1940. John Curtis Sherrin was a pork butcher at No. 63 in the early 1850s before Benjamin W. Ingram had opened it as the *Coach and Horses* pub by 1857. Seaman Edward Arnold and his wife Emma were long-term licensees there from 1861 until 1876. Others came and went before closure came in the 1890s with Ann Wyatt being the last to tender the bar. In the early 1900s it became dining rooms run by Charles Henry Williams who also used the building as a lodging house. Williams stayed until around 1920 when Mrs Margaret Smeeton became the final proprietor until World War Two bombs destroyed the building.

Bricklayer Benjamin Newman and his family resided at No. 64 through the 1850s until the mid-1860s when general dealer John Snook opened his shop there in 1871. The Snook family ran several enterprises around the town and John's business lasted until 1901 when the building was briefly dining rooms before Joseph D'Alesio founded his marine stores there from 1912 until the 1920s when it was taken over by the Hampshire Waste Collection Company. Its final function was as the Bournemouth Ice Cream factory, which was short-lived from 1939 until the 1940 bombings ended its usefulness. No. 65 was home to fish salesman John Whitmarsh for ten years from 1851. By 1863 it had become a beer house named the *Diamond Jubilee* run by George Dyett. Although owned by Southampton Corporation, the premises were leased to Lovibond's Greenwich Brewery with boatman and general dealer Richard Edwards as licensee from 1871 until the late 1880s. Another long-term landlord was Alfred Milward from the early 1900s until the 1930s with Sidney Wragg being the last of the line when the pub closed in 1956 before its demolition as part of the area redevelopment.

Next to the *Diamond Jubilee* stood the *Black Horse* at No. 65, a beer house from the 1850s under brewer John Martin who handed the keys to the King family around 1860. Robert Lock was landlord in 1863 when the pub was owned by the Winchester Brewery. Boot maker Joseph Mould was briefly serving pints there around 1870, after which the pub seems to have disappeared from the directories until Henry Gates appeared as innkeeper in 1881. The licence passed to Albert Robert Newman in the early 1900s and in 1915 his wife Annie was fined for allowing prostitutes to solicit there. The following year saw Arthur Walter Kelly as landlord. He was replaced in the early 1920s by Arthur Woodford and his wife who ran the place until its closure in the late 1930s, while Mrs Woodford remained as resident there until demolition in the 1950s.

Leather man Edward Cross and his brother George plied their trade from

No. 67 as early as 1851 and the family business ran from there until 1925. The leather goods continued to flow under merchants Cox and Dean until World War Two. In the final period before demolition the address was used by basket maker Tongs and Son (see also No. 70). Cooper John Bailey Lancaster was the occupant of No. 68 from the 1850s until the middle 1880s when George Cross extended his leather shop from next door. As with No. 67, Cox and Dean were later also at that address and from World War Two the leather business was continued by Robert Riggs until demolition.

Nos. 64–68 Orchard Lane, shortly before demolition in 1956 with the Diamond Jubilee at No. 65 and the former Black Horse at No. 66. Tongs basket makers at No. 67 had been located in various Orchard Lane premises since 1865

Boot maker Joseph Barnes was another early dweller at No. 69, listed there in 1851 but by the late 1850s carpenter Peter Pike was operating his building skills from there through to 1874 when George Cross (see also Nos. 67, 68 and 70) moved in. Cross gave up the address around 1920 when the Brown family became booksellers there until the outbreak of war when the building was destroyed. The Cross brothers also occupied No. 70 as boot and shoe makers from the 1850s until the 1880s and later the address became that of basket makers James Tongs and Son from the early 1900s until the building was lost in wartime bombing in 1940. In peacetime, Tongs moved into No. 67.

Since 1803, the *Bell Inn* had stood at No. 71 on the corner of Bell Street run by Sam Daw. By 1839 John Cross was running the bar and a long line of landlords spanned the decades until Henry Parnell arrived around 1916 and committed a string of transgressions including serving out of hours, permitting drunkenness on the premises and allowing treating. This Cooper's Brewery pub's reputation was so bad it was refused a licence in December that year and despite an appeal the pub closed in 1917. It then became a clothiers shop before becoming vacant in the 1930s and being demolished.

On the opposite corner of Bell Street was another pub at No. 72 named the *Elephant and Castle*, though not quite so old as the *Bell Inn*, being in existence since the mid-1850s with Mrs Maria Pack dispensing the pints until Mary Rose arrived in the mid-1860s. William Gates appears to have been its final licensee when closure came in the early 1890s. The building was then occupied by a wardrobe dealer, and then a hairdressers through the early 1900s before it vanished from the directories in the 1920s when house furnishers Edwin Jones extended their premises from East Street.

Early days at No. 73 saw tin man Richard Cook in residence through the 1850s until George Travers opened his greengrocers shop there and stayed until the 1870s. During the 1880s it became a bakers, grocers and an eating house, and then a drapers shop in the 1890s. The early 1900s saw Thomas Turner arrive as a taxidermist but he changed to boot making around 1911, a tradition that was continued there by William T. Murray into World War One. Reginald Strange was the final tenant before Edwin Jones Furnishing store engulfed that part of the street in the 1920s.

Block maker George Mist inhabited No. 74 through the 1850s before it became a general shop and greengrocers under Robert and Eliza Foot. The Foot family were still there in the 1870s but by 1876 George Foot had set up his smithy there and the blacksmiths firm of Foot and Son were in occupation until the 1930s. William and Harriet Curtis had their bakers shop at No. 75 from the early 1860s until the mid-1880s after which it continued as a bakery under different proprietors until Frederick Eyers set up his cycle shop there in 1911. By 1920 wardrobe dealer Mrs Caroline Lord had taken over and remained until the 1930s.

Oil and colour merchant Richard Gransden operated at No. 76 through the 1850s and 1860s when John Gransden set up there as a plumber and gas fitter. By the 1870s it had become a furniture store run by Charles and Mary Adams before Edwin Jones took over the business around 1907 and were there until wartime bombs destroyed that part of the street in 1940. In fact, Edwin Jones occupied Nos. 76 to 80 before the war. Next door at No. 77 lived builder John Young back in 1851 but from then, the premises appears unoccupied until it became a marine store under various operators before eventually being swallowed up by Edwin Jones. Tin man Thomas Pointer was at No. 78 through the 1850s and 1860s before it became a fishmongers store in the 1870s and 1880s before Edwin Jones had taken over.

Blacksmith William Weeks was in residence at No. 79 in the 1850s but there seems no other occupation there until 1871 when Mrs Caroline Cox set up her coffee house there but that venture was short-lived as it soon became a fishmongers under James Somerville. By 1887 it was a boot and shoe makers shop, along with No. 80 which in turn became part of the Edwin Jones business by the early 1900s.

ORCHARD LANE COURTS
MORSE'S COURT – Nos. 1–4

Otherwise known as Morse's Buildings, it was renamed Morris Court in

1899. The entrance to the court was off the east side of Orchard Lane between Nos. 11 and 12, just south of Lime Street and contained four houses, each were three storeys high and having the luxury of individual toilets in their back yards. Water was from a communal tap in the court but there was no ash pit provided. The 1893 report found the houses to be in fair condition, but No. 4 was described as damp, dirty and unhealthy. The court first appeared in the 1851 census, and those subsequently, but rarely featured in the directories until 1884. Its final entry came in the 1935 directory, shortly before demolition of the Lime Street area in preparation for the building of Corporation Tenements in 1936.

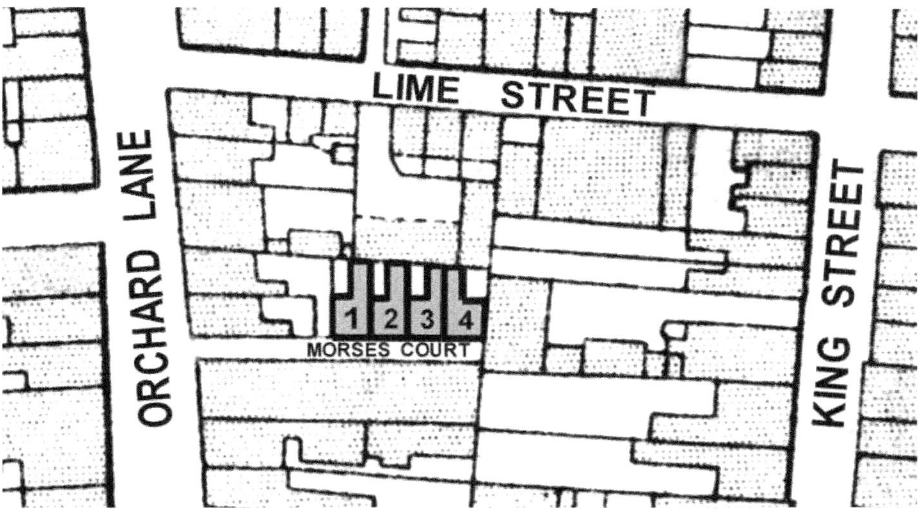

Known as Morses Buildings and Morses or Morris Court, the four houses were tucked away off Orchard Lane, just south of Lime Street

The early tenant of No. 1 in 1851 was shoemaker Joseph Barnes who was still resident a decade later. By 1871 the house was occupied by ships fireman Robert Simmons but by the 1880s coach smith William Glasspool had moved in and over the years was followed by tailor William Henry Hawkins, and ice cream maker Pietro Ragliaro. By 1911, seaman George Godley was in residence and he stayed until the 1920s when it became the home of Ernest W. Welch who was the final occupant in 1935.

Cabinet maker George Parsons was residing in No. 2 in 1851 and the house was vacant a decade later. William Budden appeared there in 1871, listed as being on parish relief, and general dealer Job Bailey was there for the 1881 census but each subsequent directory found a different tenant there, obviously not a place to stay until the Coakely family moved in during the early 1900s until the 1920s, the final inhabitant being George Annells.

Shoe maker James Holloway at No. 3 was among the first recorded tenants in 1851 and in later years was followed by barrow man Thomas Thomas, gate keeper Benjamin Bartlett, a boiler maker, a seaman and, in 1901 came Susan Buick, a woman of independent means. Cold store labourer Patrick McDonough had taken over by 1907 and stayed for around 30 years until the end came in 1935. In 1861 gun maker Samuel Cook was in No. 4 but by 1871 the occupant was nurse Matilda Perkins. The Perkins family were in occupation through the 1880s, after which there followed an assortment of renters until the arrival of John Webb in 1916 who joined neighbour Patrick McDonough as a long serving and final tenant.

Looking east from Orchard Lane along Morris Court in 1935

CHALLIS COURT – Nos. 1–6

Not to be confused with its modern-day namesake off Threefield Lane, the original Challis Court, also known as Charlie's Court in the late 19th century, was entered by a narrow alley from the east side of Orchard Lane and also via a covered passage from Russell Street. None of the six houses had through ventilation as they were adjoined to the large Phoenix Brewery that stood behind them. All were found to be damp, dark and unhealthy with all facilities to be found in the outside yard, these being also used by five other houses in Russell Street. The court suffered a lack of air flow due the proximity of high wooden buildings, one of which was a busy rag and bone store. As with Morris Court, the buildings appear to have been demolished in the 1930s, as no occupants were recorded after 1935 but the court itself survived until the 1950s

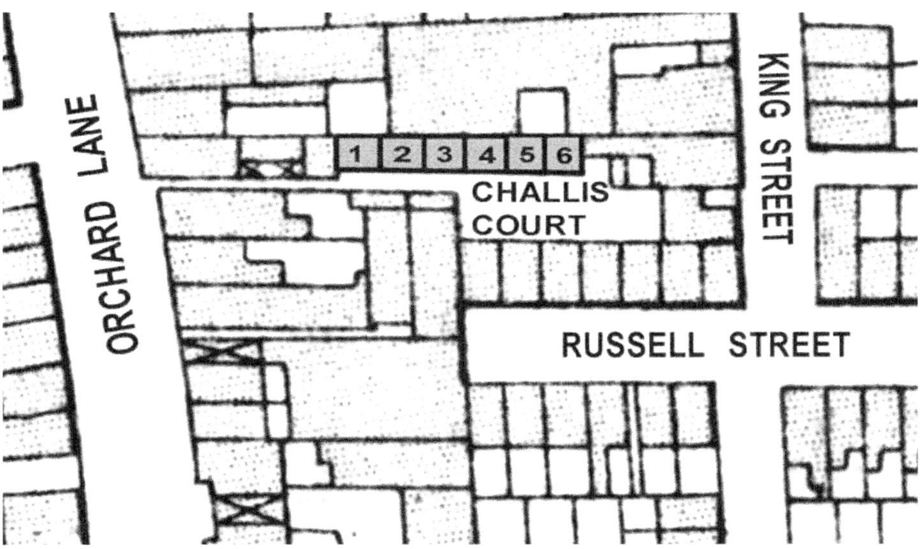

The six houses of Challis Court were entered through a narrow passage from Orchard Lane

As with many of these hidden courts, the occupants seem to have escaped inclusion in the street directories until 1871, although names do appear in the various census returns. In 1841 the only name recorded was that of boot maker George Scammell who lived at No. 3 but a full list of tenants is shown in 1851. Seaman Robert Wilson was at No. 1, followed by Ann Clark in 1861 and mariner's wife Emily Biddlecombe a decade later. From the 1880s that first house was occupied by a variety of sailors, a corn porter in the docks, and Charles William Whitlock being the final name to appear in 1935. Shoe maker Joseph Kerslake was at No. 2 in 1871 followed by a bricklayer, general labourers, a marine store dealer and finally the Tizard family from 1916.

At No. 3 was ships fireman William Elliot and his wife Caroline who lived there from 1871 to 1891 by which time she was a widow. George Albert Stevens was the final name from 1916 until demolition. Carpenter George Noice was at No. 4 in 1871 and a decade later saw waterman James Fowler living there. He was followed by a riveter, a sail maker and a ships fireman, all very nautical. No. 5 housed labourer William Matcher in 1851, laundress Mary Eames in 1861 and hawker Stephen Smith in 1871. 1881 saw boat labourer Andrew Oliver under its roof for a decade before luggage porter John Smart and his wife Sarah resided there in the early 1900s. Another porter, James Young was at No. 6 in 1851, followed by seaman's wife Susan Beaden. Seamstress Sarah Fryatt had arrived by 1871, with later tenants being a sailor, dock labourer and Miss Barbara Matthews, a laundress dwelling there in the early 1900s.

Looking west up Challis Court towards Orchard Lane

The view eastwards through Challis Court looking towards King Street

PART TWO
WEST OF ORCHARD LANE

UPPER BACK OF THE WALLS
Durkin's Passage, Southampton Place King's Terrace and Eastgate Street

Back of the Walls was an area along the inside of the old town's east wall, the upper section of which, between East Street and Bernard Street, is included in these pages. Although some of the east wall remains south of Bernard Street, virtually nothing to the north exists as the stonework was systematically dismantled through the 18th and 19th centuries, being replaced by a hotchpotch of buildings, terraces, courts and commercial premises. The numbering system was quite haphazard with various breaks in the sequence due to individual groups of dwellings and many properties having no number at all.

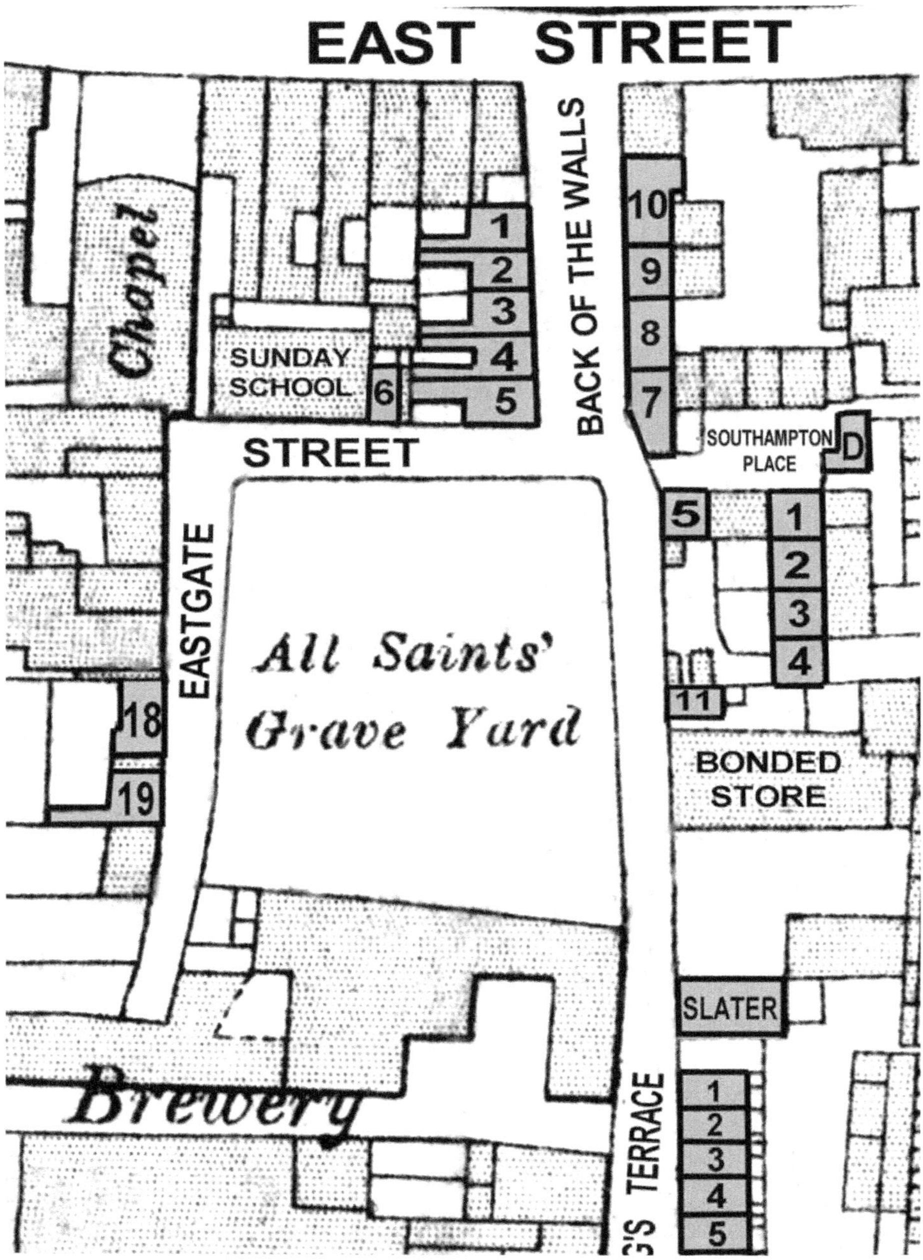

The northern section of Back of the Walls around the former All Saints graveyard showing the 11 houses near East Street, the four at Southampton Place with Durkin's Cottage shown as 'D'. No. 5 is Southampton Cottage and No. 11 is adjacent to the Bonded Store. Further south is Slaters Cottage and the six dwellings at King's Terrace. On the left are Nos. 18 and 19 on what is now Eastgate Street. The Waggon and Horses pub was part of the Star Brewery

UPPER BACK OF THE WALLS
East Side, various numbers

Running south from East Street the first group of buildings were Nos. 7 to 10 with earlier numbers 1 to 6 opposite. No. 10 was nearest East Street where its earliest occupant was straw hat maker Mrs Maria Terry, in residence from 1865 until 1884. She was followed by dressmaker Lucy Lowe who appeared in the 1891 census and seems to have been its final occupant as there is no further entry until Lankester and Son's steel store was built on the site in 1946. No. 9 was home to plumber Charles Wallbridge in 1874 followed by basket maker John Davies who was there in 1881. Mrs Hanna Chub was next in line, firstly described as a shopkeeper but later as a mangle woman. From the early 1900s it was always a shop, mostly a confectioners, until 1912, then from 1925 it was Pordage and Co. wholesale tobacconists until the address disappeared in wartime, later to be rebuilt as Eastgate Metal Works in the 1960s.

Mrs Sarah Weeks, described as a former servant, occupied No. 8 from 1865 until 1876. Next in line was a general dealer and an umbrella maker before it became a shop extended from No. 9 in 1901, later being taken over by Pordage and Co. Labourer William Harding and his wife Mary had made No. 7 their home by 1865 and remained until the 1880s. 1901 saw the reappearance of Mrs Hanna Chub, by this time described as a dock labourer's widow, who reigned supreme until at least 1925. Pordage and Co. extended there in the 1930s. Behind Nos. 7 to 10 was the yard of stone masons Garret and Haysom who traded there from the early 1900s until fellow mason David Banks took over in the 1960s as was there until quite recent times.

To the south of No. 10 was the entrance to Durkin's Court or Passage, a cut way through to Canal Walk, and leading off the passage was Southampton Place, a court containing four houses. These are visited further on. Scale maker William Wren was recorded at No. 11 Back of the Walls in 1871 and was in occupation there for at least a decade but nobody else is listed until dealer John Green in 1901. William Follett was the last in line there from 1912 until 1925. The next building on that side of the street was a bonded warehouse dating from the mid-19th century. Brewers Henry Scrase and Augustus Baker were its occupants from at least 1863 before its use by Scrase's Star Brewery from 1901 until 1925. Then in later years the site was occupied by carriers Sutton and Co. along with the Initial Towel Supply Company. Both these businesses were there until after the war. Richard Carty ran a motor repair shop there through the 1960s and 1970s and the building survives to this day.

The old bonded store at Back of the Walls still survives (Dave Marden)

A little further south we come to *Slater's Cottage* where labourer George Noice was living in 1863. Later occupants included tailoress Charlotte Leach, mail man Thomas Plomer and sugar boiler Joseph Saunders who ran a confectionery business there from 1891 until 1935. Next door was Slaters Cottage Works, a yard occupied in 1891 by coachman John Herries. From 1907 blacksmith Robert Foot set up his forge and Fox and Son were there until 1935. The site was used postwar by fruit importers Burgess, Webb and Squire along with Lankester and Son's shipping department.

The next group of habitations was King's Terrace, a row of six houses dating from the 1870s until they disappeared in the 1930s. Harness maker and saddler William Leach was in No. 1 having previously been nearer East Street in No. 6 just north of the burial ground. He was there until the late 1880s when others came and went until Richard Cartie was the last in the 1930s. Under the roof of No. 2 lived a Mrs Williams in the 1870s but she was replaced by pastry cook Mary S. Randall by 1881. Nobody seems to have stayed for long afterwards when the years saw tailors assistant John William Cook and dock labourer Alfred Gardner among the many that came and went.

No. 3 proved a little more popular. After labourer Thomas Batchelor and engine driver Walter Wilcocks were there in the 1870s, Dock labourer William George Middlewick and his family were in residence from 1911 until the very end. Charwoman Mrs King was at No. 4 in the 1870s followed by telegraph worker Edwin Emm. After the usual turnover of tenants, George Saunders arrived in 1916 and stayed until the final days. Bricklayer Thomas Lee was the early resident at No. 5 until the 1880s before later moving to nearby *Southampton Cottage*. After he left, the only householder to stay a while was George Hinkley for three years prior to World War One.

Judging by its position and separated from the others, No. 6 may possibly have been the *Golden Lion Tap*, which was listed in 1865, being the tap bar for the *Golden Lion* pub in nearby Canal Walk. Richard Turton was landlord, followed by Mark White in 1871, and the pub closed soon afterwards to become a residence, firstly inhabited by carrier William Mills in 1874, followed closely by coach builder Frank Sawyer into the 1880s. Ships fireman John Sullivan and wardrobe dealer Elizabeth Maunders were later arrivals before James Riddett and his wife saw out the final years there from 1914 until 1935.

Next door to King's Terrace stood the Royal British Schools, built in 1814 when it was named the Lancastrian School after a system developed by

Joseph Lancaster for the education of poor children. It was listed as the Royal British Schools from 1850, which had a rear entrance in Canal Walk and operated until the mid-1920s when it became a Free Meal Centre and Council School that was later demolished following bomb damage in World War Two.

The war-damaged Royal British School seen from Canal Walk in 1941

Immediately to the south of the schools stood the Phoenix Iron Works where Henry Clarkson was engineer in 1871. The ironworks site was later taken up by the Southampton Electric Lighting and Power Company, formed in 1888, but in 1896 this was purchased by Southampton Corporation and became the major source of energy to drive the town's tram network which was electrified from 1898. As demand grew, a larger generating station was built at the Western Esplanade and the old works were gone by the outbreak of World War One, with a garage and furniture factory taking its place.

Still heading south, the next building we come to was a pub, officially numbered 1A and named the *Wheatsheaf Tap* when it opened in the 1830s, being the tap bar for the *Wheatsheaf Hotel* on the corner of Bernard Street. Under Scrase's Star Brewery it changed its name to the *Electric Arms* when the generating station was built next door. As a pub it was not without trouble with landlord Aaron Rogers being fined for selling out of hours in 1909 and two years later, licensee R. Smith drunkenly assaulted a policeman. Another out of hours fine was handed to Fred Saunders in 1917 before the pub closed in 1925. Afterwards it became a private residence with several occupants through to its demolition in the 1960s with William Charles Whiting as the final resident.

The former Electric Arms pub in its days as a private residence before demolition

Between the *Wheatsheaf Hotel* and its tap bar stood a brewery run my Messrs Quick and Norman back in the 1860s, and by the early 1880s it had become a wine and spirit store under brewer Henry Welch until it was taken over by Scrase's Star Brewery in the early 1900s, lasting until the 1930s when the site was occupied by Poupart's fruit importers, Whitworth Electrical Supplies, and Simper and Co.'s sheet metal works through to 1948.

On the corner of Bernard Street we come to the *Wheatsheaf Hotel* which, at various times, has been listed as both Back of the Walls and Nos. 24 and 26 Bernard Street. Tim Dermott was its early landlord back in the 1820s while owned by the Wheatsheaf Brewery's Quick and Norman until taken over by Scrase's Star Brewery, then subsequently by Strongs of Romsey and finally Whitbread before it closed in 1976 and was demolished.

The Wheatsheaf Hotel on the corner of Back of the Walls and Bernard Street in its time under Strongs of Romsey

UPPER BACK OF THE WALLS
West Side

From Bernard Street we now look at the west side of Back of the Walls and head northwards back towards East Street. On the corner was the corn store owned by James Green in operation from the 1880s until World War One when iron merchants Lankester and Son appeared with their foundry stretching from Holy Rood Place, at the rear of the church, through to Back of the Walls. They were there until the 1970s.

In many of the early directories, buildings at the rear of some High Street premises, bordered on the old All Saints cemetery, along what is now regarded as Eastgate Street. One of these appears as Nos. 18 Eastgate Street, which was, in fact, an annexe of the Capital and Counties Bank at Nos. 20 and 21 High Street, latterly Lloyds Bank. It was listed as *Bank Messenger's Cottage* and occupied by employees of the bank. Between 1881 and 1907 it was the home of Edwin Thomas Daniels who was succeeded by William Harper Hamblyn who was there until the 1920s. The building still exists alongside the current multi-storey car park and until recent times this was in a very dilapidated state but now has been renovated. No. 19 Eastgate Street is named *Millers Cottage* in the 1911 census where the occupant was Ephraim Brown, a brewer's traveller. He and his family were also resident until 1920.

Next came the entrance to Scrase's Star Brewery, which stood at the rear of the *Star Hotel* in the High Street. The *Waggon and Horses* pub was at the brewery entrance. Dating back to the 1860s when James Gilbert was landlord until his wife Susanna took over in 1884. Henry Bear held the licence in the latter 1800s with James and Mary Sherman being the last behind the bar in 1914 when the pub was refused a licence and closed. It was then a private residence until demolished in the 1960s.

As for the cemetery, this was the graveyard serving All Saints Church that stood nearby on the corner of East Street and High Street. The church was destroyed by wartime bombing but the graves remained until the headstones were removed in 1914 and the graves were covered over as a children's playground in the 1930s. A multi-storey car park was then built on the site in the 1960s.

The bank messenger's cottage in Eastgate Street had for many years fallen into disrepair but it has since recently been refurbished (Dave Marden)

All Saints cemetery at Back of the Walls was eventually covered over and became a multi-storey car park.

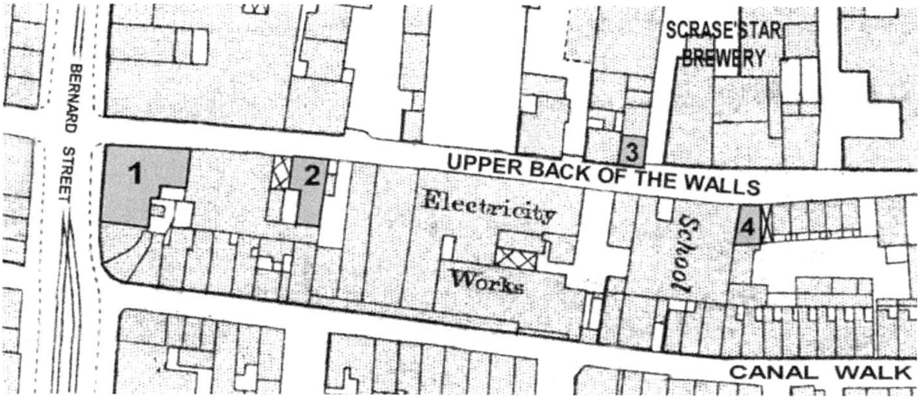

The southern end of Upper Back of the Walls showing the four public houses that were once there. 1. Wheatsheaf Hotel, 2. Electric Arms, 3. Waggon and Horses and 4. Golden Lion Tap

UPPER BACK OF THE WALLS COURTS

Two courts led off the east side of Upper Back of the Walls. These were Durkin's Court and Southampton Place (see map at the head of this chapter).

DURKIN'S COURT OR PASSAGE

This was a narrow passage leading off Back of the Walls between Nos. 7 and 11 and running through to Upper Canal Walk crossing the site of the old canal along the way. Situated in the cut was *Durkin's Cottage*. Timber merchant James Durkin had set up his business there by 1839 and was in occupation until 1855. He was followed in 1859 by John Simmonds who was a locksmith with the P&O Shipping Company and stayed until 1865. Farrier Charles Templeman was there in 1881 with nurse Sarah Hooker in the same year before the arrival of blacksmith Henry Blow in the later 1880s. He was there until the turn of the century when the cottage seems to have gone.

SOUTHAMPTON PLACE
Nos. 1–4

Southampton Place was a group of four houses in the same court as *Durkin's Cottage*, These were described as being without through ventilation. Two of them were shut in by a store behind them while the others around them were noted as obstructive buildings. They all disappeared after the 1940 wartime bombings.

Railway porter Augustus F. Dixon and his family resided at No. 1 from 1871 until at least 1920 with Herbert Henry James being the final tenant from the mid-1930s until the end. At No. 2 was paper hanger George Truss as its initial tenant. He was succeeded by the Gilbert family and then that of Thomas and Emily Sharp from the 1890s. Emily was a widow by 1911 but lived on there until the 1930s when Sydney Spanner was the last name in the rent book. The earliest incumbent at No. 3 was coachman William Kelly in 1871 and there was a high turnover of occupiers until 1911 when ships fireman Alfred Albert White stayed until the outbreak of World War One. Thomas Kendall was the final dweller through the 1930s. No. 4 was the abode of laundress Mrs Jemima Stevens for a decade from 1871. Several others came and went before shop assistant Walter Henry Chub moved in about 1911 and remained until 1925. Mrs Ashbee was the final name there just before the war.

Although the court consisted of just four houses, a No. 5 named *Southampton Cottage* does appear in the early directories from 1865 as the home of coal dealer John Orchard and is listed between Southampton Place and *Slaters Cottage* as being opposite the east side of the burial ground. The Orchards were there until bricklayer Thomas Lee appeared in 1887 and he was the last at that address in 1891.

A No. 11 also appears in the directories from the 1870s and is listed just before the Bonded Store. Scale maker William Wren lived there from

1871 until at least the 1880s and from the turn of the century, that address was home to dealer John Green and then William Follett who was the final occupant from 1912 until 1925.

UPPER CANAL WALK
Brick Court

Now almost disappeared, this street was named after a canal that ran along the outside of the town's eastern walls. Originally a mediaeval defensive moat, it was developed as a canal around 1795 that ran north from God's House Tower, across Houndwell and on to the River Itchen at Northam. Along its course, it joined the Southampton and Salisbury Canal near Kingsland. The canal was a failure and the abandoned section along the walls became a series of stagnant ditches, a reference that survived until fairly modern times. Eventually the ditches were filled in and built over, with the former towpath becoming Canal Walk.

In the early 1800s it was developed as a residential area but, as the town became more industrialised, many commercial properties began to appear until the street was completely transformed into a collection of predominantly clothiers with a host of grocers, greengrocers, butchers, bakers, confectioners and innumerable food and drink outlets but in all probability, you could buy anything you wanted there. It formed a huge attraction for locals and visitors alike and, at its peak, was a crowded thoroughfare with sellers hustling for trade and customers on guard against the light-fingered fraternity. Along with much of the lower town, Canal Walk was severely damaged by bombing during World War Two and that which survived was demolished in the 1950s.

The street was divided into two parts with Upper Canal Walk running from East Street to Bernard Street, while Lower Canal Walk continued south to the Town Quay. For the purposes of this book, we shall concentrate on the upper section only.

UPPER CANAL WALK
East Side, Nos. 1–16

This section from East Street to Mount Street was perhaps the last remaining area after the wartime destruction and subsequent clearance, with a few buildings surviving into the 1950s and 1960s. Before construction of the Holy Rood estate and the Queensway ring road, Bell Street and College Street extended as far as Upper Canal Walk.

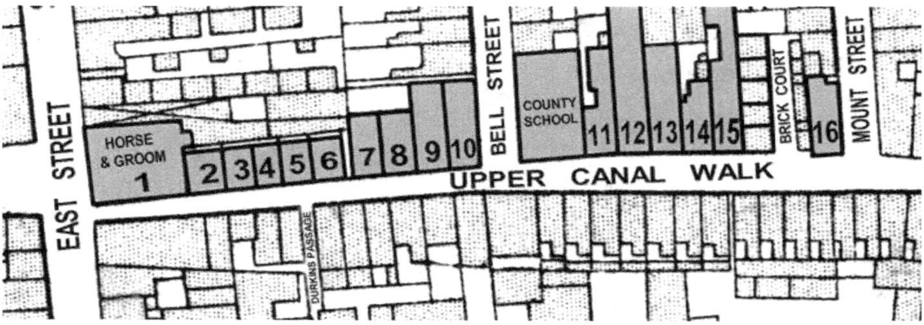

Upper Canal Walk showing Nos. 1 to 16 between East Street and Mount street. The Horse and Groom public house on the corner of East Street had a notorious history

At No. 1 on the corner of East Street was one of Southampton's most notorious pubs, the *Horse and Groom*, where fights and drunkenness, prostitution, robberies and even murders were the norm throughout its long history, being the haunt of seafarers, its reputation was world wide. Its history began in the early 1780s under landlord Joseph Wooldridge when it was known as the *Horse and Jockey* until the name change around 1820. Needless to say the pub was frequently at odds with the law and the goings on within its doors could probably merit a book on its own. Landlady Elizabeth Short did her best to keep order from 1851 until the mid-1860s after which several others tried and failed. One of the longest serving was Harry William Batten who took over in the early 1900s and somehow remained in charge until at least 1931, after which the pub's address became No. 103 East Street. For many years it belonged to Cooper's Brewery before ending as a Watney house when closure came in April 1973.

The Horse and Groom in its latter days as a Watney pub. To its right is the narrow entrance to Canal Walk (Dave Marden collection)

James Taylor lived at No. 2 from the late 1840s using his skills as a rope and twine spinner through to the 1860s when the trade was continued by William Warr until the turn of the century when Thomas Matcham moved in. The Matcham name stayed for decades and, after World War Two, they diversified as a place where you could also buy tools, fishing tackle and a few items of sports equipment while extending their premises across Nos. 3 to 6 until the 1960s. The site was then taken over by stonemason David Banks whose business survived until quite recent times.

Cabinet maker George Ellis practised his skills at No. 3 through the 1850s and greengrocer William Stone (who also took over No. 4 from 1871) was there from 1859 to 1912. The address remained as a fruit and vegetable shop under Eugene Batchelor through World War One until the mid-1930s when giving way to Matchams. The Sears family was baking bread at No. 5 in the 1840s before the premises was used for several trades as a furniture, bedding and china shop until outfitter

Joseph Hayes appeared in 1871 and extended his business at No. 6. He was then ever present until 1920 when Charles H. Meaton took over the shop. Meaton was there until the mid-1930s when clothier Bernard Morris arrived pre-war until Matchams moved in.

At this point, and to add some confusion, I will mention that Nos. 7 to 10 and Nos. 11 to 15 either side of Bell Street were once known as Nos 1 to 9 Union Terrace back in the 1840s. (In fact, several directories in the 1840s refer to the whole street as Union Terrace). The local hairdressing Biles family occupied several addresses in the locality and John Biles donned his scissors at No. 7 (Canal Walk) from 1845 until the mid-1860s. It was afterwards a confectioners run by Thomas Bricknell through the 1870s and 1880s. The trade remained as such under John Cox and his wife Emily from the turn of the century until the 1920s. Goodwins costumiers used the address before World War Two when it disappeared, probably due to bomb damage.

Early tenants at No. 8 were stay maker William Field and wire worker Charles Miller who lived there in the early 1850s. It was later a greengrocers shop run by George Channell through the early 1860s before William Mason made umbrellas there for two decades from 1871 until his wife Mary ran it as a toy shop. It was then a stationers before their son Alfred took over until the 1920s. Naturalist Samuel Wilson ran the shop briefly before wartime bombs destroyed the premises. Dyer William Holloway held the keys to No. 9 in the early 1850s but a long-term occupier was cabinet maker George Golding from 1857 until 1881 during which time he set up a furniture business there. It then became a grocers shop run by Alfred Lucas until the 1920s before a host of likewise proprietors were there until the 1930s when the address was no longer recorded.

No. 10, on the corner of Bell Street, belonged to carpenter Thomas Llewellyn through the 1840s. It then saw little activity until George Golding extended his furniture business there around 1861. After a few changes of use it became a Music Warehouse run by George William Tucker. The business passed to his son Sydney George Tucker who ran it until he enlisted as a gunner in the Royal Garrison Artillery in November 1915 but after suffering wounds in 1917 he was invalided home. Having been discharged from the army due to ill health he died at the Southampton University War Hospital in April 1919. Following his death, his wife Edith continued to run the music shop until the outbreak of World War Two when the building was destroyed.

Sydney George Tucker at the doorway of his music shop at No. 10 Canal Walk on the corner of Bell Street (Dave Marden collection)

On the south corner of Bell Street stood a Unitarian Chapel in the 1830s and by 1861 it had become a Temperance Lecture Hall. In the 1880s the Royal British Infants School had been opened on the site, which, by the early 1900s had become a Council Cookery School, and then a free meal centre by the 1930s, which lasted until the wartime devastation. No. 11 was occupied by carpenter and builder Charles Royall from the mid-1830s until the Perress family lived there from the 1840s where Thomas and his wife Ann earned a living as tinplate workers until 1871 when they were employing three men and a boy. They were followed by John George Goater who ran a toy shop there until the mid-1880s, after which the building saw several changes of use until draper Charles Millett set up stall in the early 1900s and stayed until the 1920s when Julian Chiari opened it as a confectioners. By the late 1930s it had become a general shop occupied by George Elliott until war broke out.

Schoolmaster William Simms was at No. 12 in the 1830s and from the mid-1840s the building was mostly a bakery until its wartime destruction. Samuel Ashley worked its ovens in the 1840s with Edward Ham being the last of a line in 1859 when, briefly, the shop was taken over by watch maker John Killy, currier John Dear and furniture dealer Thomas Balne before it returned to baking under Thomas Hutchings and remained as such through a long line of pastry cooks ending with Joseph William Fletcher and Sons from 1931 until 1940. The 1847 street directory records the *Horseshoe Inn* at No. 13 with Charles Warren as licensee. He served the ale until the mid-1850s and there followed the usual procession of landlords with the name changing to the *Horseshoe Tavern* in the 1880s. Time was called on this Marston's Brewery pub in 1920 when its licence was refused but the landlady, Mrs Sarah Moody, stayed on as resident until Achille Donnarummo extended his greengrocery shop from No. 14 but soon changed it to refreshment rooms which lasted until the war.

Grocer Charles Laver sold his wares at No. 14 from the 1840s until the late 1850s. Soon after, draper Edward James was there in 1861 but the shop then seems to have then been unoccupied until ironmonger William Perress and his family moved in around 1881 (they had previously been at No. 11). Tinplate workers Edward Mudge and Son took over for a few years in 1884, then it became a draper's shop before becoming a greengrocers at the beginning of World War One when Achille Donnarummo arrived and eventually expanded his businesses into No. 13. An early occupant of No. 15 was china dealer Mrs Charlotte Williamson in 1851 but her stay was brief as leather dealer John Dean had taken the premises from 1853 and remained until 1861. His place was taken by furniture dealer Henry Wiles who lasted a decade. When he left, subsequent inhabitants included a tailor, a ventriloquist, a bazaar keeper and a fruiterer but no others are listed after 1925.

No. 15A was also listed as No. 1 Brick Court which we will investigate later but from 1914 to 1920 it was a medical herbalist shop run by Jack Stanley who was founder of Stanley and Co. – famous for surgical appliances and rubber goods – in other words, condoms etc. for which they did a robust trade with visiting seamen. Business was so good, they moved to bigger premises at No. 16 on the corner of Mount Street where an associate in the business was Alfred Hawthorn Hill, father of Southampton's famous comedian, Benny Hill (whose name is actually the same as his father's). Stanley and Co. survived the blitz and continued trading until the area was redeveloped in the mid-1950s. Through the 1840s, No. 16 had been the residence of mariners and pork dealers until it briefly became a beer house named the *Windsor Castle* which appeared in the 1851 directory, run by Timothy Madden but the venture was short-lived as neither the pub nor Madden were recorded before or after.

The Stanley and Co shop at No. 16 on the corner of Mount Street was controversial in its day (Dave Marden collection)

UPPER CANAL WALK
East Side, Nos. 17–37

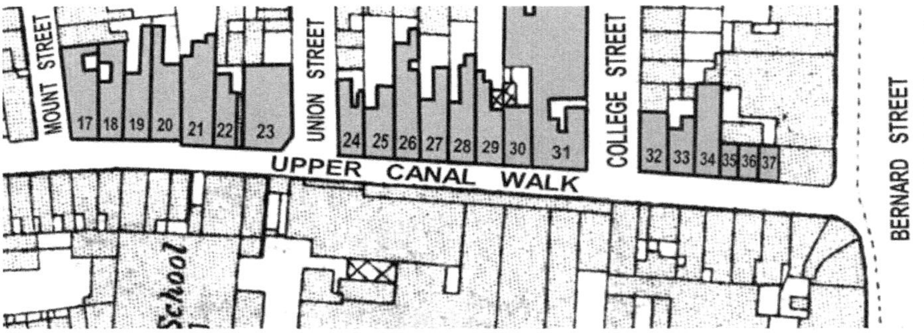

The lower eastern side of Canal Walk from Mount Street to Bernard Street showing Nos. 17 to 37. No. 17 was once the Barley Mow and No. 18 the Somerset Arms. No. 19 was the Canal Ale Stores and No. 27 the Cross Keys while No. 31 was the Hampshire House Hotel and brewery

On the opposite corner of Mount Street was a pub named the *Barley Mow* at No. 17. Early records show spirit merchant Ralph Stephens there through the 1830s and early 1840s until John Thursley was licensee in 1845. By 1849 it had closed and become the premises of pork butcher Mark Moody who remained until the late 1850s. A host of other butchers followed with Normansell and Co. being the last between 1931 and 1940. No. 18 was another butcher's shop, this one run by James Harris in the 1830s. Through the 1840s it was Thomas Chalk's tailors shop and the home of ironmonger Joseph Grose but by 1849 (around the time the *Barley Mow* closed) it had become a pub called the *Foresters Arms*. The maps and records show these were quite separate premises. The first landlord of the *Foresters* was Charles Thorn, who was also a tailor by trade. In the early 1850s it came into the hands of Samuel Sanby, a Jack of all trades, chiefly in metal working. Eliza and Charles James were hosts for a decade from the middle 1850s. The house changed its name to the *Somerset Arms* around 1863 and saw several changes of landlord before its closure around 1890. In 1891 it had become the home of the Farrell family's cutlery business. Draper John Moss traded there from 1912 to 1920 when Charles and Jessica Parkes worked in the leather trade and made boots until the wartime bombs fell.

In the 1830s No. 19 was the home of tailor Josiah Jarvis who was resident until at least 1857, after which draper Edward Hopper took up the business but by 1865 he had become a furniture dealer. Another change of use occurred in 1871 when the premises had become yet another beer house under John Maber. There followed the usual turnover of hosts and by 1884 it had become known as the Canal Ale Stores which lasted until 1892 when closure came following its reputation as a frequent locality of certain 'ladies'. Into the 20th century it became home to various businesses including a cutler, a newsagents, a greengrocers and refreshment rooms before finally listed as the Arcade Fur Stores in the 1930s.

It will be evident in our tour of Upper Canal Walk, that the thoroughfare attracted a great proliferation of businesses selling food, drink and clothing. Boot maker Alexander Colson was at No. 20 in 1834, followed by master tailor George Mitchell as one of many such traders there from 1849 to 1857, but from the early 1860s the address became a pork butchers shop through to 1901 where the main operator was William Redman. By 1911 it had returned to the tailoring business when Jacob Jeski had moved in. Jeski remained through World War One after which the premises became a fried fish shop under John Villier but by the 1930s it had once again returned to the clothing trade with haberdasher Alfred Bass being the final businessman there before World War Two took its toll.

Cabinet maker and upholsterer Alfred Jones occupied No. 21 from the 1840s until the 1870s during which time he graduated to being a furniture salesman and then a house agent but by the 1880s the address had become a butchers shop under proprietor William Hollis Damone (previously at No. 22). Then, by the early 1900s, it was briefly John Northover's dining rooms before its later occupation by photographer John Jarvis and finally being Harry Loftus costumier's emporium in the 1930s.

William Damone had been a journeyman carpenter at No. 22 back in the 1840s and his family were occasionally listed there through the 1850s until the 1870s, through which period chemist George Martin made several appearances but by the 1880s it had become a grocers shop under Charles Norton Savage who reigned until World War One when the business was taken over by Anderson and West who remained until the 1940 wartime bombs fell. Master plumber Samuel Ingram lived at No. 23 on the corner of Union Street through the 1830s to 1850s before being succeeded by fellow tradesman Daniel Brazier who also took up painting and decorating before founding the well-known building firm of Brazier and Sons around the turn of the century. By 1912 John Northover had moved his dining rooms there until the eatery was in the hands of Alex Murray in the final few years until 1940.

The premises of Brazier and Sons on the corner with Union Street (Dave Marden collection)

A busy Canal Walk in the early 1900s looking north from Bernard Street. Rose and Rogers pork butchers is at No. 34 on the right. The entrance to College Street is a little further on with a cosmopolitan mixture of locals, and visiting seamen. Scovell's Brewery with its Hampshire House Hotel on the corner of College Street can be glimpsed at the centre right of the photo (Dave Marden collection)

On the other corner with Union Street stood No. 24, which was Thomas Primer's butchers shop from the 1840s. It was afterwards a general shop run by Thomas Pittman from the 1850s through to the 1890s. At the turn of the century it was James Garney's outfitters; he also had the shop next door at No. 25 before Angel and Son took over both premises and continued the tailoring from World War One. No. 25 was originally a boot makers run by James Lucas back in the 1840s. Thomas Burridge had taken over the business by 1857 and remained there through to the 1870s when the premises briefly became a general shop before James Garney appeared in 1887 and specialised in seamen's clothing. In the early 1900s, Angel and Son had extended their business from No. 24 by World War One until the 1930s when it became Harrison's costumiers.

James Garney's shop at No. 25 specialised in seamen's clothes

Baker George Godden kept his ovens burning at No. 26 for a decade beginning in the 1840s. It then had several uses until 1884 when it became the *Cocoa Tavern* under W.J. Crockett but by 1907 it had become a Workman's Institute and Refreshment Rooms run by John (Jack) Wolfe through to the 1930s when the address was no longer listed.

No. 27 was the abode of grocer Robert Pierce in the 1830s before florist and seedsman Jonathan Wooster appeared in the late 1840s. Beer retailer Thomas Burnett had opened the *Cross Keys* there by 1851 and Henry Hoskins kept the bar for a decade through the 1850s and into 1860s. It was briefly renamed the *Evening Star* in the 1870s but by the 1880s it had a new identity as the *Imperial Inn* under Joseph Jackson which lasted until the early 1900s when James Parker set up his photography business there. In its final days in the 1930s it became Mrs S. Canter's drapers shop.

At No. 28 Charles Speck is listed as a hatter, clog maker and pattern maker between 1834 and 1843. Around 1850 George and Mary Jessop had arrived there and began various commercial ventures, including hardware and stationery through to the early 1860s. An early photographer Alfred Pilworth was in occupation in the 1860s before draper Edward James traded there in the 1870s. Mary Jessop had resurfaced as a photographer and newsagent there in 1878 but that venture ended in 1884, after which the premises became a confectioners, china shop, and then an antique dealers with the Geneen family in the early 1900s. After the antique business moved on, Mrs Canter extended her drapery there from next door.

No. 29 had seen a variety of uses in its early days. The Poole family lived there under their 'own means' in the latter 1840s until Henry Stainer began his butcher's shop, but by 1859 Ambrose Lloyd had opened his chemist shop there. That lasted until 1871 when Edward James moved in from next door before Charles Proudley opened his eating house at that address. It continued as a restaurant under several proprietors, the most notable being Tommy White, a former professional boxer, who was there from 1925 until the wartime bombs came, after which he set up his business at Queens Terrace and remained there until 1976.

Tommy White outside his dining rooms in 1934. In the late 1920s he had been professional boxer (Photo courtesy Martin White)

Looking north up Canal Walk from College Street towards Union Street in the 1930s. On the right we can see Sinclair's music shop at No. 31, Tommy White's Restaurant (Nos. 29 and 30) and Wolfe's Restaurant (No. 26) with Union Street in the distance. On the left is Lawson's Radio Shop at Nos. 41 and 42, latterly City Radio run by A.S. Brown (Dave Marden collection)

The Poole family occupied No. 30 in the 1830s when William Poole was a stage coachman (before the family moved to No. 24). Master plumber and painter Thomas Notton was there by 1851 before accountant John Brice and his family were in occupation from 1855 until 1874. In the 1870s they shared the premises with watch maker George C. Wickens but by 1884 it was Patrick Degarno's chemist shop. The early 1900s saw another change as by 1900, music dealer and phonograph salesman Frank Sinclair had set up there, a business that lasted until 1935 when Tommy White extended his restaurant from next door. The Scovell family had a brewery on the corner of Upper Canal Walk and College Street. They sold beer on the premises and by 1887 Alexander Scovell was both brewer and Wine and Spirit Merchant, selling his wares at the *Hampshire House Hotel* at No. 31 (see College Street chapter). On the opposite corner with College Street stood No. 32 which, back in the 1830s, was the butcher's shop of Johanna and George West, a family business which prevailed until the early 1860s when Francis Williams changed the premises to a grocers, remaining as such under William Lisby who was there from 1887 until its demise around 1920.

William Lisby's grocery store at No. 32 on the corner of College Street. Others in the photo are Nos. 33 to 37 Canal Walk

In 1834, No. 33 was home to builder William Morse, whose son (also William) ran a pork butchers shop there. The Morses were there until around 1850 when the address was briefly a beer house run by Henry Southwill but it had become James Bath's bakery a decade later. Moving on a further decade, dairyman John Snow had taken over before the following years saw it as a fishmongers, then dining rooms, a gramophone shop, and a greengrocers before being taken over by Rose and Rogers pork butchers in the mid-1920s. Back in 1839, George and Elizabeth Allen ran a butchers at No. 34, a business she continued until 1865 before George Henry Rose took over and established the well known outlet of Rose and Rogers from 1884, which, together with their premises next door, lasted until 1954.

Nos. 33 and 34 which was Rose and Rogers butchers shop

A variety of traders occupied No. 35, beginning with Thomas and John Fisher who were saw makers and cutlers back in 1843. General dealer Charles Bacchus had arrived by 1861 and remained until the early 1880s when the shop became a hairdressers with Alfred Coe donning the scissors. A long succession of barbers followed but by 1920 Daniel Lubel was running an outfitters at that address, then, in the final years leading up to wartime, it was Mrs R. Fox's costumiers.

Upper Canal Walk was never short of butchers shops. Alfred Gandy had opened his at No. 36 by 1839, a business that lasted until 1861, with his place taken by tobacconist Henry Haydon. Poulterer and game dealer Mary Roberts was established there by 1865 but was replaced by greengrocer Frederick Harris in the early 1880s. Come the turn of the century, Japanese fancy goods dealer Dengi Baba had moved in but several other businesses, such as Mrs Angel's drapery and Frank Sinclair's phonograph shop came and went until the address disappeared from the directories during World War One.

A girl pushes her pram towards Bernard Street as she passes the oyster bar at No. 37. Next door can be seen the Japanese sign over what was Baba's fancy goods store (Dave Marden collection)

Yet another butcher's shop had opened at No. 37 with Henry Stainer junior in 1845, followed by Joseph Boyes in 1851 but by 1857, boot maker Joseph Bailey had moved in. He lasted until 1861 after which clothier Jacob Schwartz briefly held the keys. Next in line was William Henry White who in 1871 opened a newsagent's there. The business lasted until 1887 when George H. Baker set up his oyster bar, which he ran until the shop disappeared from the directories around 1920.

UPPER CANAL WALK
West Side, Nos. 38–60

Queen Anne's Buildings stood on the southern corner of Upper Canal Walk but the several businesses that operated there were usually included under Bernard Street. This area was referred to as Cheapside in the 1840s with that a little further to the north being known as The Ditches.

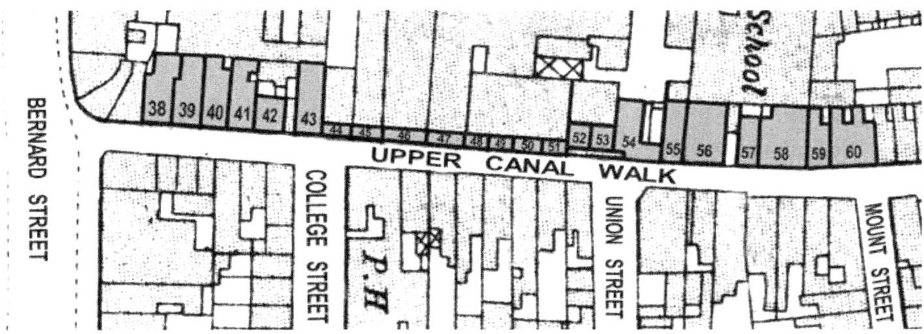

The southern west side of Upper Canal Walk with Nos. 44 to 51 shown as small lockup premises on the 1910 map. There were a couple of pubs in this area where No. 54 was the Canal Tavern and No. 60 the Golden Lion

Among the earliest traders on this part of the street were butchers James and Phillis Harris. No. 38 belonged to iron founder George Wade from the 1840s until 1881 during which time he had diversified into being a trunk and clog maker. From 1884 it had become George Mills's oyster bar but by the turn of the century was Frederick Ashley's fried fish shop; however, it became a fishmongers from 1912 and remained so until 1940, mostly run by Alice Russell and Sons. The old iron foundry site had also included No. 39 under pork butcher James Rogers back in the 1830s and William Gonk from 1850 until George Wade had extended his business from next door in the 1860s. In the 1900s it had become a greengrocery run by Mrs Snook whose family occupied many shops in the town.

In this section of the street the 1871 census describes Nos. 40 to 51 as 'Hawkers Sheds', which appear to have been lockups against established buildings. Around 1850, No. 40 was yet another pork butcher's shop, this time run by Henry Candy who successfully traded until 1884 when George Payne took over the business and then Frederick Cave from around 1901. He was succeeded by several others until 1920 when George DeGennaro opened his fried fish shop there which survived until around 1930 when costumier Mrs S. Canter briefly took over for a year before the shop disappeared. James Smith ran his greengrocery at No. 41 through the late 1840s and early 1850s but photographer George Southgate operated there between 1861 and 1871. It then became a booksellers, hairdressers and the address of a broker before George Payne opened, guess what, a pork butcher's shop in 1881. By 1912 it had become a clothiers run by J. Jeski and Sons but in the late 1930s it was the City Radio shop run by A.S. Brown (see also No. 76). Its final use before wartime bombs devastated the street.

Looking north up the lower part of Canal Walk towards College Street in the early 1900s. On the left is Frederick Cave's butchers shop at No. 40. Nearest on the right is the corner of the Scovell Brewery's Hampshire House Hotel (Dave Marden collection)

George and Harriet Musslewhite were running their greengrocery business at No. 42 back in the 1830s but when George died aged just 40 in 1846, his wife carried on the trade until 1881 before she died just six years later at the age of 82. Others perpetuated the trade there until it became Mrs M. Solomon's drapers store in 1920. Then in the pre-war years of the late 1930s it was taken over by City Radio who extended from next door at No. 41. Boot and shoe maker Samuel Honeycott did his cordwaining at No. 43 from 1851 until 1876 after which it became Hampton's Bakery, Millett's haberdashery and Daniel Lubel's outfitters, with shopkeeper Lawrence Quinn being the final occupant in 1925.

No. 44 was, for most of its early existence, a greengrocers from 1849 under Benjamin Bunday through to George Whitlock in 1887. In the years after World War One it was Mrs M. Solomon's drapery and finally Jack Carmichael's florists in 1931. Journeyman carpenter John Duhig resided at No. 45 through the 1840s and 1850s. He was followed by an assortment of tenants until the arrival of George Whitlock who extended his greengrocery from No. 44 in 1871 until 1887. Peter Millett had set up his haberdashers there by 1907 before tattooist Charles Knight was there from 1912 until 1916. It then reverted to haberdashery under the Carter family until it disappeared in 1931 when that part of the street, along with Nos. 45 to 49, was demolished.

An atmospheric study of Upper Canal Walk in the early 1900s looking south towards Bernard Street from No. 45 where Charles Knight was a tattooist with Millett's haberdashery next door at No. 44

Another early inhabitant from the 1840s and 1850s was hairdresser Henry Primmer whose abode was at No. 46 but for some reason that address was unlisted again until 1863 when boot maker William Wilcox showed up. However, he was soon gone and replaced by cutler Mark

Waterman. Whitlock's grocery had expanded still further by 1874 and now occupied Nos. 44 to 46. James and Alice Nurse had a hardware shop there in the early 1880s until outfitter James Garney moved in from the late 1880s until the early 1900s. The drapery Canter family were the final occupiers in the 1920s until the end came in 1931. Tailor Charles Skinner cut his cloth at No. 47 from around 1851 and was obviously successful as he remained in business there for 30 years. After he moved on, fishmonger William King briefly traded there but by the early 1900s the Canter family had spread their haberdashery dealings from next door, and remained until the end.

Early records show basket maker Thomas Davis weaving away at No. 48 in the late 1840s and early 1850s but before the decade was out, yet another greengrocer had emerged, this one in the shape of Henry Higgins. Higgins had gone by the mid-1860s, giving way to James and Mary Davies. By the 1870s No. 48 had become a fishmongers with Charles Nichols (or Nicholas) at the helm. He also sold eggs. The fishery business ended about 1907, then Arthur Leble began embroidering handkerchiefs there in 1912 but he wasn't a great success as by 1916, L. Angel and Son had established their drapers shop.

By 1847 No. 49 had become a beer house run by William Richards, then through the 1850s, William Howell was serving the pints. Boot maker George W. Smith had moved in by the early 1860s before the address was occupied by a greengrocer, a watch maker, an outfitter and finally Dykes newsagents from 1914. Basket maker Charles Davis was weaving at No. 50 in the early 1850s prior to the premises becoming Henry Taylor's butchers shop in 1863. Others in the trade succeeded him until the 1870s saw various changes of use until horse meat purveyor William Wilmer Holmes set up shop in the 1920s.

William Wilmer Holmes was described as a domestic pets butcher but his shop at No. 50 actually sold horse meat

No. 51 began as John Brown's butchers shop back in 1843, surviving until 1857 when Mrs Attwood sold her greengroceries there. Next in line was boot maker Thomas John Holloway through the 1860s to 1884, after which nothing else was recorded at that address. Grocer George Good set up his shop at No. 52 from 1843, then by the late 1840s it had become John Warren's leather and trunk-making business. From the mid-1850s it was a bakers shop, then a greengrocery under Caroline Coleville for three decades from 1861 until 1891 when she was the final proprietor until clothier Miss C. Morris moved in for a brief spell in 1935.

Hairdressers and tobacconists Henry and Daniel Lamont were at No. 53 from 1857 until 1867, after which Joseph Lamont set up his boot making there in 1869 but by 1871 Caroline Colville had extended her greengrocery business from next door. Tobacconist Susan Primer had taken over in 1881 and remained until 1891 when the address disappeared until resurrected in the 1920s as a clothiers run by the Hamer family. Baker Edward J. Lanning ran his bakers shop at No. 54 from 1847 until 1851. From then it seems to have been unoccupied until Susan Primer (or Primmer) opened it up as a beer house in 1859. She then went on to run the tobacconists at No. 53 when coach smith Harry Redman became mine host in 1861 on behalf of Panton's Wareham Brewery. Under his tenure it became the *Canal Tavern* and was sold to Scrase's Star Brewery in 1892 with George Pigram at the helm. He remained until the final landlord was Fredrick W. Sanders when the pub closed in 1916. It was then briefly a tailors shop before F.M. Ridgett made it his tobacco shop from 1935 until wartime bombs destroyed the building.

The Ansteads (or Ansteeds) were family butchers at No. 55 for a decade from 1839. Edward Brown carried on the trade there from 1857 until 1874 when Thomas Munckton wielded the cleaver until 1891. E. Brown and Son had returned by 1907, being the final butchers until the outbreak of World War One, during which Harry Loftus opened his outfitters there. Max Alshooter was the final draper there when the building was bombed. There was yet another butchers shop at No. 56 under Henry Stainer senior from 1845 until 1859, from then it became a second-hand clothes shop, tailors and outfitters until Edward Brown extended his business from next door at No. 55. Brown and Sons lasted there until 1887. At the turn of the century the shop was again selling clothing and remained mostly a drapers and costumiers until the war.

Between Nos. 56 and 57 was the rear entrance to the Royal British Board of Schools (see Upper Back of the Walls) and at No. 57 was Henry Wiggins greengrocers shop and you wonder how they all made a living. Henry was there from 1861 until 1887 as one of the longest serving shopkeepers. Afterwards, the trade changed hands a few times before it became Clara Miller's drapery 1916, remaining as such until World War Two saw an end to her business. Medical botanist James Ashworth was an early tenant in No. 58 back in 1859 but by the next decade it belonged to furniture dealer John Wiles for a couple of years. By 1865 James Green had opened his eating house there, changing its name to the *London Coffee House* in 1871 before leaving in 1877 when it became Thomas Long's eatery. By 1901 it was Edwin Bricknell's confectioners, which lasted until the Blitz in 1940.

Baker Joseph Pitt was at No. 59 from 1839 until 1847. He was succeeded in 1951 by fellow tradesman George Sanders who ran his ovens for a decade. The bakery continued under various proprietors until 1871 when it became, you guessed it, another greengrocers under Charlotte B. Nicholl. 1876 saw another change, this time to a confectioners and then a general shop run by Sarah Bacchus from 1881. Sarah expanded her enterprise into a refreshment establishment in 1901, specialising in shellfish for a while before Edwin Bricknell extended his confectionery shop from No. 58 next door.

Master brewer William Slater appears in the 1839 directory and by 1847 he and his wife Sarah were producing beer at No. 60 but by 1851 Sarah was a widow and, together with son William junior, they ran the family brewery which was employing seven men at that time. By 1875 their premises had taken the name *Golden Lion* which was being run by brewers manager Thomas F. Masters in 1861 while others came and went before the arrival of John Baptist Killy in 1867. Killy was a German born clock maker who had a business partnership with Arnold Schwer at No. 65 in 1855 before setting up on his own and being declared bankrupt in 1862. Having resurfaced as licensed victualler at the *Golden Lion* he remained there as publican and innkeeper until 1876 when James Cawte assumed the role. Henry King who had also been declared bankrupt back in 1864 was the pub's final landlord from 1887 until it closed upon his death in November 1892, leaving £223 11s 6d to his son Thomas. The former pub became a clothiers shop run by Philip Bernstein from 1911 until 1916 and remained as such under several others in the trade until 1931 when it last appeared in the directories.

Looking north along Upper Canal Walk towards East Street with Edwin Bricknell and Sons confectionery shop at Nos. 58 and 59 on the left. Next door at No. 60 is the former Golden Lion pub with its sign bracket still in place. The entrance to Mount Street is to the right by the lamp (Dave Marden collection)

UPPER CANAL WALK
West Side, Nos. 61–83

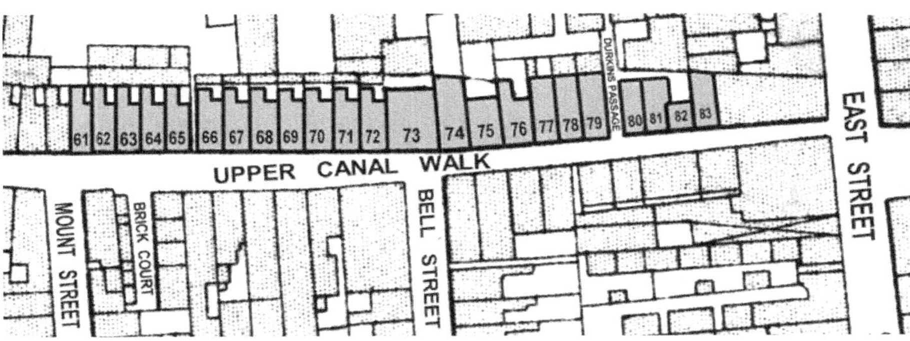

The upper west side of Upper Canal Walk with Nos. 61 to 83 leading up to East Street. No. 73 was the Lord Roberts pub, formerly the United Flags, while Nos. 80 to 82 were once the Clyde Inn

Painter David Rogers was the inhabitant of No. 61 in 1847, an address that housed a variety of uses. In 1851 its occupant was Charles Clark who divided his time between painting and glazing along with being a pork dealer. A Mrs Attwood had continued the pork dealing in 1855 before Henry Corke arrived in 1857. Corke was a builder and carpenter while still dabbling in the butchery trade until 1861 when the premises was taken over by clothes dealer Thomas Stevens but by 1869 it was once again a butchers shop until M. Holley changed it to an eating house in 1874. That venture was short-lived as it soon became home to fish dealer Jane Jackson, John Williams grocery and then watch maker Albert Henry Brazier in 1887. Clock making continued there between 1914 and 1925 under A.E. Alcock and Albert H. Pratt. The final changes came in the 1930s when Harry Fisher dealt with electrical fittings and John Mark ran a second-hand shop there.

No. 62 saw the usual procession of greengrocers and pork butchers, beginning in 1845 with Henry Candy (who did both) followed by butcher John Osman in 1851. Osman lasted until 1859 when James Knight resurrected the greengrocery business there. The return to butchery came with Henry Stainer in 1861 but he was succeeded by china dealer Frederick Stone (in 1867), clock makers John and Andrew Cross (1869) and then a line of confectioners from 1871 until 1878. They were followed by cutler Mark Waterman who gave way to Albert Henry Brazier who extended his watch making business from No. 61 in 1907, and the combined premises ended with Harry Fisher and John Mark as above.

On to No. 63 which again saw a great variety of short-lived businesses, which included grocer Martin Teague in 1847, shoe maker George Davis (1851), greengrocer Mary Leaming (1857), pork butcher Walter G. Moody (1863), Elizabeth Aston's oyster shop (1865), and hairdresser Daniel Lamont (1869–1871). It then remained as a barber shop under Thomas Doughty until Mrs Pitt and Mrs Brown ran their tobacconists there from 1912 until 1925. Next in line was costumier Harry Smith (1931–1940) and finally Normansell's butchers who saw out the final years from 1946 until 1960, being one of the last surviving businesses in the old Canal Walk.

An early tenant at No. 64 was brazier and coppersmith Alexander Parsons who worked there from 1841 until 1857. Thomas Capon was briefly trading as a tobacconist there in 1859 before the Hodgson family became one of the longest serving traders with their general and clothing businesses that ran from 1861 until 1948. Ammon Schwer was a clock maker at No. 65 from 1849, employing three men. He went into partnership with John Baptist Killy (see No. 60) in 1855 but the joint venture failed and Killy continued alone until 1859 when gentleman John Sadlier moved in. His wife Mary was a photographer who executed her artistic talents there for a couple of years, after which it was a drapery for a while until cutler Mark Walters arrived with his grindstone from 1871 until 1878 when he moved to No. 62. The Hodgson family then extended their business from No. 64 and saw out the remaining years there until 1948.

Time for another greengrocer! Step forward George Firmin who opened his shop at No. 66 in 1839 but maybe the competition was too great as he turned to confectionery in 1845. By 1851 he went back to the greengrocery business but then had combined the two by 1855 and continued as such until 1861. It remained a greengrocers under James John Nurse and his wife Ann from 1871 until 1874 when Ann became a general dealer and James a trunk maker, with a little pawnbroking on the side, before he had turned to outfitting by 1907 until World War One. In peacetime it became once more a greengrocers in several hands with James Alfred Thorn being the last in the line from 1931 until closure in 1954.

The butcher's union found another recruit in the form of Charles H. Gordon who manned the block at No. 67 in 1847 until 1853 when Joseph set up his china warehouse. That lasted only until 1857 when George Firmin extended his greengrocery and confectionery trade from next door. Clockmaker William Laishley took up the rent book in 1863 and Frederick Gaulton continued the trade there from 1867 until 1887 but by the early 1900s it had become one of the many tailors and outfitters in the locality under various proprietors until the Nurse family took over, followed by clothier Bernard Morris between 1914 and 1925 and finally by general dealer Mrs L. Levene who was last at that address in 1939.

Sawyer Ambrose Tiller was living at No. 68 in 1847 but was soon displaced by butcher Charles H. Gordon who took over from next door. Thomas Miell continued chopping the chops from 1855 until 1876. The shop remained in the trade under several more butchers, the last of which were W. and R. Fletcher prior to World War One. Bernard Morris had moved in from next door, extending his clothier business in 1925 with the final tenant being costumier Madam Conrad in 1935.

Perhaps this section of the street should have been renamed Butchers Row as No. 69 was yet another meat shop under several tradesmen from George Brown in 1847 through to Mark Russell in 1855. George Osman took over in 1857 and stayed the course until 1871 saw the arrival of fellow pork butcher Alfred Ridding. He had left by 1881 when it became a drapers, then a grocers, followed by confectioner Joseph Follett in 1887. Meyer Soloman had opened a fried fish shop there in 1901, which was taken over by Charles Hugh Gaultch in 1914 but by 1920 it became a clothes shop with Jesse William Handley being the last occupant in 1935.

Grocer and accountant Henry Simpson occupied No. 70 from 1847 but by 1851 he had swapped grocery for the pork butchers trade, while still continuing his accountancy business. His sister Mary Ann had taken over the butchery side by 1859 and continued running it until George Stevens took over in 1863 but by 1871 the shop had changed to a tobacconist run by Shadrick Pitts. That enterprise was short-lived as by 1874 the premises had become an eating house under several owners until 1891. In the 1911 census it was Joseph Goldstone's toy bazaar. Arthur and Catharine Montague were the next occupants from 1916 and by 1925 Catherine was running an amusement business which lasted until the early 1930s when wardrobe dealer Jesse William Handley took over from next door and was the final incumbent around 1935.

At last, a different tradesman in the shape of chair and cage maker James White who took residence at No. 71 in 1847. However, that was short-lived as Michael McDermot tried his hand at greengrocery there in 1849 but he was soon gone and the business had been taken up by George Firmin in 1851. Firmin had moved on to No. 66 and by 1855 the shop had become a hairdressers under Thomas Hancock who was also a newsagent. China dealer Ambrose Tiller made several appearances in the directories from 1857 until 1861. Afterwards, a succession of traders came and went, including J. and C. Ings pork butchers (of course), cutler Richard Cheetham, and then general dealer John Webb who also dabbled with eggs and fish, and (of course) greengrocery between 1871 and 1878, before giving way to clothier William Wallis. By 1912 James John Nurse and his wife had moved their outfitting business there from No. 66 but they were gone by 1939 when replaced by ice cream seller G. Chiari who lasted only until the bombs fell in 1940.

Shoemaker Edward Tiller cobbled at No. 72 from 1847 until he turned to greengrocery (surprise!) in 1851 and also worked as a sawyer. He had moved on by 1855, following which the shop was occupied by a musician, another greengrocer, a carpenter and greengrocer, a butter and pork dealer, a furniture broker, pastry cook, eating house keeper, and another greengrocer before clothier William Wallis extended his shop from No. 71 in 1876. The wandering outfitter James John Nurse appeared in 1907, adding to his other ventures at Nos. 66, 67 and 71. He and his wife gave way to the ice cream man G. Chiari in 1939.

Cabinet maker Ashley Petty practised his skills at No. 73 from 1839 until 1855 when the address became the *United Flags* public house belonging to Panton's Wareham Brewery and run by James Parkman. At last somewhere for all those thirsty greengrocers and pork butchers to congregate! Around 1900 the name was changed to *Lord Roberts* in honour of a famous Victorian soldier. In 1892 it was purchased by Scrase's Star Brewery and gained a reputation as a troublesome pub, and Eugene Goumez, its landlord of some 20 years, was dismissed. It later came under Welsh's Hyde Abbey Brewery and then Cooper's Brewery in 1929. As the *Lord Roberts*, it gained a certain notoriety as the haunt of seamen and locals of a certain persuasion. After becoming a Watney house, it underwent an extensive refurbishment in 1986 and emerged as a free house renamed *The Strand* and finally closed in 2012 when demolished to make way for a block of flats.

No. 73 Upper Canal Walk had been a pub since the 1850s when named the United Flags. After changes of name and ownerships it is pictured in its time as The Strand (Phil Warren collection)

Ashley Petty's cabinet making also took in No. 74 where he worked until the 1850s saw part of his premises taken over as the *United Flags* pub but this became a bakery at that time, first under James Osey and then Henry Ham. By 1861 it was in the hands of furniture broker William

Davis who was there until 1869, then after a time as a boot maker's shop it became the inevitable butchers from around 1881 until transformed into George Isaac's newsagents, a name that became synonymous with the trade and still lives on today with a shop bearing the name in Queensway. The vendor changed to Herbert John Ward around 1935 and remained as such until demolition in the 1950s.

No. 75, once numbered 8½, was the abode of clock maker William Ketterer in 1855 but was soon taken over by furniture broker William Davis who traded next door at No. 74. He was there until the early 1860s when it housed a variety of occupants from 1865 until 1876 ranging from an umbrella maker, fruiter and fishmonger, and a general dealer. From 1878 it became an established fishmongers, firstly under William H. Baron and then several others with John Yaldren serving from 1907 until 1925. William G. Miller was the last of the line in 1931.

There was certainly no shortage of butchers in Canal Walk. George Elias Hawkins was yet one more trading from No. 76 in 1847 until he moved to St Mary Street around 1861. His place was taken by furniture broker William Powell whose family ran their business there for around 30 years. Come the early 1900s it was time for another butcher to move in. This time it was Eastmans who lasted only until 1912 before there was another pressing need for a greengrocers, this time taken up by George Snook whose family had several shops in the town over many years. However, Snooks were gone by 1920 and the shop reverted to furniture sales under Emily Cox. The modern world finally caught up with Canal Walk in 1939 when City Radio (A.S. Brown) moved into No. 76 but sadly their time was cut short by wartime bombing.

William Hatch ran his grocers shop at No. 77 from 1841 but by 1849 it had become a beer house operated by Peter Jones. He was replaced a couple of years later by the wonderfully named Clayton Birdshead Pettit who was also a coal meter when not serving ale. By 1855 Birdshead had been replaced by Vincent Wing (try not to laugh) but that was the end of the beer shop, which, by 1861, had become a provisions dealership with

John Davis at the helm. Davis had also operated from Nos. 74 and 75 and remained until 1869. The shop briefly became a fishmongers, then a hairdressers and yet another greengrocers before becoming Alfred Woodward's pie shop in 1884. This changed to Thomas Harman's stewed eel and pie emporium in 1907. Harman's wife Karoline ran the above rooms as a lodging house which, in 1911, had another 12 people living on the premises who obviously weren't put off by the smell of stewing eels and the pie shop ran successfully until bombs fell in 1940.

Basket, cage and chair maker James White was working at No. 78 in 1845 but had moved to No. 71 by 1847 when china and glass merchant Charles White took over the premises. In 1851 Charles handed over the business to James Taylor whose family remained there until the 1890s when John Day deduced it was time for another greengrocer's shop. This one lasted until 1912 and later became a confectioners with James Hendry manning the sugar before wardrobe dealer Walter Ward saw the final two years there until the 1940 bombings.

No. 79 marked the entrance to Durkins Passage (see Upper Back of the Walls) and in 1845 was a coffee house run by Mrs Mary Roe and by 1853 she had changed the premises into an eating house, which she kept until 1859 when John Roles took over from her. He carried the same trade until 1884 when John Large took up the reins. William Pullen was the next proprietor from 1907 when he and his wife Elizabeth kept the dining rooms going until John Winter arrived to see out the early 1930s until closure in 1935. Coach builder John Lucas appears in the directories for this part of the street during the 1850s but I have not been able to determine his exact location, so possibly he may have been operating in Durkins Passage.

Fishmonger George Brown's oyster shop sees the first mention of No. 80 in 1865. Brown was resident there until the trade was taken over by George Ovens in 1881. By 1884 the shop had been taken over by the *Clyde Inn*, a beer house next door at Nos. 81 and 82 run by Charles Wiles. The early days from 1847 saw No. 81 occupied the usual variety of outlets including a grocer, confectioner and brewer Charles J. Storey, who occupied both Nos. 81 and 82 in 1853 but by 1855 both premises were in the hands of boot and shoe maker William Hopcroft. Then, by 1859, the two premises had separate occupants again with No. 81 housing dealer Henry Brown, fishmonger Emily White, greengrocer Henry Roe and carpenter James W. Roe. By 1867 William Allum and his wife Grace had moved into Nos. 81 and 82 as landlord and landlady of what became the *P&O Arms* which belonged to Welsh's Lion Brewery. The Allums remained until Grace Miller had taken over by 1874 when the pub changed its name to the *Clyde Inn* under the Old Shirley Brewery with George Lock in charge. Then by 1884 it had been extended into No. 80 but closed in 1888 under the stewardship of Charles Wiles.

As we have seen, many greengrocers came and went in Canal Walk but one who stayed the course was Joseph Kimber at No. 83 from 1851 until 1865 when carpenter James W. Roe took over with his wife Lucy who did even better by hanging on until 1887. There followed a few more greengrocers until it became a butchers shop run by Thomas Humby in 1907. Ernest Chard was briefly in charge by 1912 but 1914 saw the arrival of Giggs and Young who scattered the sawdust through to 1954.

The directories between 1861 and 1884 include a No. 84, which is likely to have been the premises on the corner with East Street. Listed there was confectioner and pastry cook Richard Ray from 1861 until 1878 with the final occupant of that address being clothier James Ireland in 1884.

BRICK COURT
Nos. 1–5

Brick Court ran off the east side of Upper Canal Walk, just north of its junction with Mount Street. No. 1 Brick Court, standing between Nos. 15 and 16, was sometimes listed as 15½ or 15A Canal Walk. The court consisted of five buildings on its north side that were still evident in the 1950s although I can find no inhabitants after 1931.

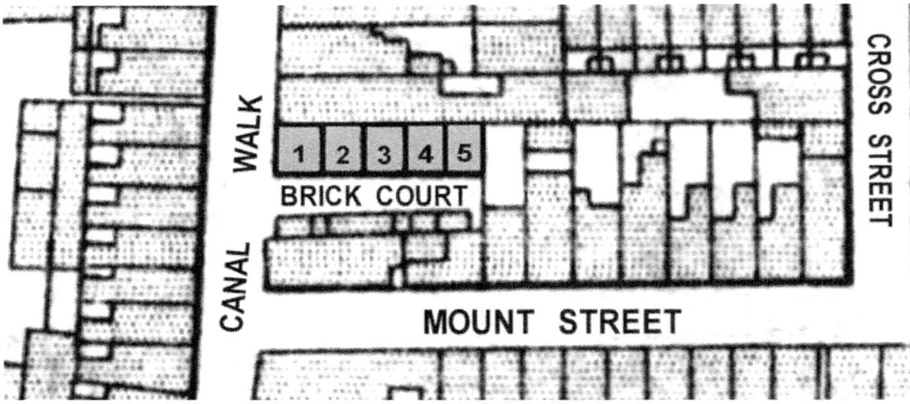

The five properties at Brick Court. No. 1 was also at times referred to 15A Canal Walk and, along with No. 2, was later taken over by the business at No. 15 Canal Walk

From at least 1841, No. 1 was the domain of boot maker William Marshman who was there until 1863, after which there seems no recorded tenant until house painter Daniel Barton arrived in 1881. Fellow boot makers James Hayward and John Thomas Holloway were cobbling there in 1884 and 1887 respectively.

The 1893 Dilapidated Buildings Report described the court as having been reduced to three dwellings with Nos. 1 and 2 taken over by the business premises at No. 15 Canal Walk. The remaining three (Nos. 3 to 5) were in a damp, dark and unhealthy condition with an ash pit and WC out in the yard. By 1907, furniture dealer Allonso W. Winter had taken over the shop at 15A, succeeded in 1914 by medical herbalist Jack Stanley (see above). Baker John Barnes was at No. 2 in the 1850s, followed by butcher James Simkins in the 1880s, who appears to have been the last occupant at that address before being taken over as 15A Canal Walk. No. 3 was home to John Thomas Turner, a glass and earthenware worker in the 1850s. The next decade saw grocers assistant George Blackthorn living there. The 1880s saw house painter Daniel Barton relocate from No. 1 then, at the turn of the century, Poor House manager George Gray was in residence.

No. 4 was uninhabited in the 1850s before a succession of seamen and labourers moved in, one of whom being dock labourer Isaac Payne who arrived in 1901 and was there as the final tenant in 1931. No. 5 was home to more of the labouring classes before coach trimmer Henry Lowe appeared in 1881 and the final incumbents were the Copperthwaite family from 1911 until the final days.

BELL STREET
Greens Court and Frosts Court

Bell Street ran from Canal Walk to Orchard Lane with some of its buildings dating back as far as 1811. The number series ran from 1 to 19 on the north side and 20 to 33 opposite. There were three local pubs, two at its junction with Orchard Lane, one being the *Bell Inn* and the other the *Elephant and Castle*. There was also the *Lord Roberts* at the opposite end of the street in Canal Walk. Almost the entire street was demolished in 1935 and then it was truncated in the 1960s with the building of Queensway as part of the ring road.

BELL STREET
North Side, Nos. 1–19

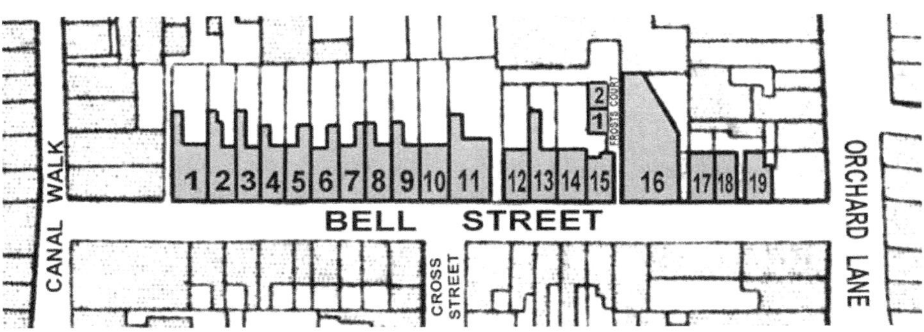

The north side of Bell Street showing Nos. 1 to 19 and Frosts Court with its entrance between Nos. 15 and 16. No. 16 was Harding's pipe works

Most of this street was populated from the 1830s but some of the earliest inhabitants are listed in the 1811 directory. Bricklayer John Andrews resided at No. 1, next to an alleyway that led to Greens Court and East Street. By 1834 whitesmith William Watts was there, then we find the Nicholas family established in 1841. Shoe binder Elizabeth Nicholas is listed in the 1841 directory as living in Bell Street and by 1851, shoemaker James Nicholas was at No. 1 where he remained until around 1870. In the mid-1850s he had given up boot making and became a coal dealer. The address returned to shoe making upon the arrival of George Scammell in 1871. He was in residence until 1884 but his son Arthur was there in 1891 employed as a school caretaker. Others came and went until dock labourer Edward Bendall took up residence in 1911 and remained until 1925, being the final occupant recorded there

Tin plater William Vining and his wife Mary were living in No. 2 from 1841 until 1861. Labourer George Golding (or Golden) had moved in by 1869 and he gave way to tailor Henry Coombes in 1876. Others arrived and departed until French polisher Ezekiel Roberts had a longish spell there from 1911 until 1925. Another shoemaker, Edward Stigant, was at No. 3 in 1834 but no others are recorded until mariner John Tizard appeared in the 1851 census. He moved out in the late 1850s, making way for customs officer Egbert Wild in 1859. He must have enjoyed his time there as he stayed until 1874. Ships stoker William Hemmett and his family spent a decade there but 1901 saw a notable return of coal porter Arthur Scammell to the street but his stay was brief. Boiler maker Frederick Read was the final tenant at No. 3 from 1907 until 1935.

Plasterer Robert Candy was at No. 4 with his wife and three children back in 1851. He died in 1866 at the age of 62 and his widow Eliza ran their home as a lodging house until 1871 when the house was let to boot maker George H. Hayward. The following years saw various types move in and move on, including dock porter Alfred Tolfree who was also a bird dealer, and fish hawker William Lacey who lived there from 1887. His son William James took over the rent book around 1912 and the family saw out the final days of the street in 1935. Customs officer Egbert Wild was at No. 5 in 1851 until he moved to No. 3 in 1857. His home was taken by the Fryer family who were dock workers, remaining there until around 1870. They were followed by whitesmith William Parsons, laundress Elizabeth Cooke, and toy dealer Richard Goodman who lived there from 1887 until the street came down.

Retired waterman Robert Perkins spent his final years at No. 6, having been recorded there from 1851 until his death in 1863. Those who came after him included several mariners and painter Thomas Smith who was resident from 1865 until 1881. Fish hawker Mary Sheen came later in 1887 through to 1916 and Frederick Goss was the final tenant there. The earliest inhabitant I have found at No. 7 is a painter named Joshua Taylor in 1851 but no others appear until 1857 when cabinet maker William Scammell and family lived there until at least 1881. Dock labourer Henry Green was also a long-term resident from 1907 until the 1930s.

Schoolmistress Ann White was at No. 8 in 1841 but in 1851 we have Mrs Sophia White, also a schoolmistress, at that address but I have not found any family connection. Sophia remained there until 1874 when she was still at the school. Later arrivals from 1887 included labourer George Golding (previously at No. 2) and his wife Edith who survived him and moved on in 1907, hotel cleaner Florence Emily Beed in 1911 and finally Albert Duncan in the 1920s and 1930s. The Tigg family of shoemakers took up residence at No. 9 as far back as 1836 and worked on until 1851 when commercial clerk John Newman moved in. An assortment of messengers, coach makers, labourers, and an engine driver followed until labourer George Tucker turned up in 1865. By 1876 he was working as a coal porter and was still there long after his retirement in the early 1900s. His wife Sophia outlived him until 1922 when the next inhabitant was Thomas Smith who was the last tenant in 1935.

Carpenter Joseph Walton occupied No. 10 in 1851 and the Nichols family spent time there from 1857 until 1865 where widow Sarah

Nichols had been on parish relief since 1851. Baker William Adams had a decade there from 1874 until 1884 and was succeeded by various others including Isabella Pim who ran the address as a lodging house around the turn of the century. James Child ran his grocers shop at No. 11 in 1834 and by 1841 it was in the hands of Thomas Godley. He was serving customers until the late 1850s when Samuel Fry took over the business and also sold coal. Stephen Duell was next in line and kept the grocery trade going until the early 1870s, after which shoemaker George Nobles dallied for a while in 1874 and some others appeared briefly but it had returned to being a general shop by 1881 when former ships fireman James Bartlett came ashore and ran the shop on and off for a while. At that time there were no less than 12 people living at that address. In 1901, Italian Frank Fuccio took over the store and switched to greengrocery, specialising in fruit and potatoes, so successfully he was there until the mid-1920s. The final occupant of No. 11 when the street came down was auctioneer Harry Brown. After the street had been demolished, farrier Henry H. Gould set up his forge on the site and shoed horses from 1939 until 1948.

Boot and shoe making flourished in Bell Street with Maria Mansbridge working at No. 12 in 1841. Benjamin Cross continued the cordwaining from 1851 until 1869 and after he departed the house was home to labourers, hawkers and seamen, one of whom was William Sheath whose family lived there from the turn of the century until the street came down in the mid-1930s. Some of the earliest tenants at No. 13 included gardener John King in 1811 and beer retailer Samuel Dawes junior in 1934 but his beer shop was gone by 1841 when bookbinder Philip Wilcox was householder, a tenure that lasted until 1855. After him, painters and bricklayers were evident until shoe making returned with George Scammell (see also No. 14) in 1865 until 1869. Furniture broker William James did his deals there from 1871 until 1881 and the final inhabitant was Thomas Sherry, a one-time fish hawker who turned to fruit and ran a shop there from 1891 until the street's final days.

Gardener Charles Pearce lived at No. 14 in the 1830s, then labourers and seamen followed him before George Scammell moved in around 1859. George and his family were quite prominent boot and shoe makers and appear regularly in these pages. The Scammells had moved on by 1865 when tailor George Stone arrived, then, in 1871, gas fitter Thomas Pointer took up residence and he and his family were long-time tenants until 1925. The final few years there were taken up by Frederick Strugnell and his wife. The earliest entry I have found for the house that became No. 15 is in 1811 when it was occupied by gardener John Robinson, one of several in that area when it was possibly still semi rural. Barrow man Joseph Tanner, seaman Christopher Martin, boot maker John Barnes and brewer John Campbell had been and gone by 1859. In fact, nobody seemed to stay there very long and the turnover continued with house painter Thomas Hardy, mariner George Merrick and dressmaker Mrs Towner all briefly appearing before the 1860s were out. The changes continued with dock labourers and a ships stoker before George Thomas Colmer and family arrived in 1916 and were the final names in the rent book.

Next to No. 15 was the entrance to Fosses (or Frosts) Court, which we shall visit shortly, but No. 16 was a building with some history. Tobacco pipe smoking was prevalent in the early 1800s and by 1834 Adam Atkinson had established his pipe making works there. The works was briefly taken over by John Short in 1841 but George Harding established a successful business there, which he and his family maintained until 1859 when he moved his residence to No. 23. Another business also prevailed at No. 16. George Goodman's was making chairs there from 1847 and a decade later he was also manufacturing umbrellas, a side of the business his wife Maria took over in the late 1850s and continued into the 1860s when she moved to No. 18. From that time, No. 16 is rarely mentioned apart from the odd occupation by labourers but they may have been in Frosts Court. By 1907 the address had disappeared from the directories until 1912 when it became Edwin Jones house furnishing store, which lasted until the 1940 Blitz.

Nos. 17 to 19 were three small cottages towards the Orchard Lane end of the street where cow keeper Mary Dawkins lived at No. 17 in 1834. The address was shared between carpenter John Priddle and bricklayer John Butler who were there between 1853 and 1865 when boot maker Edmund Tout showed up and cobbled until the early 1870s. Bricklayers and painters came through its door until general labourer Edward Walters moved in at the turn of the century and spent some 30 years there. No. 18 saw the usual short-term renters from 1834 until Mrs Maria Goodman set up shop there in 1865 (see also No. 16) but she had given up umbrella making for chair making which lasted until 1871. The family of ships stoker James Dickson had a fairly lengthy spell there from 1901 until 1916 and Joseph Edwards and his wife were the final occupants.

No. 19, next to the *Bell Inn*, had an uninteresting past. It was once a general shop with Mrs Price behind the counter in 1834 but nobody of much interest seems to have lived there. There are many blank entries in the directories until the 1880s when we have a seaman, a labourer and a tinplate worker before charwoman Mrs Elizabeth Cannon is listed in 1907 and remained as the last occupant in 1925.

Looking east down Bell Street towards Orchard Lane showing Nos. 10 to 19 on the left with the entrance to Cross Street in the right foreground. The second building on the left was the general shop at No. 11 and the tall building further along was originally the pipe making works of Harding and Son

The view westwards along Bell Street towards Upper Canal Walk with Nos. 26 to 33 on the left and the Lord Roberts pub facing the camera. The road sign for Cross Street is high up on the left

BELL STREET
South Side, Nos. 20–33

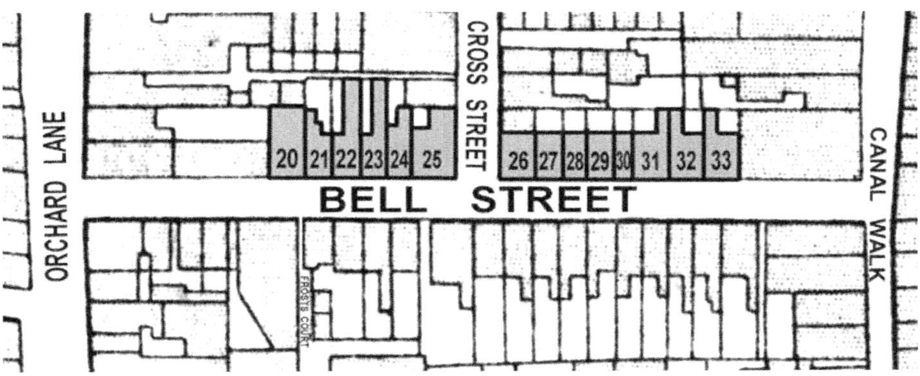

Bell Street's south side with Nos. 20 to 33 divided by Cross Street

The south side of Bell Street had fewer buildings than those opposite but, in general, people living there seemed to dally longer than those across the street. Master bricklayer John Butler stayed the course at No.

20 from 1853 until 1881 when labourer Robert Carter took his place and remained until 1912. For many years No. 21 was a bakery with John Kerley manning the ovens from 1811 through to 1843, although he is still shown there in retirement in 1851. P&O ships fireman James Herrick dwelled from mid-1850s until early 1860s, then from 1863 there were several members of the boot making fraternity, including Henry and George Scammell at various intervals to 1878. Further seamen arrived between voyages until gas service labourer John Warland appeared in the 1911 census and prevailed until the final days in 1935.

Nobody was listed at No. 22 until 1857 when painter Edwin Walker hung his hat there until 1865. Richard Goodman carried on the family chair making tradition there in 1874 (see others at Nos. 16, 17 and 18) but his tenancy was short before the usual assortment of renters arrived. Between 1881 and 1914 the house accommodated a blacksmith, seaman, cab driver and groom, a porter and a furniture packer before Edward New became the final tenant in 1916 and saw it out until the end. Carpenter Robert Prewitt lived in No. 23 from 1857 until 1861 when pipe maker George Harding moved from No. 16 across the street. Harding was there until 1871 when James Cleever took over the business. He and George Davis continued the trade until 1916 when ice cream seller Joseph Peaglia spent five years there. His place was taken by Frank Hallett who saw out the final years.

One of the earliest residents at No. 24 was coppersmith William Parsons (see also No. 31) through the 1830s who gave way to Stephen Jenkins who was sexton at the nearby All Saints Church. Jenkins was there until 1853 when ticket writer Zachariah Kerley arrived. He had previously lived with his father in John Kerley's bakery at No. 21. A mixture of carpenters, hawkers, shoemakers, painters and labourers were there from the 1860s through to around 1916 when James Henry White moved from No. 23 and became the last of the line. No. 25 stood on the corner of Cross Street and for much of its existence was a shop but back in 1834 cabinetmaker William Foster lived there. William Shears and his wife started a bakery there in 1853 and that continued under several others from 1857 until 1878 when Henry Turner began boot making there. Isaac Joyce briefly ran a beer house in 1887 before becoming a milk vendor. Coal merchant Thomas Smith arrived in 1901 and became a shopkeeper and beer retailer. When he left in the 1920s it continued as a shop under several others with George E. Stowe being the final proprietor.

On the opposite corner with Cross Street stood No. 26 where early days saw carpenter John Clark and plasterer John Parsons in residence between 1834 and 1841. Then there are no further entries until 1857 sees shoemaker James Edwards cobbling until 1871. Seafarer Thomas Walters manned the decks until 1878 saw others come and go before it became a Mission Room around 1887, which lasted until 1907 and saw painter Edward New under its roof before he moved to No. 22 in 1915. Dock labourer James Cook and his wife were the final names in the rent book.

Painter Robert Ransom was the occupant of No. 27 back in 1834 but he had been replaced by nurse Mary Forbes in 1841. A decade later, Mary was surviving on parish relief and she had gone by 1857 when there began a huge turnover of people living there. Carpenters, a sail maker, dressmaker, sawyer, painter, and a French polisher crossed its doorstep before rigger Richard May and his family resided there from 1912 until 1925 with Samuel Edward Heath being the last of a very long line. Washerwoman Elizabeth Burnett was taking in laundry at No. 28 in 1841 but the place seems unoccupied from then until 1857 when the possession of tenants saw tin plate worker Robert Ingram followed by labourers, another laundress, a general dealer, ships fireman, gas fitter, and a coach maker who all filed through its front door until 1876 when John Edward Blundell arrived, having the joint talents of painter and musician until he was gone by 1887. Thereafter, there was a return of humdrum labourers with Joseph Billows there from 1907 and his widow remained until 1925.

Customs officer James Gregory resided at No. 29 in 1851 but by 1857 he had gone to sea as a ships fireman, a job he held when he left the street in 1861. A couple of other seamen took his place until 1871 saw Richard Goodman repairing chairs there until 1884. He was the son of George Goodman who had previously made chairs at No. 16. Others of note were ships greaser William Chalk, resident from 1907 until 1914 when William Sheath appeared and remained until demolition came in 1935. From 1834, No. 30 was home to boot makers, a bricklayer, carpenters, a lamplighter and a porter before charwoman Mrs Ann Stanley held the keys from 1865 until 1876. Widow Eliza Kettle was there later from 1891 until 1911 and other widows followed her between 1912 and 1931 before John William Spooner was the final tenant.

No. 31 featured some familiar names. Coppersmith William Parsons from 1851 until 1869 (he was previously at Nos. 5 and 24) and musician John Blundell, 1887 to 1891 (earlier at No. 28). Over the years, the Goodman family seems to have occupied much of the street with china and glass dealer William Goodman at No. 31 from 1901 until 1931. Watchmaker George Plaskett spent almost half his lifetime at No.32 ticking along from 1834 until 1859, while ships fireman John Dougherty was another stalwart from 1861 through to 1884. Fanny Darman was running it as a boarding house in 1901 when she had four lodgers living there. Dock labourer David Stanley, boiler scaler Alexander Frazer and labourer George Smith were the final names recorded.

Thomas Waight was a musician who supplemented his living by ruling paper sheets by machine while he was at No. 33 from 1834 until 1876. Others who followed included an umbrella hawker, a coal porter, and various seamen until Mrs Sarah Judd was running a boarding house there in 1911. Fitters mate Ethelbert Lever was one of the last occupants from 1920 until 1931.

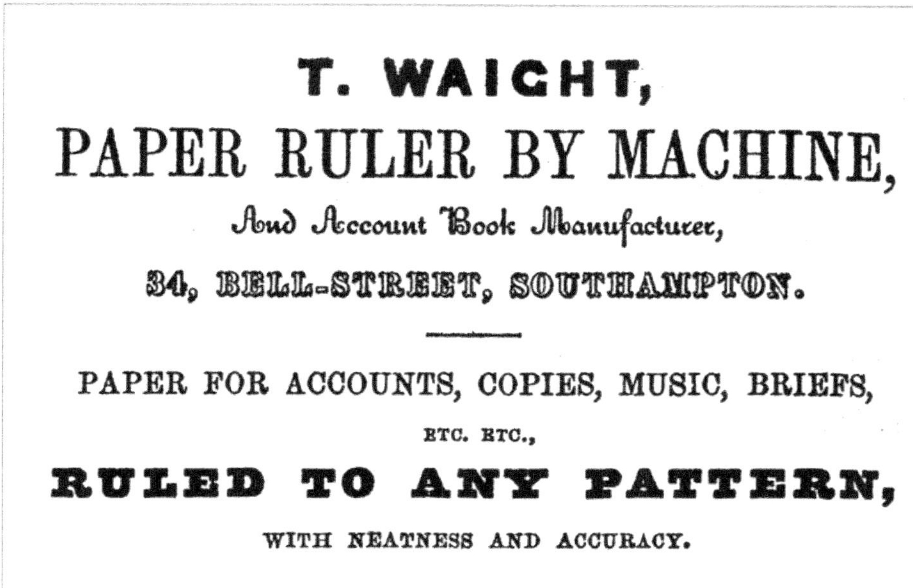

An advertisement for Thomas Waight's skills as a machine paper ruler in 1851 when the street numbers were slightly different

GREENS COURT
Nos. 1–7

This court, also known as Green's Passage, had seven houses with access via an alleyway next to No. 1 Bell Street or by a passage on the south side of East Street. The houses backed on to the yard of the infamous *Horse and Groom* pub and were built mainly of lath and plaster. These structurally defective buildings were exceedingly damp with further problems of wet caused by defective wooden guttering. None had any through ventilation and the high surrounding buildings limited the supply of air to the court. All sanitary facilities were outside in the court and a nearby slaughterhouse did not improve matters. Most of the earlier census returns show just five houses occupied but this had risen to seven by the time of the 1893 slum report and, surprisingly, the court was still listed in the directories in 1912 but had disappeared by 1916.

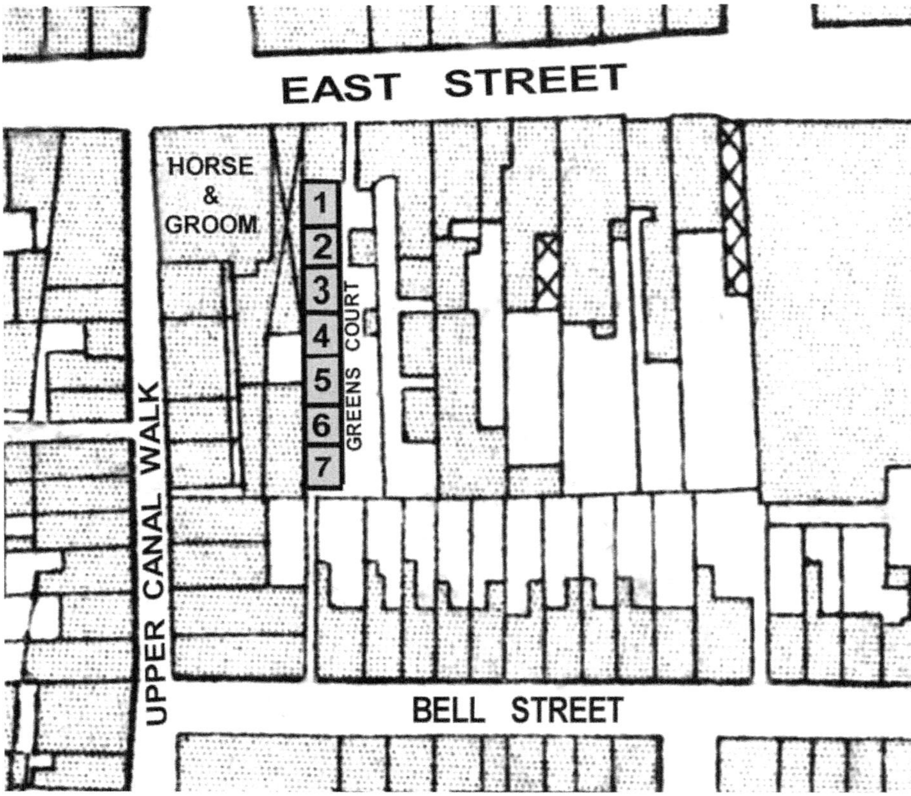

The seven houses of Greens Court tucked away between Bell Street and East Street

As with many of these isolated and hidden courts, few of their inhabitants found their names included in the various directories. However, the census returns show the buildings were occupied mainly by labourers but one tenant, Julia Payne, managed to survive there for 20 years or so, earning her living as a needlewoman.

Once again we are reliant on census returns rather than the directories that barely mention the court's existence, let alone those that lived there. Harness maker Joseph Green was resident in No. 1 in 1851, and we might assume the buildings were named after him. By 1861 seaman's wife Margaret Phillips was there. A decade later we find butcher Charles R. Payne. Nobody is listed at No. 1 in 1881 but auctioneer's porter E. Perren gets a directory mention in 1884. Back to the census and in 1891 we have Eliza Clark on parish relief followed by needlewoman Julia Payne (Charles Payne's widow?) in 1901. Julia's stay was uninterrupted until the 1911 census, listing her as an upholsterers needle hand, is the last we see of her.

Labourers galore, Robert Osbourne, George Misslebrook, Alfred Jenkins, James Thomas, Henry Priest and George Williams lived at No. 2 throughout its existence with journeyman butcher William Perry and hawker Ellen Smith being the exceptions. At No. 3 we find drayman John Paddington in 1851 and it's possible he worked in the adjacent *Horse and Groom*. Bricklayer's wife Sarah Featherstone was there in 1861, followed by butcher Richard Chaffe in 1871 and seaman John Poole in 1881. The 1884 directory found bricklayer George Over in residence with labourers William J. Hart and Thomas Stone making up the numbers. No. 4 records nurse Ann Rose in 1851 with another drayman, Harry Watkins, living there in 1871, with carman William Drake in 1884 and ships fireman Patrick Bradley in 1911 standing out from the usual labourers. In the 1891 census, a No. 4½ is listed, being the abode of corporation horse driver Richard Cross it was never shown again.

Coachman Edward Mason lived at No. 5 in 1871 followed by another drayman, William Cox who managed to stay in the miserable surroundings from 1881 until 1884. James Lance was living by his own means in 1901, then 1911 saw retired coal porter James Lahey resting there. No. 6 does not appear until 1891 with Julia Payne working in a docks linen factory and Kate Leahey (related to James at No. 5?) was the last recorded there. No. 7 has only two occupants shown in 1901 and 1911, being ships fireman John Coakley and dock labourer George Stainer respectively.

FROSTS or FROSSERS COURT
Nos. 1 and 2

Researching the smaller and more obscure courts is always difficult, none more so than Frosts Court (see Bell Street north side map). This was a small court with just two houses off the north side of Bell Street with its entrance through an alleyway next to No. 15. Appearing as Frosts Court on the 1870 map it is referred to as Frossers Court in the 1891 and 1901 census returns and is also listed as such in the 1907 directory, which shows no householders. It is not mentioned at all in later directories. The 1893 slum report names it as Frosts Court and describes the houses as being without through ventilation and had no provision for the disposal of ashes or general refuse. There was a solitary tap for water in the blind court, which was only six feet wide. References to those who lived there are mostly missing from the directories and perhaps they were just overlooked.

Of the few references I have found, the 1881 census mentions 'Houses in Court' under Bell Street and names labourer George Norris and soldier's wife Martha Newbolt as the inhabitants. In 1891 we have blacksmith John Oswald at No. 1 and next door is Thomas E. Osman, a shipyard labourer. Then in the 1901 census there is Mrs Sara Brava and dock labourer Harry Kennett, but none of these appear in any of the directories. The buildings were still standing in 1935 when the photograph was taken prior to demolition but they may have long been unoccupied by then.

The gloom and misery of Frosts Court with the two small houses set in an alleyway off Bell Street

MOUNT STREET
Mount Court

Mount Street formerly ran between Canal Walk and Orchard Lane, south of Bell Street and north of Union Street, near to where Queen's House now stands. The early records from 1811 list carpenter Richard Jordan, coachman Edward Frost, carpenter James Bampton and labourer John Bruce as early inhabitants. Nos. 1 to 18 were demolished in the 1930s as part of a slum clearance scheme and the remainder disappeared during World War Two. The street contained two pubs that were on opposite corners at its junction with Cross Street.

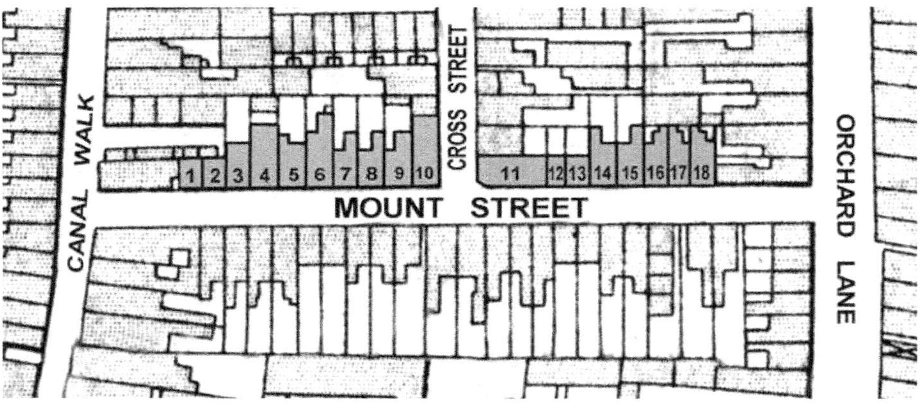

The north side of Mount Street with Nos. 1 to 18. No. 10 was the Princess Royal and No. 11 the Firemans Arms

MOUNT STREET
North Side, Nos. 1–18

Several houses in this street were three storeys high and housed multiple tenants with some in single rooms and families occupying just two. The north side of Mount Street began at Canal Walk where No. 1 was the home of various seamen and labourers with nobody staying any length of time, while No. 2 was the home of William and Mary Budden from 1841 where he was a shoemaker while she was a tailoress. Mary outlived her husband and remained there until at least 1887 and later tenants were the Such family, living there from around 1912 until around 1930 when it would seem from the photograph, the address became a store.

Anne Meill was taking in washing at No. 3 between 1841 until 1857. Labourer Edward Turner headed a line consisting of a barrow man, gas fitter, factory worker and seamen from the 1870s until William Pace arrived around 1912 and stayed until that part of the street came down in the 1930s. No. 4 also listed a variety of souls including a ships fireman, tailor, painter, grainer, boot finisher, poultry man Alfred Brackstone (1891) and paper hanger Walter Barton (early 1900s) who all came and went in quick succession, ending with Mrs Stote in 1931.

Various members of the Smith family inhabited No. 5 from 1841 with bricklayer William Smith in 1841 until Joseph Smith 1887. The house was shared with bookbinder Stephen Early and his wife Mary through the 1860s and 1870s. Mrs Farmer ran the roost from 1914 until 1935. The 1841 census sees George Henry Perkins as an optician living at No. 6. Waterman Thomas Hardy was next in line, then in 1861 came Henry Wood who rejoiced in being a window ticket writer. Laundress Mrs Sarah Harvey was scrubbing shirts there for a decade from 1871 before the usual assortment took up temporary residences with Charles White being last of the line in the 1930s. No. 7 saw some longer term tenants although journeyman bricklayer George Pearce soon packed his trowel after 1851. Stone mason John Corbyn arrived in 1859 and chiselled away until 1867 when naval pensioner William Williamson rested there for a couple of years. Carman Edward Newman trundled his cart at No. 7 from 1876 until his retirement in the 1890s. William Maloney and his family unloaded their chattels in the early 1900s for a stay that lasted through to 1925 with William Frederick Jackson seeing out the early 1930s there.

Journeyman tailor William Urry was cutting his cloth at No. 8 in 1851 and was succeeded there by his son William junior who donned his tape measure until 1859. General dealer George Whitlock traded there from 1863 until the early 1870s when Mrs Phillis Russell struck further deals until the 1880s saw others in and out until William Read spent the final decade there. Porter Edward Hilyard was an early tenant in 1851 and journeyman tailor James Young decided to stay put from 1857 until 1876. Labourers and seamen were then in abundance before Mrs Sarah Ann Ford moved in around 1912. At that time she was also the landlady of the *Princess Royal* next door at No. 10 but was soon gone when the pub lost its licence that year. John Sullivan, then Ernest Holland, were the final names after her.

Nos. 1 to 10 Mount Street with the entrance to Cross Street in the distance

At last a pub is featured, and we now come to the *Princess Royal* at No.10 on the corner of Cross Street. Its roots go back to 1834 when John Bound was a grocer and beer retailer there until around 1850 when Benjamin Vivian took over. George Whitlock sold groceries there in the mid-1850s but there is no further mention of beer until James Carter is shown as landlord of the *Princess Royal* in 1857. George Henry Scammell was selling beer and making boots there from 1871 and his wife Elizabeth was serving the pints in 1887 and then their son Henry ran the bar in the early 1900s before Sarah Ann Ford was the final licensee in 1912 when Barlow's Victoria Brewery, who were owners of the pub, were refused a licence. It was afterwards the private residence of Frederick Ford from then until demolition in 1935.

No. 10 was the Princess Royal pub on the corner of Cross Street. It was refused a licence and closed in 1912 (Phil Warren collection)

You wait ages for one pub to come along and then there are two. On the opposite corner of Cross Street at No. 11 stood the *Atlantic Arms*, which was previously the *Firemans Arms* until around 1890. Mrs Drayston was a beer seller there back in 1853 and by 1859 Benjamin Vivian was running it as a grocery and beer shop. Mariner John Sealey became landlord in the early 1860s when it took the name *Firemans Arms*. Several licensees had stood behind the bar, witnessing the antics of its customers, and if local resident Elizabeth Ainsworth was typical of the pub's clientele, it was probably a place to avoid. In April 1902, she was fined five shillings plus costs for being drunk and disorderly and refusing to leave. She had previously been convicted twice for drunkenness and four times for assault.

Alfred Brackstone was landlord in 1907 when a family tragedy occurred. His eight-year-old son Charles was with some other lads climbing over an empty railway wagon at the Platform, near the docks post office. One of the boys unfastened the heavy wagon door, which fell open and struck Charles on the head. He was rushed to the Royal South Hants Hospital but sadly died on the way. With William Fowles in charge, the pub lost its licence in 1914 due to its bar being cramped and filthy, with owners Gibbs Mew and Co. unsuccessfully appealing against the closure, citing that the *Princess Royal* opposite had already gone.

The first occupant of No. 12 was David Pearce in 1857 but few of interest passed through its door in the street's lifetime although George Barter had a longish spell there in the early 1900s to around 1925. No. 13 accommodated wheelwright John Best in 1851 and shipwright William Kinch in 1857 before the usual assortment of seamen and labourers with the exception of measure man James Gatehouse in the 1880s. Painter Charles Parsons was first through the door of No. 14 in the early 1840s then bricklayers Richard and Frederick Lee made it their home in the 1850s and the following inhabitants included a whitesmith, a couple of plumbers, and a retired laundress. None of whom stayed for any length of time and its final tenant in the 1930s was Alfred

Brackstone, former landlord of the *Atlantic Arms.*

No. 15 seemed a little more inviting as chimney sweep Arthur Black stayed on for a decade from 1851. Those who followed him were mainly seamen although musician Clement Rossi made a brief appearance in the 1891 census. The Conway family were last in line from 1916. Nos. 16 to 18 were built later and there is no record of anyone at No. 16 until tin man George Clyde in 1867, then labourer George Fielder was resident from 1869 until 1881. Dock labourers then filled the rent book until the arrival of Mrs Hack in 1912 whose family stayed until the end. Carpenter Louis Welch and his brood occupied No. 17 from 1867 to 1874 after which there was the usual succession of dock labourers with John Coalman as the last inhabitant.

The final house on the north side of the street was No. 18. Painter Edwin Walker was there in 1857 then seaman Henry Dimmick and his wife moved in around 1869, making way for more painters, George Brazier and then George Tillman, through the early 1880s.

Looking north up Cross Street the Atlantic Arms on the right stood on the corner of Mount Street

Nos. 11 to 18 Mount Street viewed from Orchard Lane with No. 18 nearest on the right and the entrance to Cross Street in the distance

MOUNT STREET
South Side, Nos. 19–39

Whereas the north side of Mount Street was demolished in the mid-1930s, the south side survived until 1940 when much of it succumbed to the wartime bombing.

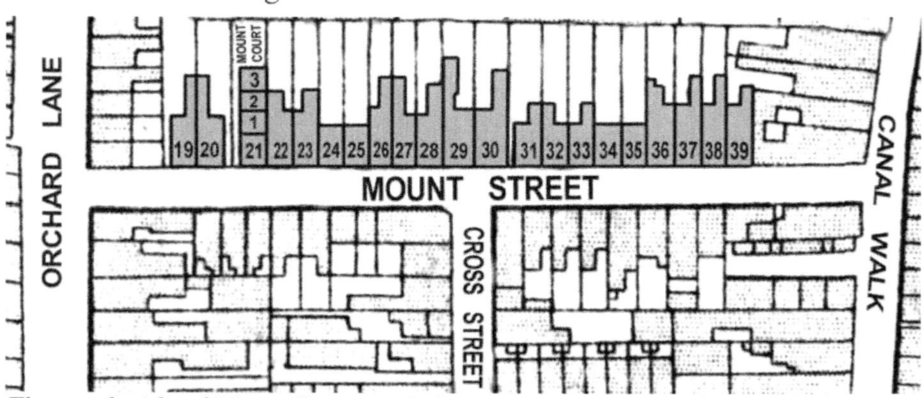

The south side of Mount Street with the entrance to Mount Court between Nos. 20 and 21

Starting from the Orchard Lane end of the street, No. 19 was home to the Budden family (others were at No. 2) as far back as 1834 when a Miss Budden was making straw hats and bonnets. Mrs Sarah Budden was a widow there by 1851 working as a laundress until around 1870. Carver and Gilder James Bickers made his frames there from 1871 until 1884. Greengrocer's storeman Joseph Baker had arrived by 1911 but had moved on by the early 1920s then George Henry Cooper was the last named there in the 1930s. Labourer William Littlecott and charwoman Mrs E. Gooden were inside No. 20 between 1851 and 1859 when the Simmons family arrived. They were there until 1871, followed by coal trimmer Henry Glasspool and dealer Maria Browning before a host of dock labourers filled the rooms from 1891, with Horace Woodford being the last from 1911 until 1940.

The entrance to Mount Court (or Mount Place) was next to No. 20, and No. 21, being at the entrance, was sometimes included in the court where the earliest occupant was noted in 1850 when tailor William Burn arrived. After him there was a constant turnover of labourers, a carriage trimmer, hawkers and a couple of military service pensioners before Henry James Gregory was the final occupant in the 1930s when the court was demolished. No. 22 had baker John Kerley there in 1834 but no further mention of anyone until sawyer Daniel Living arrived on the 1851 census. Then there is another gap until journeyman tailor Edward Ward is listed in 1859. He stayed for a couple of years before shoe makers, carters, labourers, a charwoman, seaman and a ships fireman all arrived and departed before 1914 when the Wells family moved in and remained until 1940.

1849 saw currier Benjamin Skeats at No. 23 but he soon died and his widow Sarah had gone after 1851. Street hawker George Scearff was briefly in residence before ships fireman Edward Creeden took over in 1865, followed by painter Edward Watkin who stroked his brushes from 1869 until 1874. Shipwright Lewis Welch held the keys from 1881 until 1891 and William David Wareham (1914–1925) and the Parker family

(1931–1940) were the final tenants. Mount Street was the place to go for a pair of shoes as yet another cordwainer was busy at No. 24 in 1851. This was James Holloway whose family remained there until 1891 with son William continuing the family skills. Huckster (or hawker) Margaret Scorey made a brief appearance before dock labourer William Wareham arrived in 1911 (see also the Warehams at No. 23). Frederick Brown lingered for a while there between 1914 and 1931 with Frederick Weeks being last of all from then until 1940.

No. 25 was quite exceptional in that its occupants tended to stay for longer terms than at many other houses in the street. Butcher Thomas Biggs was recorded there in 1841 through to 1871 with H. Biggs also a butcher there in 1874. There was then a period of labourers, coal porters, carmen and seamen until the threshold was graced with the seafaring Hyde family from 1907 until 1914. John George House was the final long stay tenant from 1925 until the end. Like the Biggs next door, No. 26 saw labourer William Woolford see out a long tenancy from 1851 through to 1865 and baker William Adams was there in the late 1860s until slater Henry Noyce (see him also in College Street) and his wife Elizabeth arrived in 1874. Elizabeth, a former cook, was a widow by 1881 but stayed on by her own means until the early 1900s. Ships fireman Matthew Conway was the next tenant from 1911 until 1916. Alfred Boyland came along in the 1920s, before George Wateridge became the final householder from the mid-1930s until 1940.

Bricklayer Henry Crook was at No. 27 from 1851 through to 1867 and he was followed by ships fireman Henry Fielder who remained until the mid-1870s. The later 1870s saw several labourers and seamen pass through, as did the 1880s and 1890s before coal porter George Mason was resident in the early 1900s. Mrs Wrixton donned her pinafore there from 1914 until the 1920s with Arthur Brown, William Arthur Stevens and finally John Commerford seeing out the remaining years until 1940. Town porter William Smith and his family made No. 28 their home from 1841 until around 1870. His wife Mary had become a widow by 1861 but she kept the home going until 1874. Poultry man Alfred Brackstone, general servant Eliza Rose and fish porter William Richards were all evident before 1900 and many more names were in the rent book before Robert McKenzie became the final tenant in 1939.

No. 29 has Samuel Simpson as 'Rates collector and assistant overseer of All Saints' as its occupant in 1834. He was still there in 1861 and by then was an accountant. Porter William Sanger had a slightly shorter stay from 1863 to 1874. Through the 1880s we find seaman's wife Angelina Faithful and labourer John Garner before Mrs Mary E. Brown runs the address as a lodging house from 1887 until 1901, when the Brackstone family moved in. Alfred (previously at No. 28 and later at No. 32) was a dock labourer at that time. He and his wife Phyllis had seven children but he died in 1906 with his widow running the house until she too passed away in 1912. Their son George (a fish bait dealer) and his wife continued the tenancy until 1940.

Waiter William Holloway was an early dweller at No. 30 in 1834. His tenure lasted until the late 1850s when butcher James Simkins arrived and stayed on until 1865. After he had vacated along came boot maker James Grandsen, seamen William Hallman and John Barry, boot maker Francis Rich, mariner Thomas J. Stace and labourer James Stace, all in quick succession before carver James Bickers arrived in 1887. Dock labourer William Bartlett held the keys from 1901 and all the way through until 1940.

Carpenter Robert Jordan was one of the street's earliest inhabitants when living at No. 31 in 1811. William Scammell was there later in 1834, followed by coach maker Austin White in 1841. The next named at that address were labourer Charles Southwell in 1851 and mariner William Aldridge who was resident from 1859 until 1863. Boiler maker David Gordon then had a long spell under its roof until 1874 saw Mary Williamson arrive. From 1881 until the early 1900s there was a high turnover of tenants until William Summers and his wife moved in around

1912 and the family stayed on until the last days of the street. Coachmen were still very much evident in 1811, one of them being Edward Frost who lived at No. 32 back then. Dressmaker Miss E. Jardine lived there in 1834 but no others appeared until shop man James Squibb showed up in 1851. Pipe maker Edward Harding followed on from 1859 until carpenter Edward (or Edwin) Barnes took root from 1863 until 1891. Next in line were coach porter Alex Arnold and general labourer Frank Harman before Alfred Brackstone made it one of his many abodes in 1907. The Brackstone family feature often in these pages and, as usual, they were soon gone and dock labourer Walter Bearry was in occupation from 1911 until around 1930 when Ernest Charles Clarke saw out the final decade.

Carpenter James Bampton was the occupant of No. 33 back in 1811 and between 1834 and 1836 the householder was John Goffe. An independent Hannah Goffe is in the 1841 census but, in the 1851 census, widow Sarah Goffe is named there. Painter Charles Parsons was settled there from 1859 until making way for butcher James Coffee a decade later. Labourer George Evans was next in 1874 ahead of butcher Samuel Rose who gained entry in 1881. Barman William Parker and seaman William Mallony also saw the inside of No. 33 before dock labourer Walter Wyeth was the inhabitant from 1907 until 1914 when Frederick Brackstone arrived from No. 4. However, he was gone by 1916 when Joseph Samuel began a long tenancy that lasted until 1940.

Waiter William Henning was so much at home in No. 34 he stayed there from 1834 until 1876 when butcher Samuel Rose dallied briefly before moving to No. 33. Fellow butcher James Masters was next though the front door from 1881 before corporation labourer Charles Perkins saw off the rest of the century there. 1901 found docks clerk Alfred Judd in occupation, then dock labourer Alexander Vine had a spell from 1907 to 1914. William James Cook stayed through World War One, eventually giving way to Walter Harry Bennett in 1920 to see out the street's remaining years. In its early years, No. 35 does not seem to have attracted many to stay within its walls apart from carpenter Thomas Sutton in 1841 and waterman Thomas Hardy some ten years later, before locksmith John Gordon found it desirable in 1859. Sawyer Job Williams was next to test its comforts in 1861 until 1863. Laundress Mrs Maria Hucker, mariner John May, butcher James Coffee and labourer Henry Oades (soon at No. 36) all seemed unimpressed through the 1860s. Whitesmith John Gordon and labourer Henry Hounsell gave it a try in the early 1870s until Henry Oades, by now a mariner, made a return in 1874 and spent a decade there. Fruiterer Charles Maunders, Benjamin Buckett, seaman Robert Corr and butcher James Bricknell all failed to find it homely, as did Mrs Perry, Mrs Mary Bannon, and Frederick Brown before Edwin Moody loitered there from 1914 until 1925 when Alexander Roberton found it equally to his liking and remained there until the end and was rehoused at No. 31 College Street.

Blacksmith Cornelius Morey and his wife were the early settlers at No. 36 from 1841 until china dealer John Tucker moved in some ten years later. No others appeared until dealer James Brown in 1855. Tailor Samuel Townley and Charles Pearce filled in from 1857 until butcher George Pearce arrived in 1863 and resided until 1871 when Henry Oades spent time between his spells at No. 35 and left in 1874. An assortment of characters then came and went, including mangler Ann Coe before dock labourer Thomas Roberton became householder in 1907 and his family were still there in 1940.

1841 was the year when shoe maker Samuel Warren was living at No. 37. Mariner Henry Bacon came later in 1851 and was master of his profession by the time he left in 1859 when cabinet maker Tom Hooper set up home there. Carpenter Robert Tasker was occupier from 1865 to 1869 when butcher George Pearce had a brief stay after leaving No. 36. Cook James Hart, labourer Edward Oliver and Charlotte Sealey lived there through the 1870s before Mrs Elizabeth Hayward ran it as a lodging house for much of the 1880s. John Cook was then resident through the 1890s and on to around 1930 when Bertie Mould became its last tenant.

Carpenter William Scorey and his family were under the roof of No. 38 from 1841. After his death in 1856 his widow Charlotte ran the household until she married Joseph Sealey in 1859 and moved to No. 39 in 1869. Charles Hardy was next at No. 38 until 1874 when coach wheeler Frank Sawyer and Mary Tucker saw out the remainder of 1870s. Stone mason George Morant was present in the new decade and dock labourer Joseph Harding followed on until the turn of the century, which welcomed William Summers and Emanuel Guillermin. Drapers head porter William Eades and his family were fixtures until the 1930s when Albert Brick completed the roll call.

The final house in Mount Street was No. 39 where rope maker William Campbell spent his days from 1841. He was still there in 1863 working as a labourer. Engine driver Robert Rickman succeeded him until 1869 when Joseph Sealey and his wife Charlotte came from next door at No. 38. Charlotte was once again a widow by 1871; working as a laundress and a shoe binder with her son Harry she survived until 1891 when Amey Pinkney held the keys. Frederick Noyce was the final householder from 1907 when he was a ships fireman but he had remained ashore as a chimney sweep until the final days of the street in the 1940 wartime bombings.

MOUNT COURT
Nos. 1–3

Mount Court, also known as Mount Place, contained a group of three houses in a narrow court entered from the south side of Mount Street. It was just three feet wide and the 1893 slum report states that two of the homes were unhealthy, dilapidated, damp and dirty, and were without though ventilation. Water was from a common tap in the yard. There was no ash bin provided but there were two outside sanitary conveniences. Two adjacent houses were also said to be equally bad. Nevertheless, the court survived until demolition came in 1935. Mount

Court does not appear on the 1846 map but it is shown in 1870 as three houses behind No. 21 Mount Street. Sometimes No. 21 Mount Street was regarded as part of the court but for our purposes we shall disregard No. 21, which has been visited earlier.

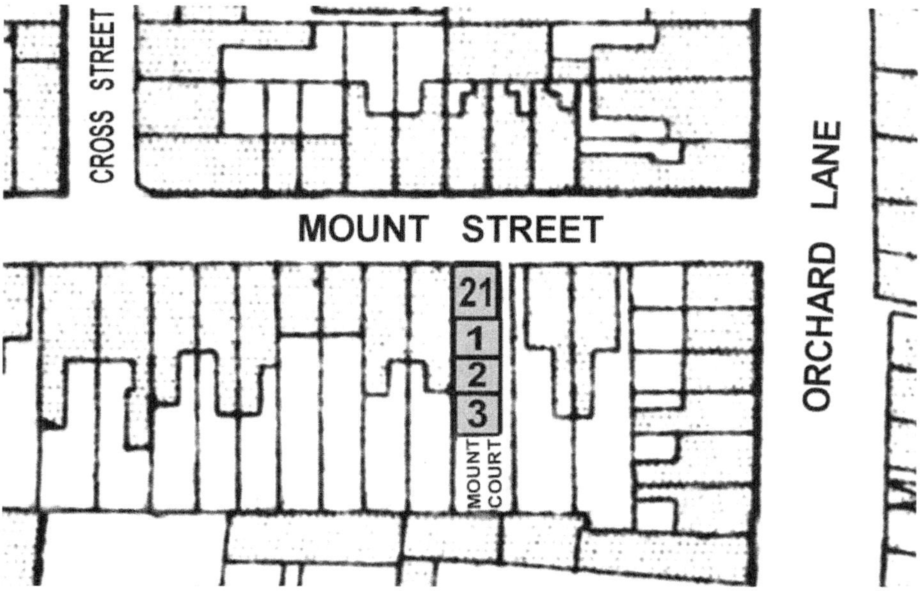

The three houses of Mount Court behind No. 21 Mount Street which, sometimes was included as part of the court

Residents of the court did not appear until the 1861 census when No. 1 was the home of shoe maker James Sloat. Seamstress Ann Fursey was at No. 2 with labourer John Hicks at No. 3. Ann Fursey was still there in the 1869 directory when listed as the only inhabitant but all three homes were occupied in the 1871 census with carpenter and joiner George Grist at No. 1, Ann Fursey at No. 2 and labourer James Foster bringing up the rear in No. 3. By 1884 there was just labourer Henry Watts at No. 2 with George Bartlett at No. 3. From 1911 only No. 2 was occupied by seaman Thomas Horton who was followed by William John Hills (from 1914 until 1921) with William Woodcock being the final name in the rent book in 1935.

A child stands at the foreboding entrance to Mount Court with No. 21 Mount Street on the right

CROSS STREET
Hawkins Court, Nelson's Place, Barry's Court and Cross Court

Cross Street ran north to south between Bell Street and Mount Street – not to be confused with another of the same name in Kingsland, or the earlier name for Lime Street. Although it was the smallest in the neighbourhood, it was possibly the most congested as it had no less than four courts leading off its short length, namely Hawkins Court, Nelson's Place and Barry's Court on the east side with Cross Court opposite. There was one other by the name of Lanham's Court (or Passage) that may have been a previous name for Hawkins Court.

There were just seven buildings listed in Cross Street, Nos. 1 to 5 on the north side with Nos. 6 and 7 opposite. There was also a No. 4½ at times. Nos. 2 and 3 at the entrance to Hawkins Court became a firewood store run by Thomas Smith from the early 1900s.

CROSS STREET
Nos. 1–7

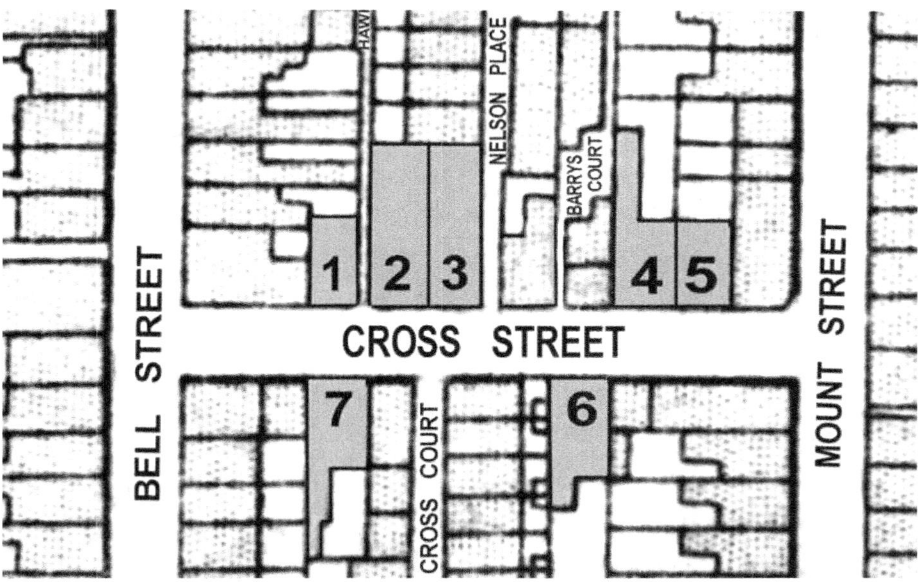

The eight buildings of Cross Street with the courts leading off on either side

Entering Cross Street from Bell Street we come to No. 1, which in 1834 was occupied by John Phillips who was listed as a beer retailer but by 1841 he is shown as a dairyman, a trade he continued until his retirement around 1861. Dock labourer Richard Fox, bricklayer John Butler and blacksmiths assistant Samuel Williams all followed through the next two decades. No. 1 then disappeared from the directories after 1881. No. 2 doesn't show until 1857 when mariner Henry White turns up but Charles Syms and then coach Smith George Sturt were there by 1861. After a couple more mariners we find clay pipe maker Edward Beadley in 1871 followed by fellow pipe maker Joseph Cleaver who set up his factory there which lasted until 1887. Labourer William Gonebeed was the last listed at that address in 1891. Boot and shoe maker John Webb was cobbling at No. 3 in 1857 for a couple of years when next we find a painter, cooper, labourer, and a boot maker before stone mason Robert Randall takes up his chisel there in the early 1880 before Samuel Lomax is the last name there in 1887. It would then appear that Nos. 1 to 3 had all gone by the early 1900s when Thomas Smith set up a firewood business on the site of Nos. 2 and 3 that lasted until 1920. Coal dealer George Gauntlett occupied the site in 1935 and the last entry was for general dealer James Sherry in 1939/40.

In 1853 we have John Petty at No. 4 who divided his time between shoe making and his duties as a sexton. He gave way to tailor Albert Rastick in 1861 and there followed a succession of seamen, a naval pensioner and several labouring types with Frederick George Noyce being the final occupant from 1925 until 1935. In 1857 a No. 4½ appears with the name of porter William Chantry living there and I can only assume this was part of No. 4, perhaps a building at the rear? Anyhow, it continued to be listed right through until the street came down with later tenants including boot maker William Titcombe (in 1861), ships fireman Thomas Smalls (1874), Charles and Mary Ann Orr (1911–1920) and lastly Mrs Winkworth from 1925.

Cabinet maker John Bounds was in No. 5 in 1849 but from 1853 we have yet another boot maker, William Herapath, who resided until 1857. Then, by 1867, fellow cobbler William Titcombe had moved in from No. 4½, remaining there until labourer James Brown arrived in 1871. A decade later, boiler maker Edward Such stayed briefly before the now familiar turnover of occupants included ice cream vendor Petro Venachia in 1901 and the final entry was Martin Devereux from 1920 until 1931. Curiously, a No. 5½ appears in 1914, as home to Mrs Jackson, and later to John Sparks from 1916 until 1920 but was never seen again afterwards.

On the west side of the street we have Nos. 6 and 7, either side of Cross Court. Boatman James Paskins had sailed into No. 6 by 1849 and had a prolonged anchorage through to 1891. He died in 1896 aged 85 while his widow Sarah stayed on until 1901. Haberdasher Simon Canter held the keys around 1911/12. The Hiscock family were there from 1914 until the early 1930s, although their name had mysteriously changed to Hancock by then. Early days at No. 7 saw coal dealer and shopkeeper Samuel Fry evident from 1853 until 1857 before John and Betsy Hyman moved in from 1859. John was a ships fireman while Betsy supplemented their income by dressmaking. By 1901 she was a widow but continued her skills as a seamstress until around 1920. Thomas Arthur Holden was then at No. 7 for the final decade before demolition came.

The west side of Cross Street with a group of people at the entrance to Cross Court

CROSS STREET COURTS

As previously mentioned, residents of the courts were often excluded from the various street directories. However, most of the courts and their inhabitants are identified in the various census returns so we do have an idea of the persons living there. The 1841 census is of little help as it lists the entire population of all the courts under Cross Street.

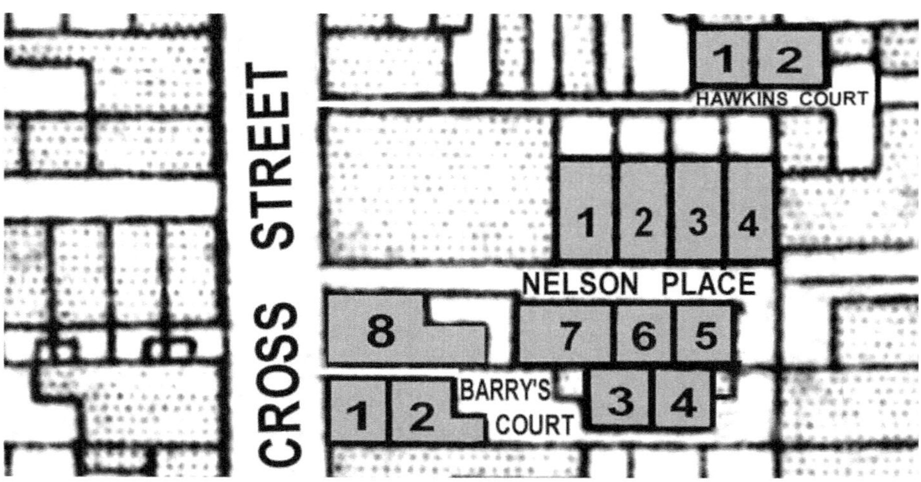

The courts leading off from the east side of Cross Street showing Hawkins Court, Nelson's Place and Barry's Court

HAWKINS COURT
Nos. 1 and 2

This was just two houses tucked away at the end of a long narrow passage on the east side of Cross Street, the court itself being just over three feet wide and the locality being described as being in an unsatisfactory state in the 1893 slum report. No mention of its residents is forthcoming in the street directories but the census returns give us a brief insight to those who lived there. The 1851 census does not list Hawkins Court but does include two houses as Lanham's Passage off Cross Street with inhabitants named as Isabella Brimmer, a mariner's wife, along with Aaron Willis on parish relief.

The earliest names I have found under Hawkins Court are labourer Henry Payne at No. 1 and laundress Elizabeth Cook at No. 2. Respectively, in 1881 we have housekeeper Mary Ann Dowell with mariner James Stone. In 1891 we see dock labourer William Dickson and shoe maker William Painter, then in 1901 we find William Dickson is still there with iron founders labourer John Watts. The final entry in 1911 has costermonger Frederick Street and charwoman Kate Farmer.

NELSON'S PLACE
Nos. 1–8

Standing between Hawkins Court and Barry's Court, Nelson's Place (otherwise Nelson Court) was off the east side of Cross Street and contained eight houses, although the 1893 slum report says there were seven. The difference is probably due to No. 8 being counted as Cross Street. Nos. 1 to 4 on the north side had small back yards but Nos. 5 and 6 opposite were back to back with buildings in the adjacent Barry's Court so had no through ventilation. No. 8 fronted Cross Street and all were said to be dark and unhealthy.

Once again we are mainly reliant on the census returns with 1861 showing master boot maker John T. Petty at No. 1. In 1871 we have labourer John Flack, then in 1874 a surprise entry in the directory finds ships fireman John McLean there until at least 1881. Labourer John Chaffe appears in the 1884 directory followed by seaman Mark Bulford (in 1891), labourer John Wyatt (1901) and carter Walter Blackman in 1911. It seems that from 1925 those who compiled the directories suddenly discovered people living there and listed them over the final decade with William Henry Platt observed from 1925 until 1935.

Bricklayer Thomas Bartlett lived at No. 2 in 1861, coal trimmer John Campbell was there from 1871 until 1884, then came labourer William Burnett, laundress Annie Atkins and dock labourer Richard Gandy before the final decade of the street found Mrs Brown, Mrs Hyslop and finally David Parish. No. 3 was home to corn merchants labourer James S. Raymond in 1861. Various mariners occupied the house between 1871 and 1884, the others being labourers, including George Prince (from 1874–1884) until Mrs M. McConnell was last through the door in 1935. More labourers were to be found at No. 4 until hawker Mary Kirby arrived in 1911 and her family was there to the very end.

Mrs Ann Jordan Roach and her two young children were in No. 5 according to the 1861 census but there is no indication of what she did to provide for them. In 1874 dressmaker Ann Fursey was resident, having previously lived at No. 2 Mount Place. Pipe maker John Cleever (of various nearby abodes) spent a few years there before 1891 saw pauper Caroline Weeks under its roof before coal porter William Aisworth (in 1901) then ships painter William Englefield (1911) made way for the final tenants, the last being William Henry Dominy Titcombe in 1931. No. 6 was home to labourer George Prince in 1871 before he moved to No. 4 but it was the domain of women from 1881 until 1901 with charwoman Ann Clark, Mrs Green, another charwoman Sarah Denham and Alice Tucker keeping order until dealer William Thomas arrived in 1911, then Frederick Penny was the last in the 1930s.

Seaman John Lund was ashore at No. 7 in 1871 and from then on came another host of ladies including housekeeper Ellen Sullivan, Mrs McLear, then Ellen Tizard in 1891. Coal porter Frederick Ainsworth, and labourer Frederick Brackstone crossed its doorstep in the early 1900s before Frederick Street saw out the final decade there. The inmates of No. 8 began with labourer Alfred Tolfree in 1871 with several other unskilled individuals until fish hawker Charles Cavell and his wife Harriett landed there in 1911. Trade must have been good as they were there through to 1935.

Nelson's Place with Nos. 1–4 on the left and 5–8 on the right

BARRY'S COURT
Nos. 1-4

Barry's Court (or Berry's Court in some early census returns) was one of three courts leading off the east side of Cross Street. It contained just four houses, two of which backed on to others in Nelson Place, so neither had any through ventilation, Only the two backing on to Nelson Place were noted in the 1893 report and they were described as damp, dark and unhealthy with flooring below pavement level, while the water supply, ash pit and convenience was outside in the yard.

Like many of its kind, Barry's Court, or at least its occupants, did not figure in the earlier street directories, with the only references to it being off Cross Street. The 1851 census names two houses as Pipe Makers Court together with one more being Berry's Court; perhaps they were all one of the same at a later date. Pipe Makers Court lists shoe binder Rebecca Barton along with mariner John Tilbury, while Sarah Evans is on parish relief at Berry's Court. The census returns are more forthcoming with entries from 1861 through to 1911. It was not until the 1925 directory that the occupant's names appeared, with 1935 being their final entry.

No. 1 faced on to Cross Street and dock porter James Hatch was an early dweller there in 1861 then, a decade later, we find laundress Sarah Garnett followed by Sarah Rice in 1874, this being the first entry I have found in the directories. Labourer George Bartlett appears in the 1881 census when the location is noted as Berry's Court and perhaps by coincidence Mrs C. Berry was running a general shop there in 1884. Could she have been there earlier and perhaps that's how the court got its name? Later census returns show pipe maker Samuel Lomax in 1891, railway porter John Sparks in 1911, while the later directories show John Fowler in 1925 and 1931 with Leonard Parker as the final tenant in 1935.

Mariner Henry Ford (perhaps not the motor tycoon) was an early name at No. 2 with plasterer Charles Tucker and his wife shown from 1871 and 1874. No. 2 was part of Mrs Berry's shop in 1884, while laundress Harriet Foley was there in 1891 and fish dealer William King held the keys from 1901 until 1911. No. 3 housed upholsterer Caroline Hatcher in 1861 before stoker Thomas Small in 1871, then cooper John Anderson in 1874, and pattern maker Charles Gilbert in 1884. There were no further names until the 1911 census listed ships fireman John Henry Jackobson. Ships painter Thomas Smith made use of No. 4 in 1861 while plumber John Barton was shown there a decade later. Another painter named John Bartlett was the occupant in 1874 with others being coal porter John Hack in 1881 and labourer Samuel Green in 1884. The final tenant I found in 1911 was Charles James Rigular, a tramways worker.

CROSS COURT
Nos. 1–12

Cross Court was a blind and narrow court leading off the west side of Cross Street, consisting of 12 houses with eight on the south side, each with a small yard, facing four more on the opposite side that had no through ventilation. The 1851 census lists only the first eight houses so we must assume the other four were built later. In most of the houses the small ground floor rooms were below pavement level and had low ceilings, not more than seven feet high. The back bedrooms of the southern eight houses were less than six feet high with none having fireplaces to ward off the damp. The gutters were made of wood and found to be defective. All conveniences were outside in the yard and the houses were considered to be unhealthy tenements.

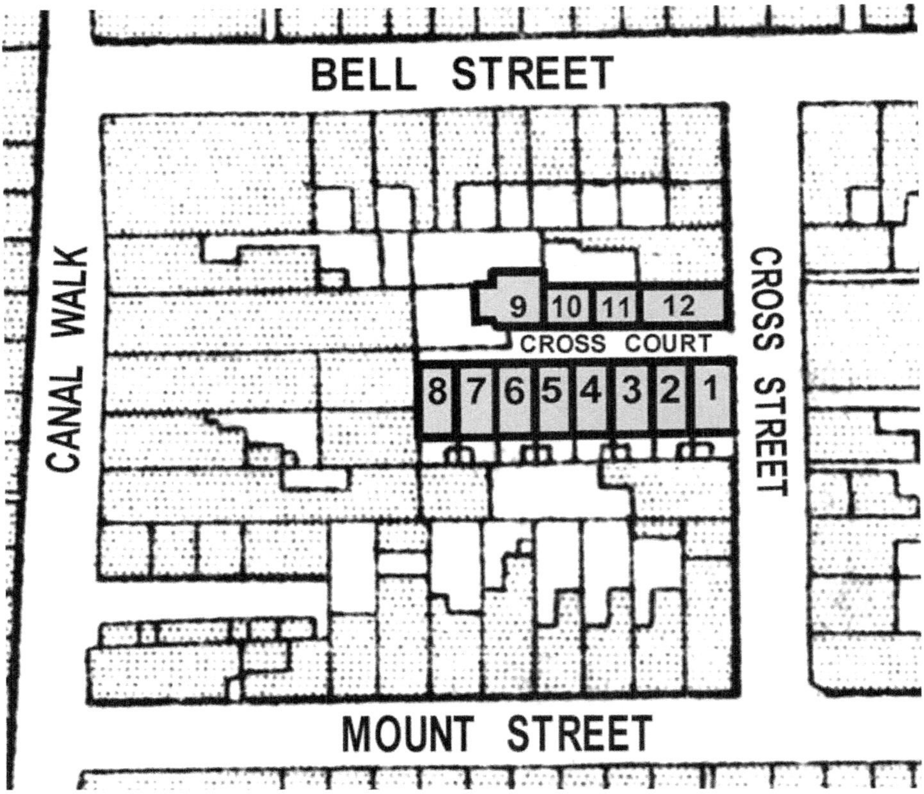

The 12 houses of Cross Court on the west side of Cross Street

No. 1 on the corner of Cross Street had porter Samuel Fry living there in 1851, ten years later we find baker William Adams, then several labourers through the years until railway shunter William J. Cook was there in 1901. Georgina and John Thomas Cook were evident in 1911 and 1914, while Alfred Hussey and his wife saw out the final decade until 1935. The first name in the rent book at No. 2 was labourer James Ward. Lucy Hawkins appeared in 1861 followed by ships fireman Stephen Morgan and his wife Susan in the early 1870s. Milkman Isaac Joyce stayed briefly around 1881 before dock labourer James Pace and his family spent many years under its roof from 1884 until 1920. Labourers were the early renters at No. 3 from 1851, the majority of others being seamen, with the exception of pipe maker Edward Edgar in 1881 and rag picker Mary Ann Alexander in 1911. Mrs Martin ran the house from 1914 until 1925 and Joseph Stafford was the last one recorded in 1935.

House servant Lucy Hawkins was present at No. 4 in 1851, then we have the usual mixture of labourers and seamen before bricklayer Harry Musslewhite arrived in 1881. James Edgar (son of Edward at No. 3) carried on the family pipe making there through most of the 1880s. Butcher Henry G. Gosney and his wife lived there through the 1890s then stableman Henry Ernest Stafford (previously at No. 8) saw out the remainder of the court's existence from 1911 until 1935. No. 5 had no occupant in the 1851 census but then saw a few seamen sail through in the 1860s and 1870s until mangler Mrs A. Sheepwash appeared in 1881. Those that followed included butcher Richard Chaffe, harness maker Harry Cleever and finally dock labourer George James Turner from 1911 until the final days. Occupation of No. 6 began with carpenter James Henry Weldon in 1851, labourer James Clark (previously at No. 8) was present in the 1870s, while seamstress Eliza J. Sutton was sewing there in 1881. Carpenter Charles Smith and his wife Matilda had moved in by 1887 but Matilda was a widow by 1911. She stayed on until 1925 and the last recorded tenant was Mrs Boyd in 1931.

At No. 7, cordwainer James Dacombe was making his boots through the 1850s and 1860s before more mariners and labourers took root through the 1870s and 1880s. One-time sailor, and later stevedore, Charles Henry Henderson (or Anderson) made his home there from 1891 then stayed all the way through until 1935. Last of the southern terrace was No. 8 where Elizabeth Hill was a customs officer's wife in 1851. Ships stoker John Whicher and plumber Charles Binstead had come and gone through the 1870s before pipe maker Henry W. Reed briefly held the keys in 1881. After him we have ships fireman George Harvey, coal runner and porter Joseph Smith and domestic groom Harry Stafford through the 1880s until the turn of the century. Dock labourer William Mann and his wife were in situ from 1911 until 1925 with Mrs Chapman seeing out the final years through the 1930s.

Moving on now to the four houses on the north side of the court that were built later than those opposite. There we have something of a mixture beginning with labourer John H. Purse at No. 9 in 1871, with shoe maker James House in the 1880s before labourer Charles Henry Brown had made it his home from 1911 until the court's days were numbered in 1935. Some names turn up at several addresses over the years. One of these is labourer John Hicks who like so many others, moved around from street to street. He was at No. 10 through the 1870s before others of his ilk passed through the door until charwoman Sophia Oliver arrived with her mop in 1891 but she was gone by the time shoe maker Joseph Kerslake appeared in 1901. Frederick Braxton bided his time there from 1916 until the 1930s when Mrs Bailes was the last name in the rent book in 1935.

At No. 11 Helen Smith's husband was away from home in 1871. The census doesn't tell us more but I would assume he was a seaman. The house then seems empty through the 1880s (at least no names appear) until charwoman Eliza Priest turns up in 1891. Through the early 1900s there were several seamen at the address before Frederick Charles Carter moved from No. 11 in 1914 with Charles Osman taking over in the 1930s. The last house in the court finds us back at Cross Street where No. 12 was the roof over yet another shoe maker, this time Isaac New in 1871. We've come across a group of charwomen earlier and now we find another two. Helen Stroud in 1874 and Georgina E. Stewart in the 1880s. House painter William A. Wheeler in 1891, then shipyard labourer William Hebb in 1901, gave way to dock labourer Anthony Marlow who was, in every sense, the last tenant in the court from 1911 until 1935.

The confines of Cross Court with most windows open to increase ventilation of the damp homes. Nos. 1–8 are on the left with Nos. 9–12 opposite

UNION STREET
Deacon's Court, Union Cut and Union Place

Union Street ran west to east between Canal Walk and Orchard Lane. Houses on the north side were not enhanced by the presence of a slaughterhouse, stables and a fish warehouse directly behind them.

The only photo of the street I have found so far features the *Builders Arms* pub which was probably the last building standing in the 1950s after the rest of the street had been demolished. The earliest records of this street date back to the directories of the 1830s and, most unhelpfully, the numbering system (where it existed) went in the opposite direction until changed in the 1860s.

UNION STREET
North Side, Nos. 1–12

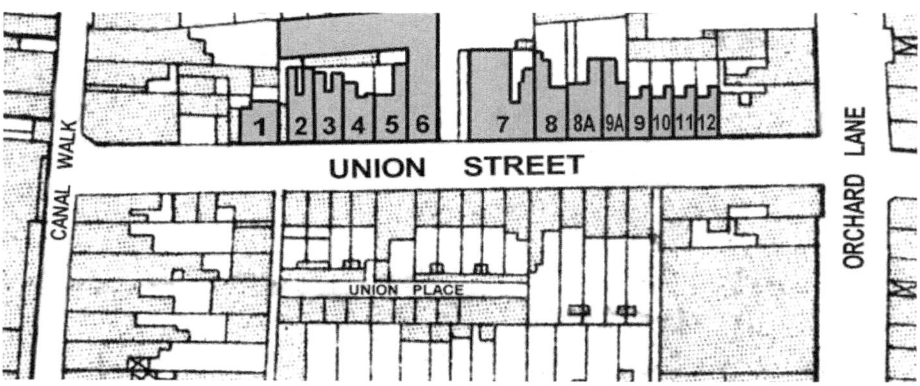

Nos. 1–12 on the north side of Union Street where the rear of No. 6 was a slaughterhouse, No. 7 was the Builders Arms pub and Nos. 8A and 9A were built on the site of Deacons Court

The 1834 directory shows a sparsely populated street with only a dozen or so inhabitants, in mostly unnumbered premises; these include baker John Borrett, beer retailer William Wills, carpenters George Pope and Thomas Young, tailor William Biles, shopkeeper Mrs James and an anonymous William Howell. Where numbers do exist it has been possible to locate them on the latter-day plan but I am never overconfident of the accuracy of some older records. Happily, some numbers were applied from 1843 so we can start to build a picture of who was where.

Coal dealer William Mills was at No. 1 in 1851 and his family remained there until the 1890s. At various times William described himself as a town porter or carrier and his son George carried on in the family tradition, along with his wife Maria who was a milliner. Not long after the Mills family had departed, dock labourer Henry Sheath and his brood arrived in the early 1900s and stayed until the mid-1930s when the Brackstones turned up. They were there until the late 1940s with Francis Hendry being the last name in 1954 when the street came down. No. 2 saw the arrival of sailor George Carne and his family in 1851. His wife Sarah was still there in the mid-1860s when barman Henry Browning came to stay until the latter 1870s. Butcher Harry Hurst was next in line and after he left in around 1890 there followed a couple of short tenancies until stevedores labourer Henry Yaldren embarked on a long stint there that lasted from the early 1900s until the late 1930s when Samuel Peacock moved in and remained until the end in 1954.

Mrs Rawlins ran a lodging house at No. 3 in 1834. Compositor George Hucker and his wife were there through much of the 1850s before cordwainer Joseph Webb set up his boot making business, which ran incredibly from 1861 until 1907. Richard Northover also did quite well to stay there from 1914 until 1939 with Thomas Albert Goodwin seeing out the final years from 1940. Henry Froud, yet another of the neighbourhood shoe makers, had set up shop at No. 4 in 1834. Seaman's wife Mary Ann Dinnick was noted there in 1851 before letter carrier Walter Cole and his family dwelled there from 1859 through to 1867. Then followed an assortment of tailors, labourers and a butcher before Herbert Payne came on the scene in 1907. He was, apparently, a hose repairer, which I assume was the stocking type rather than the garden variety. He and his family continued their time there until 1940 and Jack

Williams saw out the postwar years until 1954.

No. 5 was another early starter with stagecoach man William Phillips resting his heels there in 1834. Greengrocer George Musslewhite (in 1843), engine driver George Derrick (1851) and carpenter William Hayter (1857) all followed before ships fireman Hector Leybourn came ashore in 1861 and stayed for a decade. The Millard family were at No. 5 from 1911 until 1939 but widow Fanny soon moved to No. 24 where she ran a shop. The postwar years saw Reginald Cox as the final tenant. Customs officer George Green spent most of the 1840s at No. 6 where those that followed were the usual assortment of seamen and labourers. From around 1887 it must have been an unpleasant place to live as a slaughterhouse was built at the rear. Nevertheless others made their home there including butcher Frank Macey in 1891 and railway carman James Bennett through the 1890s then seaman Edward Fitzroy Petrony endured the surroundings from 1907 until 1914. The slaughterhouse, run by Edward Brown, remained until the 1930s by which time Mrs White was on the premises and Charles Witt was the final occupant when that part of the street (Nos. 6–12) disappeared in 1954.

Although its surroundings vanished in wartime, No. 7, the *Builders Arms*, survived into the 1950s when the remainder of the street was demolished. A number of brewers and beer retailers are listed in the early directories and they were possibly the forerunners of the pub. They included William Wills in 1834, James Hannen in 1843, Timothy Henry Egan in 1847, then James Gullicker in 1851. By 1855 it was operating as the *Union Brewery* run by John Snook and two years later it had taken the name of the *Builders Arms* with Charles Lane as innkeeper. Charles Brown ran the establishment from 1863 until 1871 with several changes of licensee thereafter including George H. Weeks (1911–1925) and ending with Mrs M. McVickers in the postwar years.

William Judd and cabinet maker Samuel Higson were sharing No. 8 in the late 1840s and early 1850s. Seaman George Wilson and his wife Mary

Ann moved in during the later 1850s but were gone by 1867 when labourer Henry King arrived and stayed on until the 1880s. Porter Henry Laney saw out the later years of the century there after which came plasterer Thomas Binstead and ships fireman Frederick Ernest Mintram who held the keys from 1911 until 1916. William George Barter saw out the final years of the house from 1931 until 1940. He was accompanied in those latter years by shellfish dealer Norman Cooper.

The Builders Arms at No. 7 was one of the last remnants of Union Street when it was demolished in the mid-1950s (Late David Goddard collection)

Nos. 8A and 9A were built in the 1890s on the site of Deacons Court and 8A was immediately occupied by fishmonger Charles W. Betteridge. Coal porter Charles Brand had taken over by 1907, remaining until 1912 when dock labourer Josiah Thomas Wilson moved from No. 14 and took root there until 1940. First in at No. 9A was ships foreman George Smoker and he was followed by James White and his wife Annie Maria in 1907 before Henry Sims embarked on a long tenure from 1912 until 1935 when Alfred Henry Wigger became the last inhabitant.

Back to the older properties and we find railway porter Henry Oliver and his wife Elinor as early residents at No. 9 in the late 1850s. Ships fireman Thomas strong was there from 1867 until 1871, giving way to stone sawyer George Maurant, then dock labourer Edward McCarthy dwelled through the 1880s before he moved next door to No. 10. A couple of tenants later, butcher John Gray and his family moved in around 1907 and remained until 1925 with William Carpenter and his family being last named in the rent book from 1931 until 1940. No. 10 was occupied way back in 1834 by master mariner John Riddett. Sailor George Cooper was there through the 1850s and 1860s when 1867 saw the arrival of ships painter William Caines who stayed until the turn of the century when Edward McCarthy moved from No. 9. Peter Brixey was last of the line there from 1931 until 1939.

The Hiscock family lived at No. 11 from 1851 with ships stoker David, wife Elizabeth and son Henry. At that time Henry was a railway porter but a decade later was following his father's footsteps. Their time there ended in 1871 when baker Theophilius Clark spent some time there in the 1870s and the next tenant to hang about for any length was baggage carrier Edward Rofe who stayed the course from 1907 until 1920. William Lines was there from 1939 until the end came in 1940.

The final property on that side of the street was No. 12, the home of butcher Henry Robinson who appeared in 1851 and lingered until 1863. Quartermaster John Culbert was next to grace its doorstep between 1865 and 1871 and there followed a succession of labourers, a butcher's assistant, a carriage painter and bill poster John Webb in 1911 before James Scorey made it his long term home in 1914 though to 1940.

UNION STREET
South Side, Nos. 13–31

Turning back from Orchard Lane we now visit the south side of Union Street, which was numbered 13 to 31 where most of the properties survived until demolition in the mid-1950s.

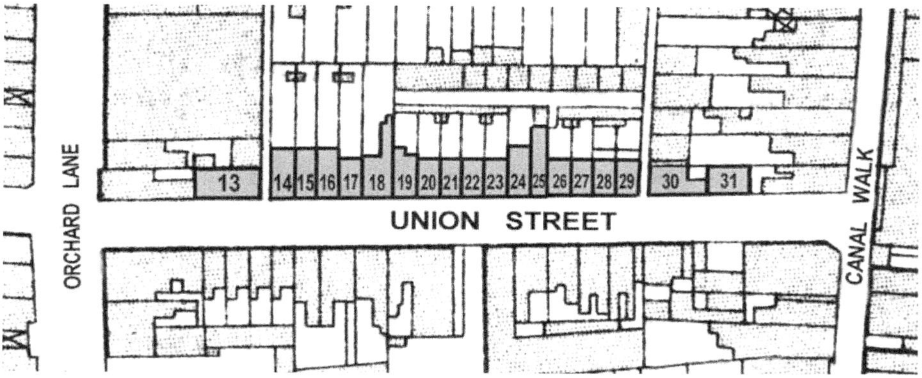

The south side of Union Street showing Nos. 13 to 31. No.13 was once a workshop and then a skittle alley

No. 13 was something of a mystery with only a few names listed there such as Mrs Camfield in 1867 and George Wilkes in 1869 and 1871. Further investigation revealed that No.13 was in fact a building at the rear of No. 50 Orchard Lane from where Mrs Maria Camfield ran her furniture and undertaker business, and George Wilkes was mine host of the *Harlequin Inn*. In 1881 it was shown as a workshop and in 1884 it was *Frazers Skittle Alley*, no doubt attached to the *Harlequin*, which closed in 1900. The only other listing of No. 13 shows coal porter Thomas Payne and his wife Alice Rosina living there in what I assume was still an outbuilding.

William Camfield (husband of Maria) was shown as a turner living at No. 14 from the early 1840s until 1855 when they moved to No. 50 Orchard Lane. The Cole family then resided at No. 14 from 1859 until 1867. Fish dealer James Dacey held the keys for a decade from 1881. Josiah Thomas Wilson (see also Nos. 8A and 22) turned up in 1911 to 1912, and then came Edward Hickman in 1914 to 1925. George Young settled there from 1935 until 1948 and Mrs Coe was the final resident in 1954.

Shoe maker John Tanner was an early inmate at No. 15 through the 1840s, then we find builder William Cosens there from 1849 to 1851. At this point I have a personal interest as Henry Crocker and his family were living there in 1857 and I recently found I am distantly related to them. Please allow me to indulge in a potted history of the Crockers. They came from Portsea where Henry served in the Royal Navy and married a young widow Eliza. Having retired on a pension in 1847, Henry moved to Southampton where he spent the remainder of his life until his death aged 79 in poverty at St Georges Street in nearby Houndwell in 1869. By 1871, Eliza was living at No. 6 Mount Street, and ten years later at No. 11 Bell Street before her death in 1886 at the workhouse in St Mary Street.

David William Crocker was the son of Henry Crocker. He had followed his father into the navy and moved to Southampton with his parents. He married a local girl, Annie Maria Andrews, at St James Church, Bernard Street, in 1866. At that time, Annie already had an illegitimate daughter, Emily, born in 1862. Initially they lived at No. 15 Union Street with David's parents, but by 1871 they were at No. 36 Mount Street. Tragedy struck in 1878 when David died at sea aboard HMS *German* due to heart disease aged 34. By that time, the family had moved to Lower Canal Walk.

By 1881 his widow Annie, who had been working as a laundress, was living at No. 1 Bridge Place, Holy Rood, with her children, and a decade later they were at No. 36 Chantry Road. She was there a decade later listed as a charwoman. By 1911 she was in one room at No. 13 Paget Street but by 1930 she had returned to Holy Rood, living at No. 13 King Street. In March that year she died in the Poor House at No. 1 Botley Road, West End, aged 84. Her daughter Emily had a given birth to a daughter, Edith, at the Southampton Workhouse in 1881 and they were living at Back of the Walls with Emily working as a shop girl before her marriage to George Stride in 1883 at Holy Trinity Church, Kingsland (see Edith at Orchard Lane). The name of Emily's father was missing from her birth certificate but upon her marriage he was named as Henry Voller, a merchant seaman from Portsmouth, then living at Northam.

The 1851 census found working jeweller John Jenn at No. 16, a place where he lived until 1867. Mariner James Wadman dropped anchor there from 1869 until 1876 and then fellow mariner Richard Rickman sailed through its doorway during the 1880s. Dock labourer Albert Edward Harding moved in from 1901 until 1912 before William Trueick arrived in 1916 and stayed until the very end in the 1950s. French polisher George Clench was applying his shellac at No. 17 back in 1843 but he was gone by 1851 when widow Mrs Charlotte Hardy and her four children made it their home until 1859. Painter James Scott Harris dipped his brush there through the 1860s before an assortment of labourers came and went from then until the early 1900s. It was 1912 when Leonard Henry Blake decided to stay until the mid-1930s and Harold Pierce was the last named occupant in 1954.

The Tanner family featured regularly in the neighbourhood during the early years. Shoe maker John Tanner had been previously at No. 15 and had moved to No. 18 by 1849. Carpenter Joseph Tanner then was head of the house through the 1850s before a transfer to No. 22. Tailor Samuel Townley was next over the threshold of No. 18 from 1855 until 1865. Barman Alfred Scorey (a member of the brewing family at College Street) found himself there in the latter 1860s before the accustomed procession of labourers from the 1870s until the early 1900s ended with the arrival of coal porter Frederick Mitchell in 1907. The Mitchell family remained in place until 1935 and they were followed by the Thompsons through the 1940s with George Appleton being the final inhabitant in 1954.

Carpenter George Pope was one of the earliest inhabitants of Union Street, appearing at No. 19 in the 1834 directory. However, nobody further is recorded there until Alice Holman in the 1851 census and then came Mrs Jane Dalton and her daughter Mary in 1853. They were dress makers and milliners around 1860 and Jane remained at No. 19 until 1867. Porter Albert Geapen stayed there from 1869 until 1871, followed by butcher Joseph Coombs, and picture frame maker Charles Bisphy before stevedore Charles Joseph Fiford dwelled from 1901 to 1916. By 1920, Albert Edward Wilkins had graced the doormat through to 1935 and Mrs MacDermott saw out the rest of the 1930s with Mrs Biles being the last householder.

John Isaac was a jeweller and spectacle maker at No. 20 from 1843 until 1853. After he had moved on, Mrs Harriet Sheppard took in washing and ironing there until 1865. Richard Waterhouse and Joseph Coombs were butchers together there in 1871 before the later appearances of LSWR ticket examiner John J. Webb, tram driver William Hudson, plasterer George Green, shipyard labourer Herbert Payne, and blacksmiths striker Edward Dollery through to 1911. The front door keys changed hands six more times before they were held by Charles William Ainsworth in 1954.

Tailor William Biles has surfaced several times in these pages and on this occasion he was at No. 21 in 1834. Somehow, No. 21 didn't seem a very popular home. Cabinet maker George Hewitt appeared in the 1850s, before we find a host of short-stay residents through the 1850s and 1860s including mariner Thomas Gray, bakers labourer George Chaffield, painter Hamlet Strong, storekeeper James Fugett then, into the 1870s, we find butcher Richard Waterhouse and mariner Joseph Mills. The 1880s reveal nurse Sarah Webb and shoe maker George Stokes, before some stability arrives with corporation carter Henry Blake who stayed from 1907 to 1920. The final years saw Arthur Thomas Parkhurst, Alfred Rustall, William Trueick jnr, Roy Wells and finally William Instance.

Tailor William Courtney heads the list of occupants at No. 22, although this house seems a little more popular than its next-door neighbour. Both carpenters, Thomas Tanner and his son Joseph stayed on for ten years from 1857. Soldier W. Harwood and his wife saw out the 1870s under its roof before we have another mixed bag of people including carpenter Elisha Warren, watchman George Smith and dock labourer Josiah

Thomas Wilson taking us into the new century. The 1911 census records George Lock who was a scene shifter at the Grand Theatre before Mrs Herd, William Dans and Mrs Crawford resided through the 1920s and on to 1940. The final incumbent in 1954 was William Trueick jnr who had previously lived at No. 21.

Tinplate worker George Elcock spent a decade at No. 23 from 1843 before mariner Thomas Strong dallied in the late 1850s ahead of moving to No. 9. Fellow sailor Samuel Hooper was there in the early 1860s before letter carrier James Grandson saw five years pass there in the 1870s. From then on there was another huge turnover with general dealer John J. Webb in 1881 heading a long list of fleeting names before the Rogers family arrived in 1920 and remained until 1940. Mrs Harris was there in the postwar years and Percy George Willcox was the last of a long line in 1954.

No. 24 was a shop for much of its time with Mrs James running it in 1834 but not many others are noted apart from shoe maker Henry Froud (previously at No. 4) in 1851, until we find tailor John W. Phillemore in 1863 and staying on until 1871. In 1874 it was a greengrocers under Henry Lock before general dealer Elizabeth Jerram arrived in 1876. Francis Parker ran his shop there in 1887 and it became a sweet shop under James Fox in 1907. Benjamin and Fanny Millard were next behind its counter from 1912 until 1925. The 1930s saw Edward Nicholas and Bertie Williams, who was the final tenant in 1940 while selling fishing bait there. Sawyer Henry Veal occupied No. 25 in 1851, then it became a shop under Sarah James who survived until plumber and painter George H. Payne moved in around 1857 and ran the place until 1871. Widow Elizabeth Jerram, who ran her shop next door at No. 24, took over and ran both premises around 1881 and from then on they were treated as one.

At No. 26 tailor Frederick Dowling was one of a handful of residents back in 1834 with pilot Joseph Oliver arriving in 1851 and porter Henry

Philpot living there briefly in 1853. Painter Herbert Martin had moved in by 1855 and stayed on until 1869 when master mariner Edward Jerram came ashore. He was the husband of Elizabeth who later ran the shop at Nos. 24 and 25. After Edward's death the house was home to fellow mariner Thomas Parker, tailor Charles Skinner and labourer James Fox through the 1880s. Later, dock labourer James Gregory and his family moved in and were there until 1931. James Miller and George Brackstone were resident through the 1930s with Arthur Hall being the final tenant postwar until 1954.

Henry Philpot was a grocers porter living at No. 27 in 1851 until he moved next door to No. 26 around 1853. His place was taken by the seagoing Ferrys (no pun intended) when Robert and William spent time under its roof with their families in the late 1850s and early 1860s. After their departure we have another period of high turnover with short-term tenants over several decades. From 1867 we see groom John Wrench, cooper William Tucker, butcher George Pierce, mariners Kingswell, Anderson and Robert Russell, labourer William Woodman, and ships fireman Charles Elkins, all arrive and depart before the turn of the century, after which things get a little more settled with John Bartlett from 1914 to 1925, Arthur Hall in the late 1930s (before his move to No. 26) and finally Mrs Bowring for the remainder of the postwar years.

Laundress Elizabeth Chamber hung out the washing at No. 28 in 1851 but no others are listed until painter and glazier Joseph Howe turned up in 1857, stopping over until the mid-1860s when railway policeman William Harrington stayed a while until 1871. Engineers labourer Charles Codd was next through the door and lingered for five years. From 1881 we see mariner George Withers, Benjamin Bartlett, cordwainer Joseph Ballem and his wife Emily, Richard Jones, and workshop labourer Charles Cross taking us into the new century. Robert Saunders was there for a couple of years before World War One, then came Bertie Williams and his wife (before their move to Nos. 24 and 25), Samuel Peacock (latterly at No. 2) and finally William Parker after

World War Two until 1954.

Mariner Edward Perkins was another of the 1851 residents, this time at No. 29. He was there until his death around 1860 with his widow Sarah staying on for another year. Porter John Reed then stayed briefly before the arrival of cooper William Tucker (previously at No. 28) in 1874 who remained until 1881 when dealer and salesman William H. Sanger became another brief entry in the rent book, when once again we see so many others come and go. These included ships cook Frederick Redman, carpenter and joiner George Hordage, and coal porter Tom Paddock. All before 1914 when William Burnett decided to spend 17 years there. 1939 saw Thomas Joseph J. Button's name in the rent book with Mrs Sigouin being the last one from 1946 until 1954. The entrance to Union Cut stood between Nos. 29 and 30 where the presence of carpenter Thomas Young was recorded in 1834 but no other names transpire until that of ships stoker John Dawkins in 1867. He stayed on until 1871 and was replaced by butcher Thomas Wheeler who, in turn, gave way to seafarer Frank Parker and his wife Eliza. In the late 1880s the house accommodated Henry Barton and coal porter William Foley. Miss Susan E. Sunderland spent the early 1900s there before dock labourer William Summers appeared on the 1911 census. Alfred Allen, John Smith, Mrs Hatch and Mrs Connolly all saw time there between 1912 and 1925 before William Stoner became the final occupant in 1931.

The final abode in Union Street was No. 31 which had Mrs Butcher living there in 1867. Francis Saunders was next in 1869, closely followed by French polisher John Gookey in 1871. Then from 1874 we have a cavalcade of casual tenants beginning with butcher George Sparkes, baker William Sanger, groom Henry Chandler, ships fireman Henry Box, mariner Edward F. Jones and dock labourer William Mark, all being accommodated at No. 31 before 1900. In 1911 the census recorded labourer Alfred Allen, before he moved next door to No. 30, with Mrs Lee taking over in 1912. There are then no other names until

Fredrick Blake arrives in 1925 and is the last occupant in 1931 when Nos. 30 and 31 were demolished.

DEACONS COURT
Nos. 1–7

This was a court off the north side of Union Street with its entrance between Nos. 8, and 9 containing seven houses built of lath and plaster, which were in a much dilapidated state by the time of the 1893 slum report. At that time, one house had already been closed and the others were condemned as being unfit for habitation. All were without through ventilation and a single tap in the court supplied water but there was no ash bin provided, leaving rubbish etc. strewn around the court. The court was soon demolished and replaced by two houses with gardens which were numbered 8A and 9A.

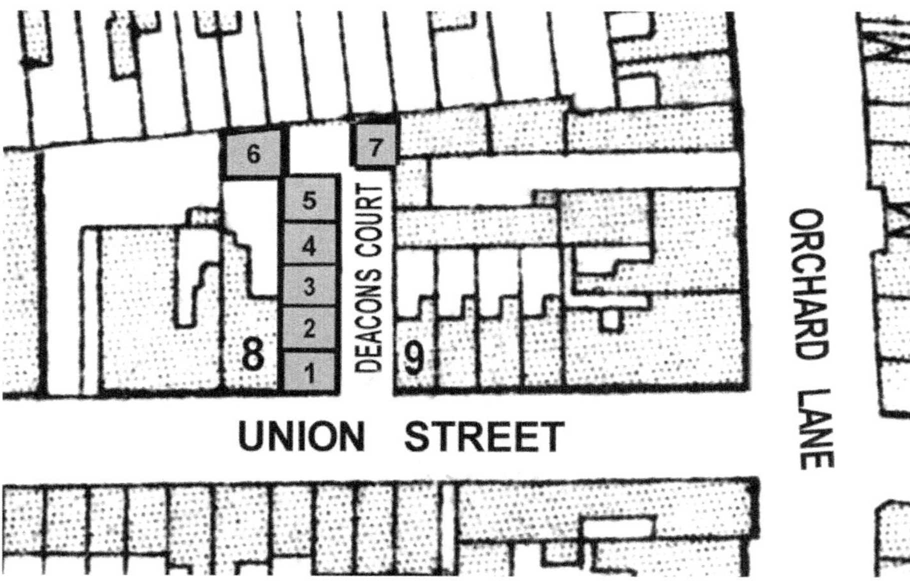

The entrance to Deacons Court was between Nos. 8 and 9 Union Street. The court had a terrace of five houses plus two others standing separately

No. 1 Deacon's Court stood next to No. 8 Union Street at the entrance to the court where once again, the earliest reference is in the 1851 census which lists boot maker Charles Johnson as living there. Johnson was still cobbling there in 1863 before seaman Charles Downer and his wife Lucy docked there in 1871. In the early 1880s Harriet Batchelor was taking in laundry while her husband was at sea, and the final names we have before the court was demolished are Robert Russell in 1887, and Elizabeth Dally, living by her own means in 1891.

Shoe maker Samuel Hallicot was yet another of the many cordwainers in the neighbourhood. Working at No. 2 in 1851, he and his family had moved away by 1871 when Henry Browning was listed as 'barman at inn' but we don't know which one. Railway man William Sparks was a porter and points man for the LSWR from 1869 to 1871 but the house was empty in 1881. However, it was inhabited again in 1884 by Mrs Gurd, then George Henry Cooper in 1887 and finally ships painter George Curtis in 1891. Louiza Davis graced the interior of No. 3 in 1851 but her place had been taken by unemployed tailor John Newman by 1861. Labourer and carter William Hendy had arrived by 1871 and dock labourer Edward J. Lowe in 1881. Edward had worked his way up to steward by 1884. George Curtis was resident in 1887 before moving next door to No. 2 and Robert Vear was his successor by 1891.

Tailor Charles J. Skinner was perhaps the court's longest resident, his tenure at No. 4 lasting from 1851 until 1881. Steward Charles Welch and then Charles Smith came and went in 1884 and 1887 respectively before the house was vacant in 1891. This was probably the one referred to as closed in the 1893 report. Labourer John Hicks was an early dweller at No. 5 in 1851 and butchers assistant Thomas Ponsford had moved there by 1861. Railway porter John Webber appears in the census for 1871, as does sugar house labourer Patrick Kink in that of 1881. Mariner Charles Lake (1884), and William Brown (1887) were next and Jemima Tizzard was the last recorded in 1891, living on parish relief.

As far as I can determine from the old maps, No. 6 and 7 were separate from the others with No. 6 being the abode of Mary Whitlock who is described in the 1851 census as being a 'churn woman' but she was gone by the time joiner Thomas Olding arrived in 1861. Painter Joseph Selby appears in the 1871 census, but not in that year's directory. Eliza Selvy is listed in 1881 before we find labourer Charles Codd in 1884 who was previously living a short distance away in Union Street. Mrs Paine and labourer George Voller are the last names at No. 6. In No. 7, the court's final house we have tin worker James Bascome in 1851 and school mistress Fanny Axford is there a decade later. Mariner William Brine comes later in 1871 with fellow sea dog William J. Hayes in 1881. One time bargeman and later general labourer, John Nichiolas is the final name in the court from 1884 through to 1891.

UNION PLACE
Nos. 1–11

Union Place was a terrace of 11 small houses that were hidden away in a court that was tucked between the back yards of Union Street and College Street. It was only accessible via Union Cut, a narrow passage only four and a half feet wide that ran between those two streets. In the 1893 slum report the houses were described as being damp and unhealthy with the only water supply from a single tap in the courtyard where there was also a toilet and an uncovered ash pit. Being surrounded by other buildings meant the circulation of fresh air through the court was minimal.

Once again we are reliant on the early census returns to discover who was living there as the directories did not include Union Place until 1884, although a few names were listed under residents in 1863.

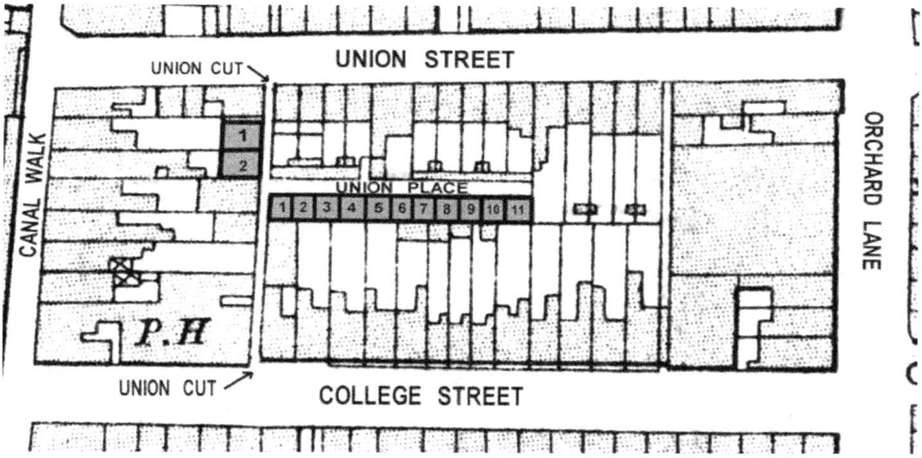

Union Place, tucked away between Union Street and College Street, was only accessible via the narrow Union Cut, which had two houses of its own

The earliest record of the inhabitants of Union Place appears in the 1851 census where at No. 1 we find chair maker Amos Powell. Then we have nothing more until 1861 where steamboat fireman James Wadman is in the first house. He was gone by the next census, which lists seaman's wife Sarah King, and by 1881 her husband William is home. William appears to have stayed ashore as in 1884 we find him occupying both Nos. 1 and 2 as a general dealer but he had moved on by 1887 as boot maker Joseph Ballem was living at No. 1 (having moved there from No. 3). Mariner Charles Elkins, hawker William Street, and boiler scaler Thomas Cox all followed on until Mrs Hampton arrived in 1912 and remained there until 1925. Alfred John Penfold and finally Dennis Degnin saw out the final years until demolition came in the mid-1930s.

Sarah Morgan lived at No. 2 back in 1851 but in 1861 dock porter James Gray is there, although by 1863 he had become a ships fireman. Bricklayer James Short was in residence according to the 1871 census and apart from William King in 1884 there are no others recorded until 1887 when shopkeeper Charles Elkins turned up. He was followed in 1891 by general dealer William Nest, and then came hawker Henrick Thomas in 1901. Thomas Payne was householder from 1916 until 1925 with Alfred W. Rackett and Mrs Coles seeing out the final years.

At No. 3 lived ships labourer Edward Headland in 1851 but boot maker Joseph Ballem had arrived by 1861 and cobbled away there until 1884 before moving to No. 1. The 1890s saw Julia Cummins living there under her own means although the house was empty in 1901. The early 1900s saw occupation by John Fryer and coal porter Charles William Freak before Harry Ashford and his family held the keys from 1914 until demolition came in the 1930s. In 1851 engineer George Hearn was the first recorded inmate of No. 4 with boiler maker's wife Jane Jennett present a decade later. Costermonger and general hawker George Brookman had an extended stay from 1871 until 1887 before needlewoman Rose Sheppard arrived with her sewing box around 1891. Marine store assistant George Thomas had a brief spell there before coal porter George William Freak moved from No. 3 in 1914, while George Richard Gandy and family were the final tenants from 1920 onwards.

Labourer John Burton and butchers assistant Henry Phillips were early settlers at No. 5 in 1851 and 1861 respectively. Seaman's wife Ann Gray was at home a decade later before labourers David Hansell and David Mann covered a few years before fish salesman and general dealer James Sherry held the fort through the latter 1880s and into the new century. John Scaun saw out the years from 1912 to 1920 before John and Arthur Hearden lived there through the 1920s with George Snooks jnr following on and Jack Charles Manly bringing up the rear in 1935.

William Withers at No. 6 was one of several labourers who occupied the court in 1851. Next in line was shoe maker George Brice, there in 1861 to 1863, followed by Chelsea Pensioner Richard Mayler who enjoyed his retirement there in 1871. Dock labourer George Edwards resided there from 1881 to 1884 and dressmaker Lucy Williams sewed her garments there in 1891. General labourer Thomas Billows and his family rented the place from 1907 until 1920 with George Snooks snr living next door to his son from 1931 and seeing the final years of the court.

No. 7 was the home of several seamen with ships fireman James Davis in 1851 along with mariners Enery Newman and Henery Bartlett there in 1861 and 1863 respectively. Porter William H. Grace was noted in 1871 while the 1880s saw labourer John Adkins, Mrs L. Light and Thomas Parson. The 1890s produced something of a mixture including laundress Agnes Dean, licensed hawker Sarah Pope. Then in the early 1900s came Alfred Tolfree who, according to the 1911 census, was 'unable to work'. He had gone by 1916 when Richard Gandy moved in but Mrs Goddard had arrived by 1920 and stayed on until the end. No. 8 welcomed labourer Henry Grant in 1851 and, a decade later, Ann Whitingstell was running it as a lodging house. Dressmaker Elizabeth Whitcher was sewing away in 1871 with fish hawker James Sherry selling his wares in 1881. The pick of the following years produces painter Henry G. Barton, widow Jane Hicks, costermonger Edward Risden (1900–1914) Arthur Edward Gong (1916–1925). Mrs Dack and finally Ernest Hooker who saw out the 1930s.

We find another dock labourer by the name of Philip Delaney at No. 9 in 1851 and a decade later the house was unoccupied. James Gray had previously lived at No. 2 and by 1871 he had become a shipwright, then through the 1880s dock labourer George Living, seaman Richard Kent and William Nutbean had all been resident with painter Henry S. Linton and coal porter Thomas Medley there in the 1890s. James McIntosh was away at sea in 1911 but was back home with his wife Mary in 1912. Thomas Henry Scorey's name was in the rent book from 1916 until 1931 and Frank Peers was later and last in 1935. Mariner James Kelly spent time ashore at No. 10 in 1851 but by 1861 dealer Charles Bartlett had moved in. Bartlett was still there a year later but by 1871 he had moved to No. 11 and made way for seaman's wife Matilda King who was awaiting her husband's return at No. 10. Fruit dealer and costermonger Henry Cook was next in the 1880s ahead of William Grant who spent at least 35 years at No. 10 where once he was a licensed hawker but later became a Town Quay labourer.

The final house in Union Place was No. 11, which in 1851 gave shelter to labourer Richard W. Olney before cordwainer George Thomas Cook made his boots there in 1861. As we have seen earlier, Charles Bartlett had moved from No. 10 around 1871 and remained there until 1912 over which time he was described as dealer, general merchant, hawker and fish dealer. James Edward Williams enjoyed a shorter spell there from 1916 until 1925 when Edward Barnes was the very last tenant, in every sense, when demolition finally came.

The cramped conditions of Union Place are apparent in this view looking east from Union Cut

Another view looking east along Union Place from Union Cut (Dave Marden collection)

UNION CUT
Nos. 1 and 2

Union Cut, known earlier as Union Court, was a narrow passage just four and a half feet wide that gave the only access to Union Place. At one time, it had two houses of its own, these being described as extremely dark, damp, and unhealthy, with their structures defective in places and their floors being below pavement level. Despite those conditions, they all remained inhabited until demolition came in the 1930s. (For map see Union Place).

Once again details of the people living here are sadly missing from the directories until 1884. Before that, we have only the various census returns but even those do not show Union Cut in 1861 and 1871. The 1851 census records labourer Charles Gifford at No. 1 with shoe maker William Dickman at No. 2. Onward now to 1881 where we find dock labourer John Campbell at No. 1, then in 1884 there is labourer Joseph Silvester, followed in 1887 by Thomas Moody. Labourer Colin Campbell makes an appearance in 1891. From then until 1912 we have casual labourer George Voller and finally Edward Smith and his wife from 1914 until 1931.

Back at No. 2 we find the Gray family, where James Gray is a shipwright in 1881 along with his son James jnr who was coal porter in 1901. James jnr died aged 40 in 1908 and his widow Bessie remained there working as a charwoman until the house came down in the 1930s.

Looking north along Union Cut towards Union Street. This narrow alley was the only way in to Union Place and contained the two houses shown here

COLLEGE STREET

Latter-day College Street was once in three sections. The first was a relatively short stretch running from Canal Walk to Orchard Lane. The street then continued to Threefield Lane as Winchester Terrace and the final part from Threefield Lane to Terminus Terrace was Cambridge Street. As they eventually merged in one thoroughfare, the haphazard and duplicated numbering system was changed several times until around the turn of the 20th century when the entire length from Terminus Terrace to Canal Walk was renumbered 1 to 100 on the south side with numbers 2 to 96 opposite. For the purposes of this book we will look only at the two sections that ran from Threefield Lane to Canal Walk. The south side numbered 31 to 101 with the north side numbered 34-96. Considering its length, College Street was unusual in that there were no courts leading off it, apart from the entrance to Union Cut next to No. 96. Except for the small terrace near Threefield Lane (Nos. 31 to 39), nothing survives today as most of the area to the north is now redeveloped as the Holy Rood estate.

COLLEGE STREET
North Side, Nos. 34–70
(Originally Nos. 1 to 21 Winchester Terrace)

This section of College Street between Threefield Lane and Orchard Lane was originally Nos. 1 to 21 Winchester Terrace, with No. 1 being a workman's hall. All the surviving postwar buildings were demolished in the 1950s redevelopment.

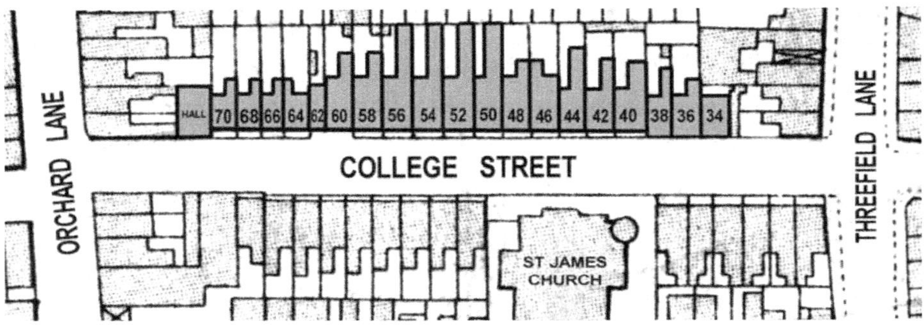

The north side of College Street between Orchard Lane and Threefield Lane showing Nos. 34 to 70 with No. 38 being the former Gladstone Inn and the workman's hall next to No. 70

We begin our tour of College Street heading west from Threefield Lane where we find No. 34, which like much of the street dated back to the 1830s with Mrs Watts in residence in 1839 and 1843. This section of the street seems a cut above the rest of the neighbourhood and looking at some of the more notable tenants we find baker Thomas Downs in the early 1850s, mariner George Lyne and his dress maker wife Tryphena through the 1860s, coal dealer George Eastham in 1871 and chimney sweep John Hawlett 1891. Mrs Birmingham was running it as a boarding house from 1907 until 1916 when she was succeeded by Mrs McGuirk who was there until 1940. Thomas P. Anderson spent the postwar years there with William Charles Smith being the last named in 1954 when demolition came.

Andrew Lamb Esquire was present at No. 36 in 1843 and upholsterer William Scammell was there in 1849. Engineer John Coleville followed in 1851 and a decade later we find sawyer George Bolton who probably worked at the large sawmill nearby in Threefield Lane. Cab driver Albert Adams was there through the early 1870s then we have the usual mixture of labourers and seamen until William Dix who was a telephone man in 1901. Dock labourer Alfred Higham and his family were long term tenants from 1907 to 1931 with Albert Edward Baker a close second from 1935 until 1954.

No. 38 was a pub named the *Gladstone Inn*, which was a residence until converted to a hostelry in March 1866 under Welsh's Lion Brewery. Richard Adams was joiner and beer house keeper there in 1871 (but strangely, by 1887 he had moved to No. 50 which at one time had been a temperance hotel). By 1878 the *Gladstone* had been taken over by the Shirley Brewery whose tenure later gave way to Gibbs Mew and then Welsh's Hyde Abbey Brewery. The pub closed in 1921 when it lost its licence and the premises became a grocers shop with Mrs Zoe Rose running it in 1931. By 1939 Sydney Arthur was behind the counter with Frederick Matthews in charge through the postwar years.

Flyman Richard Veal parked his carriage at No. 40 in the early 1840s and widow Mary Osman was an annuitant there in 1851. Engineer Andrew Scott followed her into the mid-1850s and then, at the end of the decade, P&O steward Stephen Warren and his wife Eliza arrived from Portsmouth and had stepped over the threshold. Sadly, by 1861 Eliza was a widow and running her home as a lodging house but by 1871 she had become a school mistress and remained as such until the mid-1870s when she returned to Portsmouth and saw out her old age as a needlewoman. Coal dealer George Dyer and his wife were next in the rent book through the 1880s. Others had short stays but cook Alice

Maude Barnes had arrived in the early 1900s and rattled her pots and pans there until the late 1920s when Alfred Mills saw out the final years of the street from 1931 until demolition in the mid-1950s.

No. 42 was, for much of its early existence, a lodging house, first run by Mrs Ann Mouncher from 1839 until 1847 when Mrs Jane Moody welcomed boarders until the 1850s, then engineer John Paul made it his home for a few years but by 1859 it had once again become a lodging house, this time under Mrs Deborah Bracher who kept house until the late 1860s. The address then appears to be vacant for a decade until dock labourer James Kinch shows up in the 1881 census, followed by Mrs Dyer (from No. 40) and then boat builder William Symes. Hydraulic crane driver George Henry Davis had parked his jib by 1901 and settled until around 1930 when Harry Thomas Crook unpacked his bags and remained until the last days of the 1950s.

Nos. 44 to 62 disappeared after 1940, as a result of wartime bombing. Cabinet maker John Badcock was French polishing at No. 44 through the 1840s before draper George Foster and his family settled there from 1849 before making way for joiner Joseph Dominy in 1857. He stayed for a decade until the keys were handed to tailoress Mrs Ann Masson who sewed her garments until 1874. Sawyer William Smith tended his splinters there through the early 1880s and Margaret Knight was living on her own means in 1891. Housekeeper Harriet Phillips was there a decade later when it was possibly back to being a lodging house. However, seaman William Curtin had sailed in by 1907 and dropped anchor until 1925. Rudolph Schwicker and his wife were the final inhabitants until 1940. Like its neighbour, No. 46 was for many years a lodging house and from 1839 it was run by young widow Mrs Sarah Wilkinson who was still there in 1884, although her daughter Sarah Rennie, also a widow, was head of the household by then. Lucy Bentley had assumed the role of housekeeper by 1901. Fish salesman William Edward West was renting the house out as apartments in 1911 and had also spread his enterprise next door to No. 48 by 1912. No. 48 had also been a lodging house under Mrs H. Rubie from 1839 until 1847 when Mrs Garnett took over. From the 1850s the house was rented to various people including mariner George H. Hooker, the Salter family who were engineering seafarers, Chelsea Pensioner William Baiss and tailor Samuel Townley by 1871. The frequent changes of occupation continued until general dealer William West arrived in 1901 and, along with No. 46, let it as apartments with both buildings disappearing from the directories after 1931.

No. 50 had a quite interesting history, starting out as home to tea dealer John McCormick in 1834. By 1843 it had become a temperance hotel under John Withers but that was short-lived and by 1849 Thomas Haddon and his wife Emma were running it as a shop selling groceries and beer. Trade must have been good as they incorporated Nos. 52 and 54 into their business from 1851 until 1857. Shoe maker Henry Mussell had taken over at No.50 in the 1860s while the others were separately let. Carpenter and joiner Richard Adams was present from 1874 until 1887 and marine engineer Alfred Ernest Elliot enjoyed a long residence from 1911 until 1940.

There was an ecclesiastical beginning for No. 52 when the Reverend A.C. Wright made his home there in 1839 and by 1843 engineer Samuel Wright was in residence but I have not found any family link between them. Mariner Joseph Smithers is there in the 1851 census before Thomas Haddon spread his empire. Ships chandler James Campbell was next, arriving in the late 1850s before the coming of tin man Edward Tizard and marine pattern maker William Barnes. Laundress Emma Cable appears in the 1881 census but a decade later, the house was occupied by labourer John Davis and his family. His son James, a corn porter, was head of the home in 1901 but the Davis's will have been sharing the house with others, and at this moment I will divert to a little more of my own family history.

My maternal great grandmother Josephine (nee Scott) lived briefly at

No. 52. She and her husband Jesse Kitcher Hillyear had moved to Southampton with their son Jesse Hillyear jnr from their native Brighton. Jesse snr had gained employment as a dock labourer in 1899 but sadly, in February 1900, he died in the house from a combination of influenza and pneumonia at the age of 32. Josephine had previously given birth to two illegitimate boys in Brighton Workhouse, one of them being my grandfather Robert Scott (1883–1953). Jesse jnr, who was born in 1891, was killed in World War One at the age of 26. Josephine lived with my grandfather and his family for a while at Ryde Terrace, Chapel, and later at Lower Bridge Road. After a long and hard life she died at a nursing home in Poole, Dorset, at the age of 89.

The early 1900s saw house painter Walter Barton take residence there but by 1914 the building had become let as apartments by William West until 1931 when Mrs Pamela Davis, widow of John Davis, was still living there and remained until the end came in 1940. Groom Benjamin Wallis lived at No. 54 through the 1840s before Thomas Haddon had extended his grocery and beer sales there but after Haddon had gone, wine cooper William Mason had settled in from 1861 until 1876. He was followed by brass finisher James Ellisold Harman, boiler riveter William Radford and Mrs Martha Dyer through the 1880s. Mrs Dyer, a lodging house keeper, had previously let rooms at Nos. 40 and 42 and had later moved into No. 56 by 1891. Crane driver William Knight was the next tenant from 1907 until 1920 with John Lahey being the final householder from 1931 until 1940.

For some reason (unknown to me) Nos. 56 and 58 do not appear until the 1861 census, which shows Susanna Ludgate at No. 56. Her occupation states she is assisting her father, Isaac Spencer, who was a collector of rates and taxes. We shall find him shortly at No. 60. Susanna was a widow by 1861 and remained at No. 56 until the late 1860s when tin man and former tinker John Dilworth set up shop and stayed until 1887. Martha Dyer then ran her lodging house there in 1891 and Sophia Drake continued the business in 1901. By 1911 the householder was ships painter Percy Thomas Bunker who was working for the Union Castle Line and by 1912 he had been joined there by his father Thomas, late of the *Gladstone Inn* at No. 38. George Richard Slater was next in line from 1914 until 1925, when James Johnson, and latterly Edward Barrett saw out the remaining years until 1940.

Like its neighbour, No. 58 was absent from the records until the 1861 census when tallow chandler John Dilworth was probably annoying others nearby with the odours of his work. He had departed to No. 56 by 1865 when Mrs Elizabeth Best arrived but she had moved to No. 52 by 1867. In fact, nobody seemed to stay in No. 58 for any length of time as no fewer than nine occupants came and went before the turn of the century when ships painter Richard Slade managed to hang on until Walter Blackman turned up in 1914 and surprisingly stayed put until 1940. No. 60 was home to possibly the most unpopular man in the street. He was Isaac Spencer whose role in life was collecting rates and taxes. This he did from his humble abode from 1843 until 1865 when the Stride family ventured in. Baker Jesse Stride and his wife Emma Mary made it their home until 1881. Labourer George Gregory had opened a general shop there by 1887 but by 1901 his wife Elizabeth was running it as another of the many boarding houses in the area until the mid-1920s. In the 1930s it was home to Charles Septimus Pattison (previously at No. 64), then finally to Mrs Salter who saw out the final couple of years there.

Master mariner Richard White had sailed into No. 62 in 1843 and was later commander of the *Ariadne* and *Monarch* in that decade, after which carpenter John Best and his family settled until 1861. Shoe maker Josiah Whitehorn spent the mid-1860s there before another succession of short-stay tenants ticked over until the early 1900s saw the address run as a shop with Henry Tutt behind its counter until the mid-1920s with George Flooks seeing out the final decade. Nos. 64, 66 and 68 all survived the war but were gone by the 1950s. Printer Edward M. Kingdom, painter Charles Chandler and a dressmaking and millinery duo of M. and E. Maton all saw the inside of No. 64 through the 1840s then engineering smith Henry Sunderland was based there from 1853 until 1867. 1871 saw the return of dressmaking there under Miss Martha White. Mariners, labourers and seamen moved in and out with widow Rosetta Smith present in the early 1900s before Charles Septimus Pattison held the keys from 1914 until moving to No. 60 by 1935. James Martin survived the war years there and was the last name recorded in 1948.

Stonemason Uriah Warren wielded his chisel at No. 66 from 1843 before giving way to carter Henry Fry and his wife Mary in 1847. The Frys remained until the 1860s when the normal turnover of inmates included hawker Horatio Philpott, ships fireman Jesse Townsend, boot maker Edward Hoskins and seafarer Henry Smith by the turn of the century. General labourer Walter John Joyce dallied for a couple of decades from 1911 with Richard J. Dawkins resident pre-war before Mrs Atkins arrived in peacetime and was the last at that address in the 1950s. I can find no occupants of No. 68 until the Legg family who are listed in the 1851 census. William and James Legg worked variously as iron foundry labourers during a long stay that lasted until 1874. Next in line were seaman James Penny and his wife Mary Ann, who was a widow before 1891 when pork butcher Frederick Wareham moved in. He stayed put until 1912, giving way to a long spell of tenure by the Morris family. William, his son James William and wife saw the years pass by until the final days in the 1950s.

The final dwelling in this section of the street was No. 70, which, as with its neighbour, saw nobody listed until the 1851 census when brass worker John P. Ford was recorded. Others later included whitesmith John Ralph and army pensioner James McGuire before 1863 saw the arrival of the Gandy family. Widow Mary Ann was 'dependent on her children' to make ends meet until they had moved on by the mid-1870s. Dock labourers and ships firemen were among several others listed there until Thomas Atkins and his brood appeared in 1916 and lasted until

1940 when bombs fell on the street. The final building which stood next to No. 70 was a workman's hall, which dated from around 1867 but had vanished after 1887.

COLLEGE STREET
South Side, Nos. 31–57
(Originally Nos. 1–6 and 22–30 Winchester Terrace)

The six houses between Threefield Lane and St James Church were originally Nos. 1 to 6 Winchester Terrace. They were described as New Buildings in the 1887 directory. Upon renumbering under College Street, No. 1 became No. 68 Threefield Lane and the others were Nos. 31 to 39 with Nos. 41 to 57 (formerly Nos. 22 to 30 Winchester Terrace) running west from the church. Of these, only the first five (Nos. 31 to 39) remain today (plus No. 68 Threefield Lane) and I have recorded those living there up to the 1970s, while Nos. 41 to 57 were swept away in the 1950s redevelopment of the area.

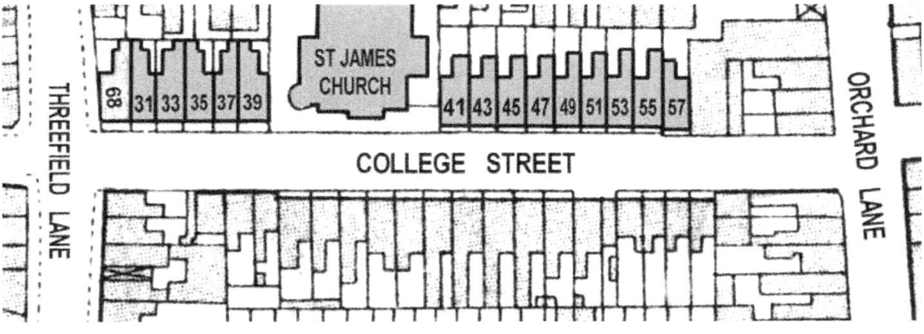

The south side of College Street between Threefield Lane and Orchard Lane was latterly numbered 31 to 57 and included the original St James Church

Mrs Collins was one of the first residents at No. 31 in 1887 but nobody was listed there in the 1891 census. Then in 1901 we have barrow porter Thomas Fielder but he was gone before 1911 when William Head's wife Annie was running it as a boarding house where two of the lodgers were divers in the docks. The Heads remained until the 1920s, which saw

William Demley reside for a decade before William Amos Oakley moved in on the eve of war with the Roberton family taking over in the postwar years through to the 1970s. Widow Annie Stainer was first in at No. 33 in 1887 before another widow, Fanny House, arrived in 1907. During World War One, Ivor Gray had taken over and lived there for an incredible period until around the 1960s when Alfred S. Hellen saw the 1970s arrive. No. 35 was home to whitesmith George Burt (or Burge) before the 1900s saw labourer William Gilbert as householder through to the 1930s and Albert Holness and his wife moved in postwar with her still being there in the 1970s.

Henry Stewart and Kate Maxwell were early renters at No. 37 before mariner Abraham Jones and fish merchant William George West saw in the new century. West remained until 1935 before Ethelbert Lever arrived in wartime and William Halford was there from 1946 with his wife remaining until the 1960s. The last of these 'new' houses was No. 39 which was inhabited by timber merchants foreman Henry William Charlton into the 1890s then marine deckhand James Hall was under its roof from 1911 until the 1920s, when a mission hall was attached to the adjacent church and its keeper was housed in No. 39. It became known as the Mission House with the Reverend Horace William H. Molyneux in charge from 1925. Other churchmen continued there until the church itself was destroyed in wartime bombing. Reverend George Alfred Blunt remained there postwar until Hubert Edwards arrived in 1954, with Mrs M. Burch as tenant in the 1960 and 1970s.

St James Church stood between Nos. 39 and 41 College Street. It was built in 1857 with its entrance fronting on Bernard Street but it was destroyed in World War Two. In its place, a new church was built on the site in 1956 but in 1965 it was sold and converted to the Greek Orthodox Church of St Nicholas.

Unlike their newer neighbours, Nos. 41 to 57 dated back to the 1830s as some of the older buildings in the area and, at that time, it seems none were numbered, so it has been my best guess as to who exactly was in which house. In 1834 I have placed pavement rate collector William Lomer at what became No. 41 as he is the first mentioned in this section of the street. He was followed in 1849 by mariner James Grant, then came basket maker Stephen Martin in 1851 with dock policeman John Harper in 1853. There followed no end of changes until 1871 when butcher Thomas Gale stayed through much of the 1870s after which the turnover was high once again until the early 1900s saw coal porter Alfred George Leggett and his family take residence which lasted until 1940. Mrs Wyatt spent the immediate postwar years there with Edward Charles Cray being the last name in the 1950s.

In No. 43 I have placed wine merchant William Weeks who was listed next to William Lomer in 1834. Moving on to the 1850s we find painter George Churchill, mariner George Dyer and William Stroud and then into the 1860s we have shipwright Joseph Pearce, tailor Robert Snow and Henry Axe. Locomotive driver Edwin Hendy had steamed in by the 1880s before dock labourer Arthur J. McLennan made it his long-term home from 1891 until 1935. William Pragnell saw out the war years there and Ernest Bray was last of the line postwar. Early inhabitants of No. 45 were the Ward family where cabinet maker Stephen and his dressmaker wife Eliza lived from 1845 until the mid-1850s when they were followed by railway policeman John Ostler and his wife who stayed a while before William H. Saunders, a P&O Line steward, arrived in 1859 and hung on for a couple of years. Baker George Heath did likewise and then ships steward Josiah Beavis spent his time ashore there from 1871 until 1884. The only other tenant of note was town sergeant William H. Gardener in 1901 before dock labourer Albert Ernest Smith spent around four decades there from 1907 until 1946 when the final few years housed Miss Smithers.

The boot-making Gandy family appear often in these pages and the 1840s saw James Gandy at No. 47 until the mid-1850s before Charles Barnes, at various times a painter and carpenter, arrived in the late

1850s. We then have Mrs Emma Miell as householder in 1861. One-time mariner and latter-day army pensioner Rolla Ross spent a decade there from 1865 while a longer stay was achieved by Albert Hayes, who from 1891 earned his keep by being a brewers labourer, carman, and a fish merchants carter during his extensive tenure that lasted until 1935, while Miss Smith was the final holder of the keys from 1940. Boiler maker William Hill and his wife were the early names at No. 49 in the 1850s before the 1860s residents included butcher Charles Hunt, marine engineer Thomas Archibald, engineer James Chick, fish and potato salesman George H. Bulpit and mariner Francis J. Brewer. Brewer held on until the arrival of Mrs M.A. Rogers and her daughter Caroline appeared in the mid-1870s before sailor James Tapp dropped anchor in 1881. Brewers assistant John Robert Smith was the householder in 1901 and by 1911 he was working as a laundry man on the Union Castle Line. He, and his later widow Agnes, were there until World War Two when Miss Bailey resided in peacetime.

Gardener William Hiscock looks to be the earliest resident in 1834 at what became No. 51 but no others are recorded until the 1850s when mariner James Lovelock, clerk Thomas Payne and shipwright John Thorn made their way inside. The Thorns endured until 1867 with needlewoman Sarah giving way to ships steward Thomas Snelgrove and his wife Ann, who occupied until seaman's wife Mrs Julia Payne arrived in the mid-1880s. Joseph Willis Summers was a crane driver in the docks when he began his long stay there from 1901 until 1940, after which Leonard James Cannon was the tenant in the postwar years. Charles Eyles was first in at No. 53 back in 1851 but he was gone by 1853 when clerk and timekeeper Edward Oakshott clocked in. Several changes occurred in the 1860s when house painter Henry Banks, baker George Rice and mariner George Talman moved in and out before cooper Edward English and his wife Fanny set up home in 1874, raising their children under its roof until around 1900 and from then on the house welcomed several other short term renters until Thomas Henry

Clitheroe settled in from 1920 until the war years, with William Sullivan and his wife seeing out the remainder until 1954.

No. 55 was another of the earliest inhabited houses when, in 1834, it was occupied by cabinet maker Mr Griffiths. Carpenter Benjamin Gage was next in 1847 followed by tailor Henry Burbage. After several further changes through the 1850s, house painter Henry Perkins and his dressmaker wife Elizabeth arrived in 1859 and survived until 1881. The latter 1800s welcomed mail cart driver Robert Orris and clerk Charles Wyatt before general labourer Henry James Fielder crossed its threshold in 1907. His widow Sarah Eliza remained until 1939 when Mrs Dawkins lived through the war years until the street came down in the mid-1950s. The last property in this section of College Street was No. 57 near the corner of Orchard Lane. Coach maker Andrews and Co. were listed near that location in 1834 and No. 57 was occupied by wheelwright John Tiller from 1843 until 1855. Plumber George Hartnell wielded his blowlamp there in 1857 and there followed a lengthy association with the beer industry beginning with brewer Thomas Stickland's tenure through the early 1860s which later saw fellow brewer Alfred Brown in occupation from 1871 until 1876, brewers assistant and drayman Samuel Wallbridge 1876 until 1891 with brewer's cellarman Robert Curtis keeping the connection alive until 1901 when fish salesman George Channel broke the chain. However, the link was restored when brewer's topman William Henry Helbert moved in around 1911, remaining there until he died in 1920 while running the *Cyprus Hotel* at No. 4 Royal Crescent Road. George House was the next inmate from then until 1940 and the final tenant was Harry Bellows in 1954.

All that remains of the College Street houses is this short terrace viewed from Threefield Lane. No. 68 Threefield Lane is on the corner with Nos. 31 to 39 College Street beyond (Dave Marden)

COLLEGE STREET

North Side, Nos. 72–96

(Originally Nos. 1–15 College Street)

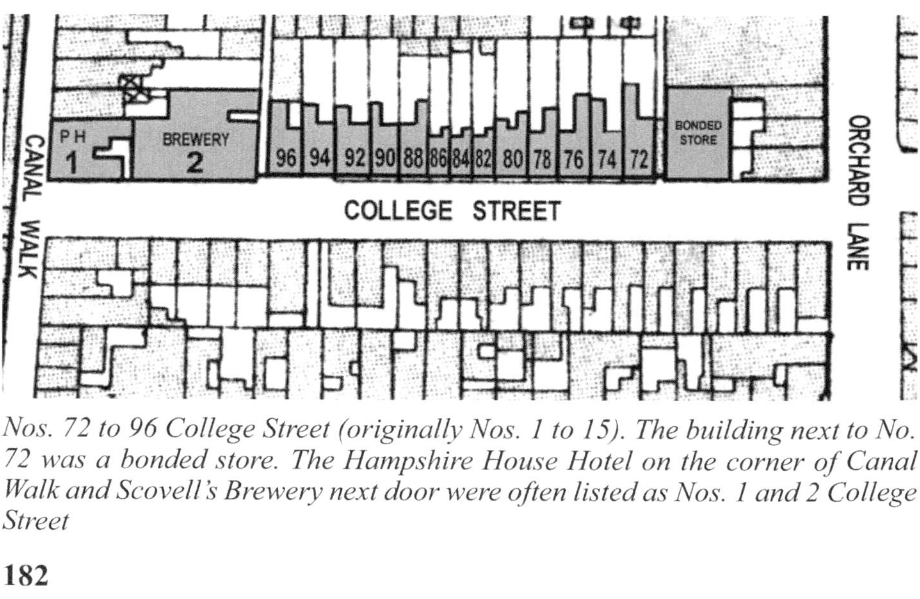

Nos. 72 to 96 College Street (originally Nos. 1 to 15). The building next to No. 72 was a bonded store. The Hampshire House Hotel on the corner of Canal Walk and Scovell's Brewery next door were often listed as Nos. 1 and 2 College Street

Much of this part of College Street dates back to the 1830s and there was also a building at its eastern end near Orchard Lane, standing next to No. 72. In 1874 this was George Valder's corn and hay store then in 1884 John Smith was selling coal and firewood there. In 1891 the building was just listed as a store but by 1907 it had become the Winchester Brewery's bonded vault and remained as such until around 1930 when it became a fruit merchants store under Innes and Helliwell. The final record was in 1935 when shown as belonging to provision merchants Aplin and Barret and the Western Counties Creameries.

No. 72 was once the home of builder John Beavis back in 1834 but 1843 saw the arrival of Ann Smitham who survived until 1855 living off an annuity. Mariner George Nichols and his wife Mary then moved in and stayed until 1861 when fellow mariner William Shears arrived and was earning a living as a boiler maker by the time he left in 1884. Sail maker John H. Bury and his wife Ann were next but Ann was a widow by 1901 and her place was taken in 1907 by Frank Thomas Tizard, a hydraulic crane driver. He was there until at least 1925 and there followed a further quartet of names ending with Charles Attard in 1940.

Mrs Jane Shephard, of independent means, held the keys to No. 74 from 1834 until around 1851 when ships stoker Frederick Morgan moved in. His tenure lasted until 1857 when tailor William Bateson arrived and was quickly followed by boot binder Elizabeth Grose and cabinet maker Thomas Strong. Railway guard James Cooper was next in 1863 and stayed on until 1871 but after he left there was the usual turnover of mariners and labourers throughout the 1870s to 1890s. Things were more settled in the early 1900s when labourer Charles Cook a long-term occupant from 1907 until 1935, then Henry Lowe and his wife were there pre-war with William Chorley seeing out the postwar years.

The early years at No. 76 saw Mrs Smith and tailor Thomas Powell resident, before another tailor, John Gandy, arrived in 1843 but by 1845 he was working as a cook which was still his calling in 1847.

Bookbinder Thomas Bradstreet was renting there in 1851, followed by dealer Jacob Rogers, mariners Jacob Cheek and William Wilson, and customs officer George Martell, all before 1860. The 1860s were not much different with greengrocer Harriet Musselwhite, labourer James Talbot and baker George Smith adding to the list. The doormat must have been pretty threadbare through the 1870s, 1880s and 1890s as nobody seemed to stay for very long until engine fitter George Richards and his wife settled there from 1901 until 1916. Mrs Simpson was then householder until the 1930s and then George Lee stayed on from 1939 until the end in the mid-1950s.

Draper Robert Clougg spent a decade in No. 78 but the house appears to have been empty for five years after his departure in 1845. Cabinet maker Edward Webb was more than happy there as, after his arrival in 1851 he stayed the course through to 1874. Dock corn porter George Harding and his wife Bathsheba presented themselves in 1887 but by the turn of the century, Mrs Harding was a widow and died in 1907. In her place came Francis Peter Bailey, a plate layer with the LSWR, but he was gone by 1914. Mrs Coombs and her family saw out World War One there and stayed until the mid-1920s. Others came and went through the 1930s with Frank Diamond being the last when the house disappeared after 1940.

It does seem that cabinet makers were in plentiful supply in and around College Street. Adding to their ranks was Thomas Franklin at No. 80 from 1834 until 1851. Hardware and general dealer George Wade was next over the threshold and millwright James Gilbert succeeded him in 1861. Bricklayer Thomas Jenkins (previously at No. 87) had a spell there in the 1870s, as did wine cellarman William May in the 1880s. Then followed the familiar turnover of short-stay residents until the arrival of dock labourer Robert Thomas Sevier who was present for most of the early 1900s until William James Paisley and his family were resident from 1911 until World War Two. Norman Walter Barnard was there for the remaining postwar years.

James and Elizabeth Noyes were the early settlers at No. 82 in the 1830s and by the mid-1840s the door was welcoming barman Joshua Scovell, no doubt related to the brewing family at the end of the road. He died in 1853 and his widow Elizabeth remained there until the late 1850s. Throughout the 1870s and 1880s nobody stayed very long until charwoman Elizabeth Kinch donned her apron there in the early 1900s. After her departure the list of tenants seemed endless until George Avery was custodian in the 1930s with Percy William Allez as the last recorded tenant in 1948. No. 84 was the abode of watch maker George F. Jones throughout the 1840s then in 1851, pilot Edwin Waters had a brief stay. Mariner Charles Strong junior graced its interior in the early 1850s and the 1860s welcomed shoe maker William Wareham and cabinet maker Charles Clift before whitesmith John Gordon spent the 1870s there. A host of seamen passed through during the 1880s and 1890s then, in 1907, furniture packer John Taylor was key holder through to the mid-1930s and William Griffiths was there postwar until 1948.

In 1834 No. 86 was where watch maker John Yon called home but in the 1840s it gave shelter to cabinet maker Stephen Ward (who had moved to No. 45 by 1845) and cordwainer Charles Cummins before coal meter John Bishop rested his bones there in the late 1840s and early 1950s. Brewer John Osman no doubt saw many new neighbours in his two decades there from 1857 until 1876. In the 1880s, sawmill jointer Frederick Domone and his wife spent a few years there, as did railway porter Joseph Henry Mason from 1891. Coal porter John Boniface had his name in the rent book from 1901 until 1920 then Norman Walter Barnard lived there through the 1930s and John Goodman in the postwar years until 1948. Hatter John Bailey and cordwainer James Nicholas were the earliest names at No. 88 in the 1830s and 1840s before mariner George Robert Mason sailed in around 1851 and remained there until his death in 1889. His son, a porter of the same name, kept the family home going until 1891. Tailor William Doncom and his family then spent 25 years there from the turn of the century and

William Henry Gull was present for the rest of the street's days until 1954.

John Wiseman and his son Joseph were tailors at No. 90 in the 1840s before mariners John Warren and John Whittle were there through the 1850s. Ships steward Robert Spearpoint and his wife Mary had moved in by 1861 but Mary was a widow by 1863 when their son George went to sea at the age of 14. They had vacated by 1874 when carman George Self and his wife Sarah ran it as a lodging house until drayman Edward Carter stayed briefly around 1881. Dock corn porter Henry Arnold appeared in the late 1880s and 1890s before baggage carrier George Edward Friend was a street stalwart from 1907 until 1925. Frederick Albert George Moody spent time there pre-war but the house was unoccupied between 1940 and the early 1950s before demolition around 1954 when Eric Sills was resident. Harbour master William Tubbs carried out his maritime duties while living at No. 92 from 1834 until his death in 1853. His son Henry, a county court bailiff, moved away soon afterwards then waiter Benjamin Goater stayed briefly before railway porter George Bessant had a couple of years under its roof. Through the 1860s the inhabitants were P&O cook John Simpson, cabinet maker Joseph Applin, laundress Rebecca Mitchell and carpenter William Reeks (later at No. 79) from 1863 until 1867. Customs officer George Martell (previously at No. 76 in 1859) had a brief stay around 1874 before sawmill carman George Garrett was present in the early 1880s. A few others arrived and departed before boiler maker James Boyle and his wife Mary Jane arrived in 1911 and widow Mary left there in the mid-1920s. George Edward Friend (previously at No. 90 in 1925) had moved to No. 92 by 1931 and remained there until the wartime bombing of 1940.

I have not found any record of No. 94 until 1871 when it was occupied by W. Thick. Tailor James Donkin had found his way there by 1874, as had bricklayers labourer John Rogers in 1881. There seems nothing further until David Whitfield is listed in 1907. He was previously at No.

78 in the early 1880s. Fishmonger Harry Darley was at No. 94 from 1911 until the wartime bombs fell in 1940. The premises that became No. 96 was referred to as 'back of public house' in 1881 and I've found nothing else there until the Coventry Radiator and Presswork Company set up their business there in 1931.

At the western end of the street, where it joined Canal Walk, stood a brewery and a pub named the *Hampshire House Hotel*. These were numbered 1 and 2 and were separated from the rest of College Street by the cut way, which was Union Court. Philip Scovell is listed as a brewer and beer retailer at No. 1 back in 1834 while No. 2 appears as separate accommodation in the early directories with a host of tenants over the years. By 1851 a larger brewery had been set up under Scovell and Sons, becoming A. and H. Scovell (Alexander and Henry) by 1871 and known as the Hampshire Brewery. In 1876 it had been expanded as the College Street Brewery with the pub at No. 1 and the brewery at No. 2. Senior partner Henry Scovell died in 1884 leaving an estate worth over £6,500.

In later directories the *Hampshire Hotel* (as it was from 1898 when owned by Strongs of Romsey) became renumbered as No. 25 Canal Walk. By the early 1900s there was an extension of Strongs brewery across the entrance to Union Court. This was next to No. 94 and was numbered 94A or 96, which later became a vegetable warehouse in the 1940s. The *Hampshire Hotel* closed in 1921 as there was a glut of pubs in the area and the building afterwards became a milliner's shop, while the adjacent brewery was demolished and replaced by garages.

COLLEGE STREET BREWERY,

SOUTHAMPTON.

ESTABLISHED 1824.

A. & H. SCOVELL,

BREWERS,

WINE AND SPIRIT MERCHANTS, &c.

Families and Shipping supplied in Casks of 4, 6, 9, 12, and 18 Gallons, &c., &c.

REID'S LONDON STOUT IN CASK OR BOTTLE.

An 1871 advertisement for the Scovell Brewery at College Street

The photo is from around 1920 shows the last days of the brewery at the west end of College Street looking towards Canal Walk with a glimpse of the Hampshire Hotel on the far corner. Nearest the camera are Nos. 96 and 94 (Dave Marden collection)

COLLEGE STREET
South Side, Nos. 59–101
(Previously Nos. 15–36 College Street)

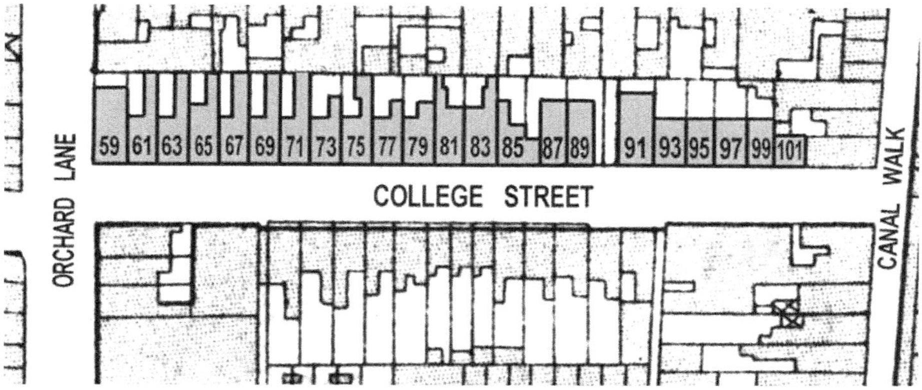

The south side of College Street showing Nos. 59 to 101 between Orchard Lane and Canal Walk. Nos. 59 and 61 became a pub named the Napoleon Tavern and was renumbered 43 Orchard Lane

This side of the street was well established by the 1830s when No. 59 was a shop run by Mrs Giles in 1834. By 1845 it was still a shop but then in the hands of Mary Ann Leake who was proprietor until Ambrose Tiller ran it as a beer house in 1855. Named the *Napoleon Tavern*, Charles Judd was serving the pints there from 1857 until 1871 but by 1891 the pub had extended into No. 61 and the pair became No. 43 Orchard Lane (see that chapter for later details). No. 61 had been the home of master mariner Samuel Summers from 1834 until 1851 when coal merchant John Croft and his wife Eliza were briefly in residence. By the mid-1850s tailor Thomas Jesse had spread his cloth there, remaining in the house until it was absorbed into the *Napoleon Tavern*.

Ironmonger Thomas Osman was at No. 63 from 1834 and on into the late 1840s, then the house had nautical inmates through the 1850s with shipwright Thomas Dunn, and mariners William James, William Hill and Edward Legg. That changed in the 1860s which saw joiner Walter Perkins, grainer Charles Colewell, painter John Donaldson pass through its front door. Blacksmith William Maynard was present through the

1880s while the 1890s found dressmaker Milly Everett and coach painter Walter Monk. Into the 1900s we find George Frederick Metcalf from 1914 until 1925 and Arthur Peckenham through the 1930s with Albert Edward Elliot the final name in 1940.

Schoolmaster Samuel Elgar lived at No. 65 in 1834 and painter William A. Golding was there in the 1840s. Tallow chandler James Hatch, previously at No. 67, had moved from next door by 1853 but he didn't stay long as John German, an engineer with the Royal Mail Steam Packet Company, had taken his place by 1855. Further arrivals through the 1860s were boot maker Richard Sharpe, lamp lighter John Halford, blacksmith Thomas Guy and Slater Henry Noyce. Edward Tizard's combined talents included gas fitting, plumbing and being a tinsmith while at No. 65 through the 1870s. He had earlier been a ships fireman when living at No. 70. The turnover at No. 65 continued with ships cook John Summers (1884), fruit dealer Charles Maunders (1901) and hawker B.H. Hampton in 1911. Thomas Biggs was the new tenant from 1912 until 1920, followed by William Prewitt until 1925, and latterly Albert Baker from 1935 until 1940.

Shoe maker Walter Bennett was cobbling at No. 67 in 1834 and by 1841 charwoman Elizabeth Reed had made her home there. Sarah Ball was next in 1845 before butcher Thomas Primer jnr made his entrance in 1847. Charles Hatch had arrived in 1851 (before moving to No. 65) and engineer Alexander Steadman by 1855, then mariner Edward Legge in 1857. Engineer Joseph Hinks and his wife Mary Ann were present in 1859 but by 1861 Mary was a widow and working as a dressmaker. Coastguard William Campbell and his wife Mary Ann had moved in by 1863 but by 1871 Mary was yet another widow on the street and had left by 1876, after which the house saw several changes until coal porter William Macey settled there from 1901 until the mid-1920s when Emanuel Monte Macey was recorded until the final days of 1940.

In 1834 No. 69 was home to a dying breed with Richard Wooldridge being one of the last generation of stagecoach men. Excavator John Little was there in 1841 as was waterman William James in 1847. Customs officer Charles Forder was resident from 1849 until clerk William Roberts arrived in 1855. The early 1860s found printer and compositor Frederick Horton as tenant before ships fireman Edward Tizard (later at No. 65) was present for the second half of the decade. Various members of the Summers family inhabited No. 69 through the 1870s and 1880s until seaman Charles Rand moved in from 1891; 1914 saw Michael Edward Farnan stay there until the mid-1920s. Casimiro Teglio is recorded there in 1925 and George Frederick Metcalfe in the 1930s before Richard Carty became the final name in the rent book in 1939.

Yet another shoe maker, this time Richard Malser, was at No. 71 in 1841 but by 1845 his dressmaker daughter Mary Ann was head of the house. Pilot Edwin Waters was next, before he moved to No. 84 in 1851, making way for master turner Henry Camfield. Painter William Mears had dipped his brushes there from 1859 but by the time he left in 1863 he was working as a slater. Labourer William Macey had arrived (from No. 73) by 1874 and remained until 1891 by which time he had become a coal porter before moving again, this time to No. 67. Fellow coal porter Frederick Wyatt, his wife Eliza, and their ten children were next at No. 71 from 1901 where the family remained until that part of the street vanished in 1940.

William Garland was a tailor and habit maker in 1834 when he lived at No. 73. Shoe maker Richard Marsh was there in 1841 but by 1845 Mrs Mary Bevan was running it as a lodging house until 1849 when ships fireman John Hurst arrived. He was gone by 1851 and brewer Thomas Prior was present from 1855 until mariner William Moody sailed in around 1863. Labourer William Macey had made it one of his several homes through the latter 1860s before mariner John Gill appeared in the mid-1870s. Several more names entered the rent book before that of seaman John Macey (son of the much moved William) in 1911 and

William Frederick Binham who was the last from 1931 until 1940.

Picture dealer George Bell was at No. 75 in 1841 before mariner Charles Rook and his family embarked on a long stay from 1845 until 1871. Charles had died by 1863 and his widow Emily carried on, earning a living from mangling. There then came a series of mariners and labourers with one exception: Albert Frederick Lawrence, a traction engine motorman, in 1911. Richard Smith was the final resident from 1920 until 1940. Dressmaker Susan Birks was busy sewing at No. 77 in 1841 and Mrs Mary Wakeling was running a lodging house there in the late 1840s. The 1850s saw pilot William Bullmore, sawyer George Dawkins and cabinet maker Frederick Books all cross its threshold before mariner Leonard Hawkins and his family docked there in 1861 and lasted over a decade. Carman George Stonadge was another for the long term, being there from 1881 until 1901, only to be outdone by brewery scalder Mark Gorton who was there from 1901 until 1935, with his widow remaining to the final days in 1940.

One-time waiter and later news vendor John Hart was at No. 79 in 1934 and enjoyed his long stay until shipwright Edward Pearce moved in around 1857 and left in 1863. Joiner William Reeks was next until he moved to No. 92 in 1871. Railway porter Albert Martell carried his luggage there in 1876 with his wife Mary and, a while later, the rent book recorded two unusual names, being Bishop Fodringham in 1887 and seaman Thaddues Griffiths (from Barbados) in 1891. Thaddues had died in Australia and his widow Sarah had moved on by the time boiler scaler Edward Lacey turned up in 1911. William Frederick Robert Sevier was the last to live there in the latter 1930s until the final year of 1940.

Early names at No. 81 include John Callen of the Academy in 1834, customs officer James Dixon in 1843 and William Cutler of independent means in 1843. Tailor James Martill was evident through most of the 1850s. The Hendersons (previously at No. 83) were doing well there around 1860 with James being a draper and his wife Ann being a 'Proprietor of houses'. In the late 1860s and on through the 1870s were the Jordan family with mariner Henry and his wife Annie and then into the 1880s and 1890s there was an assortment of labourers, bricklayers and ships firemen until in 1911 we have fish hawker James Olive who stayed on until the mid-1930s when William Albert Halford was the final tenant in 1940.

Cabinet maker and upholsterer Benjamin Woodford lived at No.83 in the early 1840s and draper James Henderson saw most of the 1850s there before moving to No. 81. Coachman John Barber had a couple of short spells there, the first being back in 1851 before returning in 1871, but he was soon off again, making way for boat builder Alfred Dumper in 1874. The Dumpers were there until Cornile Riggs ran a lodging house there in 1891. The early 1900s welcomed pork butcher Edward Scott, fishmonger John Holmes and blacksmith Louis Harris who remained until 1916, which saw the return of John Holmes. The 1920s featured a number of changes with Mrs Callaway being the last of them.

No. 85 was also home to another upholsterer in the 1840s, this time to Nicholas William Foster. Printer Robert Thomas Russell had arrived by 1851 before the late 1850s and early 1860s saw a flurry of changes with mariner John Warn, cabinet maker John Foster, watch maker Robert Snook, boiler maker Alexander Irvine and another watch maker by the name of John Edwards. The 1860s and 1870s were not much different with mariner James Eve, tailor Henry Spring, ships fireman Emanuel Summers and plumber Edward Hemming all treading the doormat in quick succession. Things settled down a little in 1901 when coal porter George Summers stayed for a couple of years and then shipping company labourer Alfred Barton's family reigned from 1907 until 1940. For some reason Nos. 85 and 87 outlasted their neighbours into the 1950s demolition. Arthur Diaper was the last at No. 85 from 1940 until the end.

Shoe maker Thomas Mountfield was turning out his footwear from No. 87 in 1841 and later that decade there came bird dealer Joseph Bailey and beer retailer John Fitch. Upholsterer Nicholas William Foster had moved from No. 85 by 1851 with shipwright Edmund Denyer replacing him in 1857. The 1860s then witnessed multiple changes that included sawyer and broker Aaron Whitmarsh, waiter John Maliche, dealer George Dugale, mariner James Fenn and bricklayer Thomas Jenkins (later at No. 80 in the 1870s). Engineers assistant G. Tollman and his wife Harriet were next in line from 1874, then, in 1884, porter Henry Beare appeared before labourer Thomas Slightman brings us up to 1891. Dock labourer Thomas Anderson enjoyed a long sojourn from 1901 to around 1930 when Albert John Smith, Charles White and Anthony C. Wilson witnessed the final years until 1954.

No. 89 was recorded as a beer house run by William Read in 1834 then labourer Soloman Hill was recorded there in 1841. The house was empty in 1851 but inhabited once again by blacksmith Charles Eden in 1853. In 1855 it was a beer house again, this time under James Arwood, then carpenter Edward Fielder and ornamental turner Samuel Batchelor saw out the 1850s with cabinet maker and upholsterer Thomas Sturdy in place from 1861 until 1863. Butcher Robert Edney Jewell and labourer Charles Hoare seemed to share the premises between 1867 and 1874 before labourer William Mason (later to Nos. 82 and 93) and his family arrived in 1881. His son Francis was householder there in 1891 living under his own means until photographer Charles T. Ford made a brief appearance in 1901. Carpenter and joiner James Payne then took up residence from 1907 until 1940.

There was an alleyway alongside No. 91, a property that does not appear in the directories until 1867 and looks to have been a workshop for most of its existence. Joseph Tucker, glazier Marcus Spiers and tailor William Randell were listed there before 1871 but in the 1881 census it was described as a store. Cabinet maker James Ferbridge and greengrocer James Boyce were key holders in 1884 and 1901 respectively then by

1907 it had become the gas fitters works of George Vivian and Son and carpenter James Payne (from No. 89) also had a presence there. Vivian and Son remained until at least 1925 before wholesale fruit merchant Louis Frank Helliwell arrived in 1935. In the final years to 1940 the building was used by decorators A. Wright and Son.

Butcher Edward Rogers was one of the early names at No. 93 where cabinet maker (yes, another one) Soloman Norman and his dressmaker wife Matilda lived through the 1840s. Blacksmith Thomas Thatchell spent a decade there from 1849. Bricklayer Isaac Wills had a stopover in 1859 before the arrival of letter carrier John Godley whose abode it was between 1861 and 1867. From 1871 the address was a lodging house run by Mrs Emma Keep until around 1890. Brewers labourer William Mason (possibly the same William Mason who was a cooper previously at Nos. 54 and 55) spent a decade there in the early 1900s before widow Isabella Donaldson moved in for a couple of years. At the outbreak of World War One, Joseph Ernest Button was resident until 1939 when Mrs Perrone was the final tenant at the eruption of World War Two. She then moved to No. 97 when peace returned.

John Hayes was a brass finisher and gas fitter at No. 95 for a decade from 1841. He was succeeded by dressmaker Ann Sweatland in 1851, while she in turn gave way in 1853 to John Cox who ran a pistol and rifle gallery. Whitesmith John Milsom saw out the 1850s before Mrs Eliza Culverwell set up her lodging house, which lasted until 1874 when she moved next door to No. 97. Afterwards, several short-term renters moved through its door until fish hawker Edward Mason settled in from 1891 until the early 1900s, then came more changes until Mrs Judd arrived in 1916 and held the fort until the mid-1930s. The 1939 register lists widow Mrs Florence Fella and her son Alphonso who was still there in the 1950s. He worked at an electric cable factory along with his brother Gerald.

Whitesmith John Watkins was at No. 97 in the early 1840s and porter

Henry Headland saw out the rest of the decade. Carpenter William Powell was next in 1853 but had become a barman by the time he left in 1859. Labourer William Lewis appeared in the 1861 census but had been promoted to foreman by 1863. Painter Edwin Elgar had moved in by 1865 but was gone by 1874 when Mrs Eliza Culverwell had moved her lodging house from No. 95. She remained until around 1890 when dock labourer Frederick Ridges became key holder through to 1911 when butcher Timothy Callaway arrived and stayed until the 1920s. The following years saw several changes before Mrs Perrone was the tenant in the postwar years, having previously lost her home at No. 93 in the wartime bombing.

Possibly the last cabinet maker in this section of the street, Thomas W. Waller was in residence at No. 99 from 1841 until 1871 when being unemployed, the household relied on his son George who was a solicitors clerk. Master butcher George Henry Rose had arrived by 1881 and he was followed in 1884 by Mrs Ives, seaman Alexander McClean in 1891 and dock labourer Samuel Baker in 1901. By 1907 Nos. 99 and 101 had become Rose and Rogers butchers store, which it remained as such until demolition came in the mid-1950s. No. 101 was a small building that was mainly in use as a shop. Bookseller Isabella Ron was there in 1841 but a decade later it was uninhabited. Milliner and dressmaker Jane Philpot had set up there in 1857 and the Callen family had followed her by 1859 with Elizabeth Callen being a greengrocer. The Callens had gone by 1863 when tailor Thomas G. Gallaway was selling clothes there. Next in 1865 was hat maker Horatio Philpot (later at No. 66). Joiner William Maidment was briefly resident in 1871 before pork butcher Henry Rogers had it as his store before combining it with No. 99 in 1907.

PART THREE
EAST OF ORCHARD LANE

At one time referred to as the Rookery, this was once a notorious area dating back to the early and mid-1800s which was shown as such on various Ordnance Survey maps and contained some of the most appalling slums and fearsome inhabitants. In many towns and cities the term Rookery was used to describe heavily populated slum areas whose inhabitants included such undesirables as thieves, felons and prostitutes. As such, through the darkest Victorian period, many of its inhabitants rarely appeared in the earlier street directories. Charles Dickens went on several escorted visits into the underworld of London's Rookeries, horrendous slums inhabited by the dregs of mankind that made up the local population. Such places existed in other cities and towns, including Southampton, which was apparently just as notorious as those observed by Dickens. As for Southampton's Rookery, I would think many of the locals who featured in the directories and census returns were honest and law abiding; it's the anonymous ones who weren't.

LIME STREET
Youngs Court, Bee Hive Buildings, Campbells Court, Spring Court and Cozens Court

Until the turn of the 20th century, Lime Street was known as Cross Street, which ran west from Orchard Lane to Threefield Lane. There was also another street named Cross Street off nearby Bell Street – and a third of the same name in Kingsland! At one time, King Street Rookery stood on the north side of Cross Street between Orchard Lane and King Street, consisting of several unsavoury courts accessed by alleyways, isolated from the outside world where possibly few people entered, other than the poor residents themselves. Many of these properties, and their owners, came in for severe criticism in the slum report that was published in 1893. The Rookery was a warren of blind courts, dark passages and crumbling tenements known as Young's Court, Bee Hive Buildings, Campbell's Court and Spring Court etc. By the time of the slum report, the neighbourhood was a little more orderly but for the poorest people still living there, life and conditions must still have been atrocious.

Much of the old Rookery was replaced by commercial and industrial premises, but amazingly, some of the old buildings of the area survived until the 1930s when many of the wretched hovels were swept away and replaced by Corporation Tenements. The area bounded by Lime Street, King Street, Russell Street and Threefield Lane was replaced by four-storey blocks of Corporation Tenements that were begun in 1936 and occupied by 1939. These were quite poor by modern standards but infinitely superior to that which they replaced. Even so, they deteriorated to such a degree they were replaced in the 1970s by what is now Challis Court.

There are many photos of the old streets as they were, including Orchard Lane, King Street and Lime Street etc. but, as yet, I have not come across any images of the old Rookery buildings themselves. Presumably, the local photographers stayed away! As with so many of the old streets, the numbering system was, to say the least, haphazard, changing many times as the street evolved and much altered over the generations. For the purpose of (relative) continuity, I have used those allocated around 1900 as a guide, with references back to some of the earlier numbers.

Lime Street, like many others, has changed beyond recognition and the records of early residents are somewhat lacking. Some are not mentioned at all, while others are more sparingly noted. Of those who actually made it into the directories or census returns there is a lack of information as to their locations on the street due to so few house numbers, or in many cases, none at all.

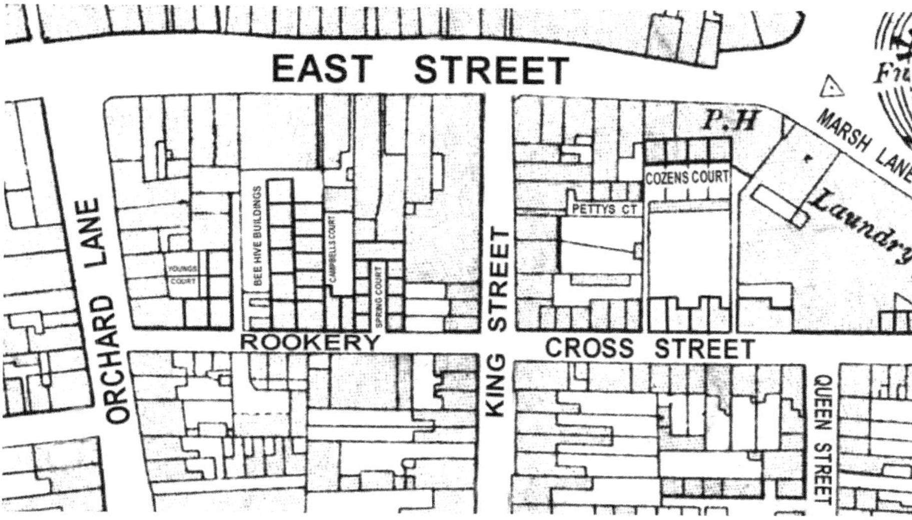

The Rookery area and its courts in the late 1800s, which later, along with Cross Street, was renamed Lime Street

LIME STREET
North Side, Nos. 1–4

Much of this area was taken up by various courts, which we shall visit subsequently (see Rookery and Courts below) but apart from those, there were only a few numbered buildings along this section of the street itself. Between Orchard Lane and King Street there were just five, although it seems several changes took place around the 1890s when some of the old Rookery buildings were demolished. At one time back in the 1700s, part of this area was named Spring Gardens, a green and pleasant space that probably gave its name to Spring Court, which followed around 1840.

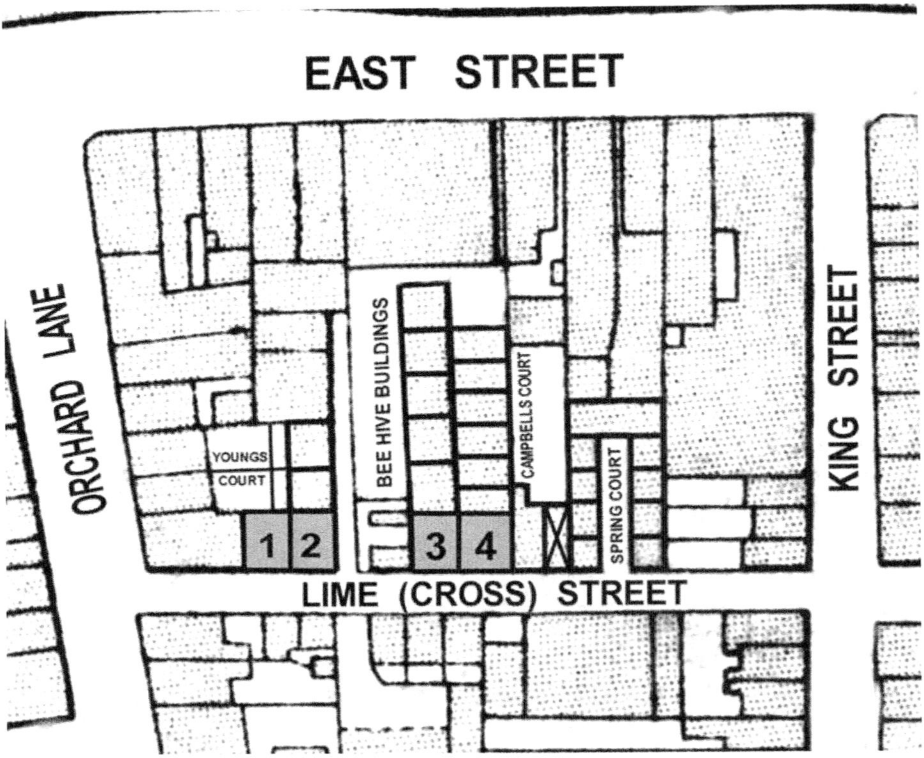

The north side of Lime Street showing Nos. 1–4 in relation to the old Rookery Courts. No. 3 was once the Cross Keys, and No. 4 the Oriental Tap

One of the earliest names at No. 1 is ships fireman John Alexander in 1857. He was followed in 1859 by labourer John Sullivan who was previously at No. 11 running the *Shamrock* public house. He had disappeared by 1869 but more about him later. Shopkeeper John Brown was there afterwards but in the 1881 census he was listed as a fish hawker. Boot maker Henry Seward arrived in 1884 and others at that address in the early 1900s included hairdresser Lorance Rosoi and toy maker George Locke in 1907. No. 2, in 1851 was the home of Jane Tubbs, wife of an agricultural labourer. The address later housed an assortment of ships firemen, carters and labourers in the early days. Pipe layer John Punch was there in the 1860s and 1870s, followed in later years by washerwoman Eliza Blake in the 1890s. Then, in the early 1900s, came labourer James Harrison who was the last person at that address.

No. 3 may have, at one time, been No. 6 Bee Hive Buildings, which disappeared about the same time as the emergence of the *Cross Keys* beer house, which in 1851 was run by Michael Joy, subsequently handing over to carpenter Joseph Pike, before fireman Angus McCarthur took charge in 1861 and remained until the 1870s. By that time McCarthur was a Royal Mail Shipping Company stoker and the premises had become a public house under Mew Langton's Newport Brewery, lasting until closure in 1907 with Thomas McGrath at the helm. The address then became a private residence until the latter years saw redevelopment with one of the new premises on the site becoming Stanley Godwin's fish and chip shop.

In 1861, William Kent is listed as a beer retailer at No. 4, which stood near the entrance to Campbell's Court. This had become the *Oriental Tap* by 1871 under Henry Lampard, being the tap bar to the *Oriental Arms* in East Street. A decade later, its name had changed to the *Anchor Inn Tap* under the Anchor Brewery with carpenter Charles Jacobs as host until it disappeared in 1884.

LIME STREET
North Side, Nos. 5–15

Originally numbered 1 to 6, the buildings between King's Street and the entrance to Cozens Court were renumbered as 5 to 10, and those east of Cozens Court became Nos. 11 to 15. Nos. 11 to 14 were pulled down in 1891, while Nos. 5 to 7 were demolished around 1901 and were replaced by utility flats in the 1930s. At that time, Nos. 8 to 10 were also demolished. Also, in the 1930s, the area occupied by No. 15 was replaced by the Octavia House flats.

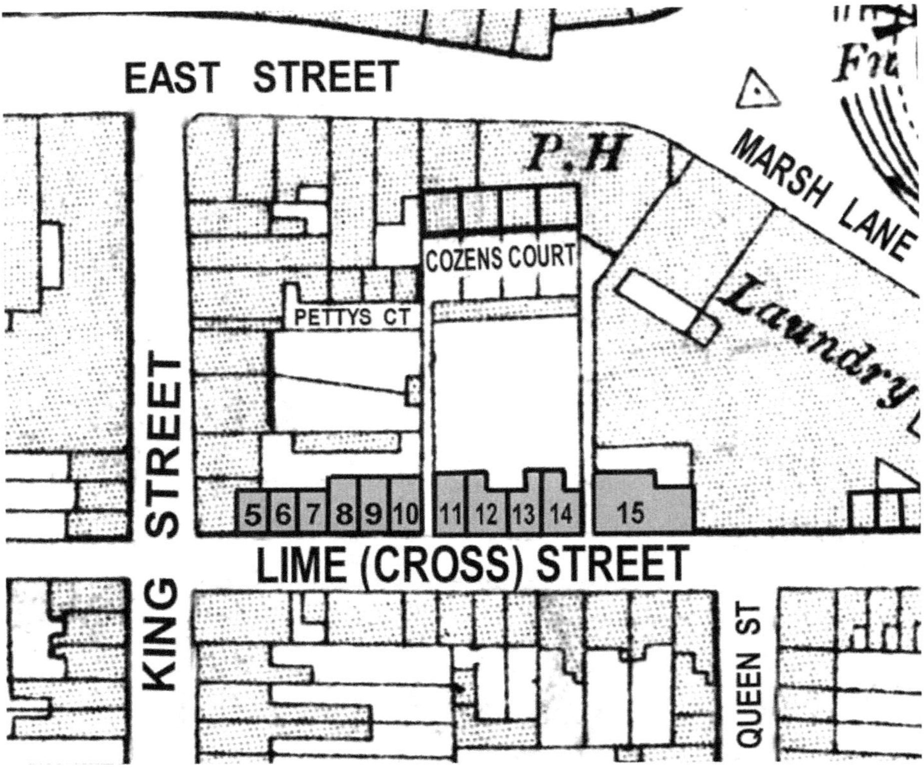

The north side of Lime Street with Nos. 5 to 15 east of King Street. No. 11 was once the Royal Tar and No. 15 the St Mary's Hotel Tap

Labourer John Price was an early resident at No. 5 in 1851, being followed by several of his kind until Alfred Webb as the last in 1901. Draper Henry H. Brookman resided at No. 6 in 1851. He was followed by coal burner John Thomas and then, over time, by labourers, a shoe maker, and finally, scissor grinder Henry Cole in 1901. Boot closer Hugh Jones at No. 7 in 1851 gave way to dressmaker Mary Ann Dawkins, bricklayer James Drudge, butcher Henry Tuffin and charwoman Mary Ann Walters were among others until that premises also vanished after 1901 with general labourer Benjamin Young being the last of the line.

No. 8 was the abode of builder Richard Cozens who was no doubt associated with nearby Cozens Court, which we shall visit shortly. He was evident there from 1841 and at one time was a business partner to renowned builder Joseph Bull until 1852. Cozens had moved away by 1857 and died a pauper at the local poorhouse in 1861 aged 77. An assortment including labourers, laundresses and boiler makers followed until the Miller family of chimney sweeps arrived in 1881; they then moved to No. 12 in 1884 before returning to No. 8, where they remained until the 1930s when the utility flats were built on the site.

No. 9 saw butcher Walter Davis in residence in 1851 before the Mansbridge family arrived in 1859. They were bricklayers and stonemasons, followed by the usual assortment of labourers, seamen and dock workers until Horace Shave was the final tenant in 1931. In 1841, porter William Purkiss was living at No. 10, which stood at the entrance to an alleyway that led to Cozens Court. Purkiss was there until around 1857 and the address was home to the familiar variety of painters, seamen and coal porters until Percival Ellis became the final name in the 1930s rent book.

On the other side of the alleyway, at No. 11 stood the *Royal Tar* with Henry Adams and his wife Mary Ann running the pub through the early 1850s until around 1855. That was when labourer John Sullivan took over and renamed it the *Shamrock* but his venture was not a success. Early in his tenure the house was subject to a prosecution for allowing drunkenness. Police found two men and seven women in the tap room, all drunk and fighting. The same disorder with the same parties reoccurred the next afternoon and following night. Despite his pleas of innocence, Sullivan was fined ten shillings plus costs, with an alternative of ten days in jail.

The beer house had closed by 1859 and the address then became the residence of bricklayer John Martin who was followed by dairyman William Nineham from 1861 until 1865. Next came an assortment of labourers until this section of the street was demolished around 1891. George Noyce was at No. 12 from 1841. He was a carpenter whose wife ran a boarding house next door while his son Fredrick was a chimney sweep. The family lived there until 1859 when stone mason Edward Dommitt (or Dommot) arrived with his wife Fanny. A number of labourers came and went before chimney sweep James Miller moved in from No. 8 around 1884, and went back there after 1891 when No. 12 was pulled down.

Mary Noyce was running a lodging house at No. 13 in 1841, which subsequently became a home to labourer William Palmer and later to boot maker Henry Fry in the late 1850s. Labourer and one-time boot maker George Martin had arrived by 1861 and stayed on through to the mid-1870s. Brass founder Frederick George Benham and labourer Isaac Mason were among the last there until demolition came with charwoman Sarah Hurnes being the final name in 1891. No. 14 does not appear to have been occupied until 1851 with labourer John Coghlan under its roof. Dairyman William Bartlett was there in the latter 1850s before ships fireman George Skates and his family were resident from 1853 until the mid-1870s. Frederick George Benham had moved there from No. 13 by 1884 and George Simmonds was its final tenant.

No. 15 was the *St Marys Hotel Tap*, which stood at the end of a long passage leading from the hotel itself in East Street. The tap dated back to at least 1841 when landlord Henry Blandford was in charge. John Pope and his wife Jane were there in the 1860s before William Soper and James Bishop headed a lengthy list of licensees under Strongs Brewery ownership until, in its final throes, it became the *Green Dragon*, run by Henry Hammond in 1891.

In the late 1860s and early 1870s, Nos. 15A and 16 are recorded but I have not been able to locate them. No.15A was occupied by carpenter and joiner Joseph Jones and No. 16 by cellarman George Wallis, so perhaps they were in close proximity, or attached to, the *St Marys Hotel Tap*. The final building towards the end of the street was the rear of the South Hants Steam Laundry based in Marsh Lane from around 1881 and lasted until the early 1930s. The previous occupant of that site since the 1850s was that of John F. Hattat's Brewery and Vinegar Works. Last of all was the iron store of William James Axton and Co. from 1914 until it disappeared with the laundry.

LIME STREET
South Side, Nos. 2–20
Orchard Lane to King Street

As with those on the north side of the street, the south side underwent several changes of numbering. In this case I have used those from 1891, which remained until demolition came in 1935 and the King's House flats were built over this part of the street.

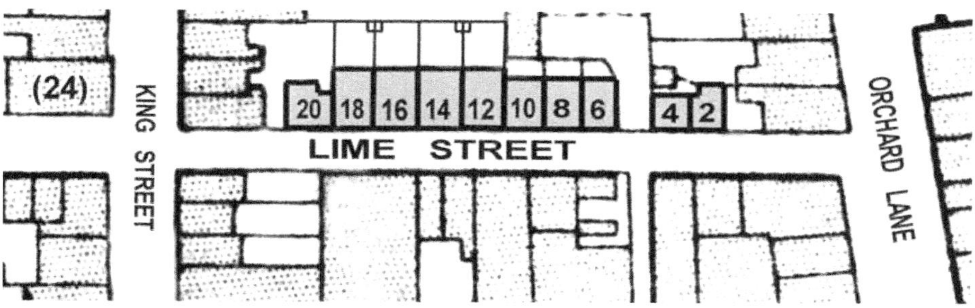

The south side of Lime Street as it was in 1891. Nos. 14 to 20 disappeared soon afterwards and were replaced by a warehouse. No. 24 was once the Carpenters Arms pub and previously included in King Street

The first name I have found at No. 2 is boot maker Thomas Jones in the mid-1850s and the next is George Preston, a hawker and labourer in 1871. In the 1890s we find charwoman Eliza Brady, Mrs E. Scorey and fellow char Mary Simmonds. Then into the new century we have boot maker Pascal Spacagna and boiler scurfer Thomas Henry Marlow. John Kennett arrived in the mid-1920s and Charles McGuire was the last in 1935.

Boot maker John Stickland was working at No. 4 in 1859 and no others were recorded until Ann Kneller in the late 1860s. Mrs Gannaway and coal porter William Cole were both there around 1871, followed by coal trimmer Henry Moore (previously at No. 8). General dealer William Ashley was longer term from 1907 until 1920 and the last at that address was William Richard Goodman whose family were involved in a regretful scene in advance of their home being demolished. Ahead of the transfer to their new homes, the occupants had been ordered to put their belongings out on the pavement by early morning, ready to be loaded and transported to new accommodation at Coxford. However, the Goodmans from No. 4 discovered their goods would be carried on a lorry partially loaded with coal. The deservedly proud family objected to this and after a ten-hour wait were informed they would not be moving that day. Neighbours rallied round in support while providing food and tea to the beleaguered family.

The Goodman family with their neighbours and meagre possessions outside Nos. 2 and 4 awaiting transport to their new homes in 1935 (Dave Marden collection)

No. 6 seems to have evaded the directories until 1867 when Dennis Murphy was in residence. Labourer James Brown was next in 1871 before baker Henry Bates in the same year. General labourer Jesse Mecarty and seaman Charles Anderson graced its interiors in the 1880s and by 1907 fish dealer Thomas S. Sherry embarked on a long stay that ended in 1931. By that time he had become a fruiterer. At No. 8 sawyer John Davis was one of the street's early settlers in 1851. He was followed by general dealer James Dacher (or Dacey) whose name appears in the early 1860s. Coal porter Robert Giles was there in 1871, as was Henry Moore (see No. 4) in 1876. However, Moore was back at No. 8 by 1891. General dealers James Smith and George Clark did their deals between 1901 and 1920 with Walter Chalk being the last inhabitant from 1931.

Under the various renumbering schemes, No. 10 did not appear until 1887 when George Arney was the householder. Marine foreman William Edmonds surfaced in 1901 and William Kearey held the keys from 1804 until Bert Baker became the final inhabitant in 1931, remaining until 1935 when the buildings came down. Dealer James Dacey (see also No. 8) was at No. 12 in 1867 until around 1870. Then a few others came and went before general labourer Thomas Anderson crossed its threshold in 1881 and remained for a decade before boot repairer Charles Ainsworth applied his soles and heels from 1901 until 1925. James Diaper and Joseph Croucher saw out the 1930s there before demolition came. The remaining houses from Nos. 14 to 20 were demolished around 1900 and replaced by the premises of wholesale druggists F.W. Wride and Co.

No. 14 had been a lodging house run by Mrs Julia Burton from 1861 until 1867 when costermonger Henry Cook wheeled his barrow there. Coal porter William Hillier was the next occupier in 1871. General labourer and hawker John Jamieson was the last tenant there from 1881. The occupants of No. 16 seem to have evaded officialdom until 1887 when Mrs Coakley was listed there. She was replaced in 1891 by fish saleswoman Harriet Sillick and I can find no others at that address but No. 18 looks to have had a longer existence, beginning with labourer

George Haskins in 1841. He was there in 1851 and his daughter Jane Haskins (also Hoskins and Hoskings) was running it as a lodging house from 1861. Carpenter Charles Morgan and labourer George Holmes saw out the latter 1860s before labourer James Beavis moved in around 1881 and was still there when demolition came.

The final house in this group was No. 20 with labourer James Scammel under its roof in 1867. Fellow labourer and coal runner Michael Chrimans (or Crimmins) was next from 1869 until the 1870s when chimney sweep William Noyce wielded his brushes there, but labourer Thomas King was the last in line from 1881 until the street came down, by which time he had turned his talents to hawking fish.

LIME STREET
South Side, Nos. 24–39

Nos. 24 to 39 were all demolished in 1935 to make way for new Corporation Tenements, known locally as Lime Street Flats, which were themselves demolished in the mid-1970s and redeveloped as Challis Court.

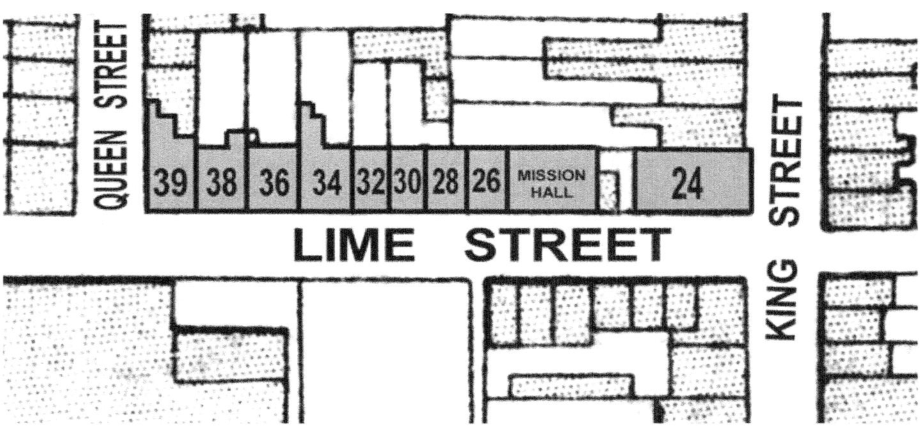

The south side of Lime Street between King Street and Queen Street. No. 24 was the Carpenters Arms and the Mission Hall was earlier part of the Carpenters until the pub closed. No. 39 was a shop, which later became No. 29 Queen Street

No. 22 does not appear in the directories and may have once been the building on the corner of King Street but we now continue with No. 24. This was originally the *Carpenters Arms*, which dated back to the 1820s with Tom Frost as landlord. Like many street corner pubs the address of the *Carpenters* flitted between Cross Street and King Street during its existence. Thomas Barnes ran the place from 1847 until at least 1871 and by 1876 William Knight was in charge. Mrs M.A. Lott looks to be its final landlady in 1884 shortly before it closed. General dealer William Sparks was based there in 1891 with seaman Henry Monahan following him in 1901 but by 1907 it had become a lodging house with the rear portion of the building in use as a congregation mission hall. Edwin Mutton had taken over the lodgings by 1911 before it came into the hands of Mrs Mary McLean 1912 until the 1930s when James Flynn was the last to let its rooms in 1935. The mission hall was gone by 1914.

Masons labourer Walter Ling was at home in No. 26 back in 1851 and labourer George Alexander had taken over a decade later; by 1881 he was running it as a general shop until he left in the late 1880s. It continued as a shop under Alfred G. Axton in 1901 but by 1911, coal porter Joseph H. Billows and his wife had moved in and remained until 1935. Seaman Joseph Ball was between voyages at No. 28 back in 1851 and a decade later it was home to journeyman butcher Henry Duffin. Labourer Mark Ford was the tenant from 1865 until 1887 and by 1907 Alfred Axton had extended his shop there from No. 26. Frederick Penny had moved in by 1912 and remained there until 1935. Turner Charles Brookman was sharpening his chisels at No. 30 from 1851 until 1853. A later occupant was boiler maker Charles Macey from 1861 until 1865. Labourer James Woods had his feet under the table there from 1869 to 1871 and after him came charwoman Sarah Ann Biddlecomb, labourer William Bessant, corn porter Charles Moor and ships fireman William Wilton. He and his wife stayed from 1912 until the mid-1920s when Alfred James Lofts became the final name in the rent book. Tailor Benjamin Byles was an early householder at No. 32 in 1851 but no other names appeared until that of ships fireman Henry Wheeler in 1867. An assortment of firemen, labourers and painters came and went before charwoman Mary Brown donned her apron there in 1901 and stayed until the mid-1920s with Frank F. Lockyear being the final tenant in 1935.

No. 34 was one of the better homes in this part of the street as its inhabitants seemed to stay on much longer. Stonemason George Mansbridge was there from 1841 until the mid-1850s when bricklayer William Willis wielded his trowel through to 1871. Labourer John Payne settled there from 1876 until around the turn of the century when ships donkeyman Robert Potter was evident until 1914. Then William Billows and his wife saw out the final years there. Town porter Thomas Bartlett was at No. 36 in 1851 and after him came stonemason Jabez Brown and his wife Jane followed by Mrs Mansbridge, shipwright Charles Graves and coal porter Thomas Smith who turned up in 1876 then stayed with his family until the early 1900s. Fellow coal porter Frederick Fulford rested his limbs there from 1911 until William Scammell saw out the final 15 years of the house.

For some reason No. 38 was listed as unoccupied in 1851 but the 1865 directory shows laundress Elizabeth Randall at home there. She remained until at least 1871 and was followed by labourer Michael and Caroline Sheen. The house obviously had connections with the nearby laundry as it was home to laundryman Henry Leggett in the 1880s and steam laundry foreman William Harman in 1901. Street hawker William Joseph Dart was the final occupant here from 1907 through to 1935. No. 39 was for many years listed as No. 23 Queen Street where James Balls had been a grocer since 1881 and served behind its counter until around the turn of the century when another link with the nearby laundry came about with the arrival of Maria Green who was a washerwoman there in 1901. General dealer Thomas Harman sold his wares there from 1907 until the mid-1920s when George Slaymaker presided over the final years of the shop.

LIME STREET
South Side, Nos. 40–52

This row of buildings between Queen Street and Threefield Lane was known as Fielders Cottages in the 1869 directory and numbered 1 to 7. In the 1881 census they were named as Cross Street Cottages.

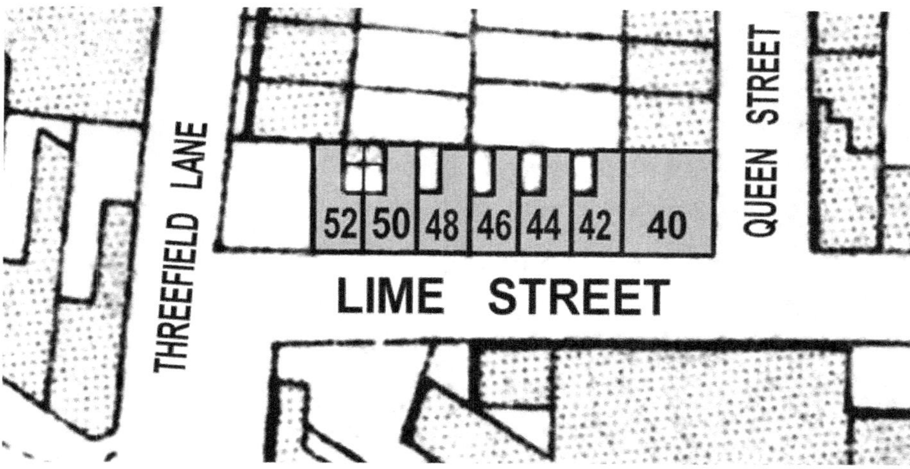

Nos. 40 to 52 on the south side of Lime Street with the Nelson Inn at No. 40. These buildings were previously Nos. 1 to 7 Fielders Cottages

No. 40 was the *Nelson Inn*, at other times listed as No. 1 Queen Street. Charles Olm was landlord back in 1867 and there was the usual steady turnover of hosts before George Wheeler pulled the pints in 1884. He was still there in 1891 but in 1901, dock coal porter Frederick G. Palmer had taken over prior to Alfred Poulter who was the final licensee when it closed in 1907 and became a lodging house operated by Robert Rose. By 1914 it had become the home of William Brown and later Alfred Greenwood in 1920 and its final years in the 1930s were shared by Frederick Linford and John Kennett, previously at No. 2.

Sweep William Noyce appears at several addresses over the years. In 1861 he was at No. 42. Mrs Elizabeth Hoare was there in 1865 followed by mariner John Aley in 1869. In 1871 Nos. 42 and 44 were both vacant for reasons unknown but No. 42 was occupied in 1881 by labourer and army reserve Frederick Burge. Nobody seems to have stayed there for any length of time before labourer John Henry Stace showed up in 1911 and remained until Arthur Barnes moved in around 1931, but the house was empty by 1935. Charwoman Ann Reason was at No. 44 in 1861 as was carpenter George Noyce in 1865. Then, after mariner Richard Tunstall stayed briefly, there was no-one else until labourer Charles Ware had moved in around 1881. Among the various others who followed were dressmaker Catherine Radford in 1891, marine fireman George Bagley in 1901 and Mrs Beatrice Brown in 1911. Frederick Henry Brackstone lived there from 1916 until 1931 when he moved next to No. 46. James E. Shillimore was the last renter at No. 44 in 1935. Laundress Elizabeth Broomfield had her wash tub at No. 46 in 1861; seaman James Penny and his wife Mary Ann were present in 1871. Coach builder and wheelwright George Passmore's family embarked on a long journey there in 1881 which lasted through to his widow Mary and son Alfred ending the family stay there around 1925. Robert George Robinson and then Frederick Henry Brackstone (from No. 44) were the 1930s residents. The early 1860s found Mary Ann Weston, followed by painter George Silvey, at No. 48. Carman Joseph Headley lived there in 1871. Fish hawker Richard Sainsbury appeared in 1881 while general hawker John Brown was next in 1884. The next couple of decades saw yachtsman John Martin, journeyman butcher Walter Leadbitter and blacksmith Charles Matthews enter its front door, with Matthews and his wife Mary Ann being the last inhabitants from 1931.

Pennah (or Pricilla) Hodges was charring from No. 50 from 1861 until 1865 and later arrivals were butcher Henry Bath in 1869 and dressmaker Mary Brown in 1871. The 1880s witnessed mast maker Charles Pepper and boot maker James Hayward while the 1890s welcomed dressmaker Jane Witcher and coal porter Alfred McWilliams. Labourer Henry Broarer enjoyed a long stay there from 1911 until 1931 when William Prosser saw out the final years there. On the corner with Threefield Lane stood No. 52 which was always a general shop with Mary Butt serving in 1861 and E. Edwards in 1869. Edwards was also a commission agent but we don't know what for. Nobody was minding the shop in 1871 as it was vacant and by 1881 labourer Charles Betteridge had taken accommodation there, as did painter Thomas Smith in 1884 with his wife running the shop. The same setup was repeated with coal porter Charles Brown and his wife Ellen in 1891 and the family business continued with son John until 1931. Mrs Flowers was the last person in there in 1935 when that side of the street made way for the Lime Street flats.

Nos. 40 to 52 Lime Street known as Fielders Cottages between Queen Street and Threefield Lane. No. 52, once a general shop, is nearest the camera

THE ROOKERY AND COURTS

The Rookery and its various courts were to the north of Cross/Lime Street but the term was also applied to parts of King Street and Queen Street. References in the 1893 slum report include 11 houses in the King Street Rookery and Cross Street (later Lime Street), all of which were in a very unsatisfactory condition. Two of them were improved after the service of a notice preliminary to a Closing Order. Two more are described as houses let out in separate rooms that were repeatedly overcrowded, where "the owners appear to have no other object in view than to crowd in the houses as many lodgers as they can, totally disregarding space and ventilation. They have a common yard, where the sanitary conveniences are situated, and these are used in common with six others in Cross Street". It was recommended that such houses be subject to the same bylaws that apply to common lodging houses as they had the effect of creating a poisoned atmosphere.

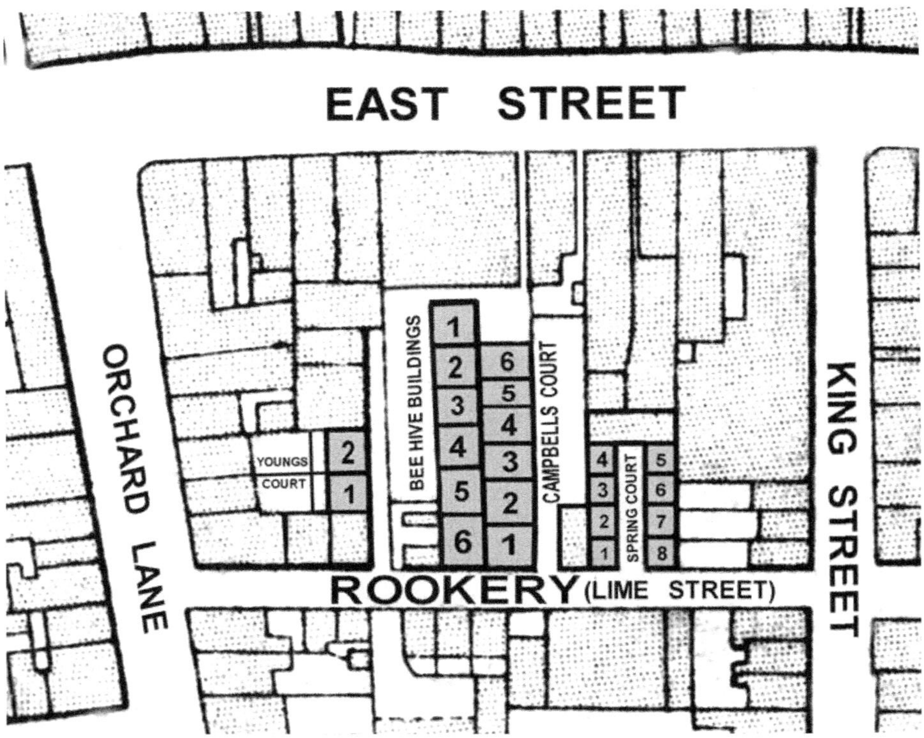

As best as I can determine, the Lime Street Rookery area with its associated courts in the mid-1800s. This was much changed in the later decades

YOUNGS COURT
Nos. 1–2

This was a court off Cross (Lime) Street that contained just two small houses, both having back yards that had taps and water closets but no ash bin was available to them. The first mention of Youngs Court appears in the 1841 census that shows labourer William Inns in residence. No more is recorded until the census of 1851 that has sawyer James Inns at No. 1 and labourer Charles Head at No. 2. 1861 sees labourer John McCarty and marine stores dealer Ann Driscoll living there. Another labourer, William Carter, appears at No. 1 from 1869 until 1884 and, likewise, Timothy Murphy from 1871 until 1884. William Tizzard (No. 1) and John Gannaway (No. 2) are the final recorded tenants in 1907 although the court was still listed but unoccupied until 1920.

BEE HIVE BUILDINGS
Nos. 1–6

Bee Hive Buildings, also known as Beehive Court, was a row of six houses on the north side of Cross Street (present-day Lime Street) that formed part of the old Rookery; one of these may have been included in Cross Street after the others had been demolished. There was also access to the buildings via a narrow passage from East Street. During the early 1800s, some of the residents had respectable occupations but the later clientele degenerated to hawkers, labourers and charwomen. Prior to the slum report there had been several families living in each house but, by 1893, the buildings were described as being in a ruinous condition and having been closed by the magistrates due to a lack of ordered improvements. One house is described as having first-floor rooms occupied by various persons who were situated over a stable and again being without through ventilation and having a single sanitary convenience. Two other houses were let out in separate rooms and repeatedly overcrowded. They had a common yard, where the sanitary conveniences were situated, but these were used in common with other houses in Cross Street. Another was described as an exceedingly bad property, where the owners appeared to have "no other object in view than to crowd the houses with as many lodgers as they could, totally disregarding space and ventilation, and having the effect of a poisoned atmosphere". Bee Hive Buildings were still listed in the 1907 and 1912 directories but the 1911 census recorded no occupants and the derelict buildings seem to have disappeared soon afterwards.

The 1851 census has road surveyor George Lane in No. 1 with labourer Daniel Sullivan there in 1861. The address was vacant in 1871 but pilot George Watts was recorded in 1881. Labourers Samuel Hill and William Carling were the last when the building was closed. No. 2 was the home of Royal Mail seaman John Squires in 1851 and he was succeeded by labourer Dennis Folley, hawker John Calice, sailor's wife Charlotte E. Gandy and labourers John McCarthy and Thomas Reeves. No. 3 lists railway porter Thomas Springer in 1851, followed by labourer John Welch, charwoman Mary Grant, fish hawker Michael Sullivan and labourer Alfred Hounsem. Back to 1851 when No. 4 was graced with the magnificently named Charlotte L. Littlecote Hooker, a widow with five young children and no evident means of support. In later years came labourers Cornelius Brown, David Sullivan, David Felarthy, Joseph Amey, John McCarthy and George Hounsem. No. 5 was the abode of more labourers, these being Michael Egan, Charles John Bowers, Robert Barry and John Bishop. This house was vacant from 1884. Catherine Dunn lived at No. 6 in 1851 but the address no longer existed afterwards and it is my belief this became the *Cross Keys* at No. 3 Cross Street, which appeared about the same time.

CAMPBELL'S COURT

Nos. 1–6

This was a row of six buildings shown and named on the 1846 and 1870 maps. They were immediately east of, and backing on to, Bee Hive Buildings, and were almost certainly those previously named as Scammell's Court in the 1841 and 1851 census returns that were listed between Beehive and Spring Courts. The 1841 census included cabinet maker William Scammell at No. 3 and it is presumed the court took its name from him. Although Campbell's Court appears on the 1870 map I can find no references to it after 1861.

The 1841 census showed most of the houses had a dozen occupants or more but I have only listed the heads of the households, beginning with gardener James Hawkins at No. 1, and by 1851 the tenant was washerwoman Elizabeth Smith. By the time of the 1861 census the name had changed to Campbell's Court and Elizabeth Kelly was living there with her three children. Back to 1841 again and we find pipe maker William Norton at No. 2 and a later occupier in 1851 was labourer Charles Rickman. The house was empty in 1861. No. 3 was the abode of cabinet maker William Scammell as mentioned previously. This, along with No. 4, was unoccupied in 1851 but labourer James Nineham was in residence in 1861. Labourer Moses Mabbet inhabited No. 4 in 1841 and the only other name listed there is that of Hizziah Nineham in 1861. Dressmaker Ann Boyer was sewing her seams at No. 5 in 1841 with later arrivals being labourer William Haskin in 1851 and shoe maker George Thomas a decade later. In 1841 No. 6 housed Jane Tubb who is undoubtedly the same Jane Tubb(s) living in Cross Street ten years later. Labourers James Daisy and George Billons were present in 1851 and 1861 respectively.

SPRING COURT

Nos. 1–8

The 1811 directory lists Spring Gardens and Spring Place in the vicinity of King Street. Dating back to the late 1700s this was probably a green and pleasant place that later included a pub named the *Turk's Head* dating from at least 1797 with Edward Rolph and his wife in charge. They were followed by William Allsop in 1811. The area was much changed by 1841 when the census recorded the many occupants of Spring Court, an obscure collection of eight dwellings that formed part of the rookery and stood between Orchard Lane and King Street on the north side of what became Lime Street. Its houses appeared in the 1851, 1861 and 1871 census returns and only three, at Nos. 6 to 8, were recorded in 1881. It was never included in the 1893 slum report, so must have disappeared by then.

In Spring Place, the 1811 directory included gardener Robert Norris, tailor George Oakshot, carpenter J. Rogers and a shoemaker by the name of Smith. However, from 1841 residents appeared only in the census returns when No. 1 had labourer Thomas Young as tenant. Labourers Thomas Wilson and Edward Brien were listed in 1851 and 1861 respectively with domestic servant Mary Sullivan there in 1871. Back to 1841 and at No. 2 we have blacksmith James Orchard followed by pauper Isobel George, labourer Dennis Murphy and fish dealer Margaret Ireland. No. 3 was the home of labourer William Turner which later housed agricultural labourer George Margam, Kate Murphy and labourer James Barry. At No. 4, labourer William Constead was resting his boots in 1841 before giving way to fellow labourer Thomas Watkins and laundress May Ann Andrews in 1861. In 1871 Nos. 4 and 5 were both vacant. No. 5 saw carpenter William Scott there in 1841 and later, hawker Eliza Haskins in 1851. She was the last listed at that address and only Nos. 6, 7 and 8 made the 1881 census. Shoe maker Isaac Brown was cobbling at No. 6 in 1841 and was succeeded by labourer James Harriman, Stephen Jameson, labourer Thomas King and finally Joanna Sullivan in 1881. Labourer William Foster was living at No. 7 in 1841 and others who later graced its interior included agricultural labourer Richard Remnant and labourer John Jameson who stayed on until 1871, with docks coal porter Robert Giles being last in 1881. The final dwelling at No. 8 had labourer John Casbourn in residence from 1841. Fellow labourer George Cooper had arrived by 1851 and stayed for 20 years before dock labourer James Barry was the last occupant in 1881.

COZEN'S COURT
Nos. 1–4

Variously spelt as Cozens, Cosens or Cussens Court. Originally four houses occupied this court and were accessed by a long narrow alley from Cross Street (latter-day Lime Street). None had through ventilation as they backed onto the *St Mary's Hotel* public house. In the 1893 report they were described as being damp and unhealthy with sanitary conveniences out in the yard. Builder Richard Cozens lived nearby in Cross Street from the 1840s and was most likely involved in its construction. The court ceased to exist after 1940.

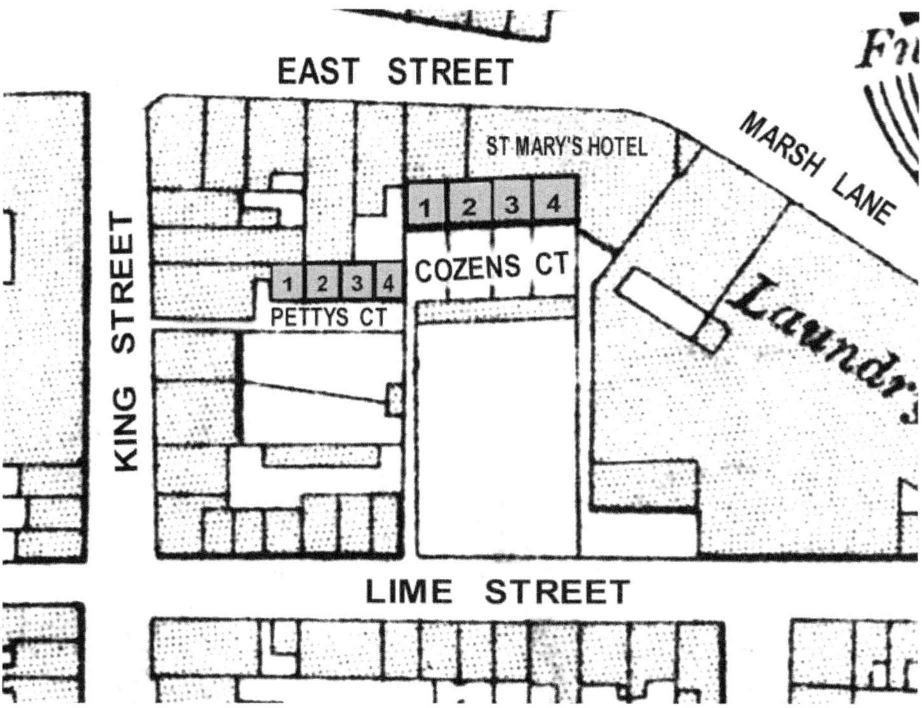

The four houses in Cozens Court were reached via a long alleyway from Lime Street. The nearby Pettys Court was entered through a covered passage from King Street

Like so many other courts, this one was only mentioned in the early census returns from 1841 until included in the 1884 directory. The line-up in 1841 was blacksmith William Edmunds at No. 1 while No. 2 housed painter William Martin, and at Nos. 3 and 4 were Henry Ailwood and Ann Watts, both of independent means. By 1851 railway porter Hugh McGarrah had moved into No.1 with the Macey family present there from 1871 until 1925. Mrs Beech was the last at that address in 1940. Boiler maker and plater John Horner was at No. 2 from 1871 to 1884 with James M. Bungay being the last at that house from 1925 until 1940. No. 3 saw labourer Abraham Midhurst behind its door before ships fireman Charles W Cook was there in 1884. He was followed by rag sorter Elizabeth Wilcox before another ships fireman, Henry Durman, and his family moved in around 1901 and stayed until the very end. No. 4 was the home of hairdresser Henry Balls in 1851 and a decade later tailor James Nineham had moved in. By 1871 the place was vacant but reoccupied in 1887 until 1891 by laundress Elizabeth Macey, after whom no-one else was listed.

KING STREET
Coombs Court, Petty's Court, Russell Court and Miller's Court

King Street ran south from East Street down to Chandos Street and while it was not quite as infamous as the adjoining Rookery (which stood in what became Lime Street), it did have its unsavoury features. Throughout the Victorian era it contained a good many common lodging houses with various individuals packed into rooms that were of a very basic standard and no fewer than 13 buildings were used as such. Landlord Walter Brown and his wife ran at least seven such establishments at Nos. 8 to 12, 23 and 32 in the early 1900s, while two others, at Nos. 2 and 4, survived into the 1930s. Most of the buildings in the King Street area were demolished in the 1950s to make way for the present Holy Rood estate with blocks of flats named after the old streets and neighbourhoods.

KING STREET
East Side, Nos. 2–8A

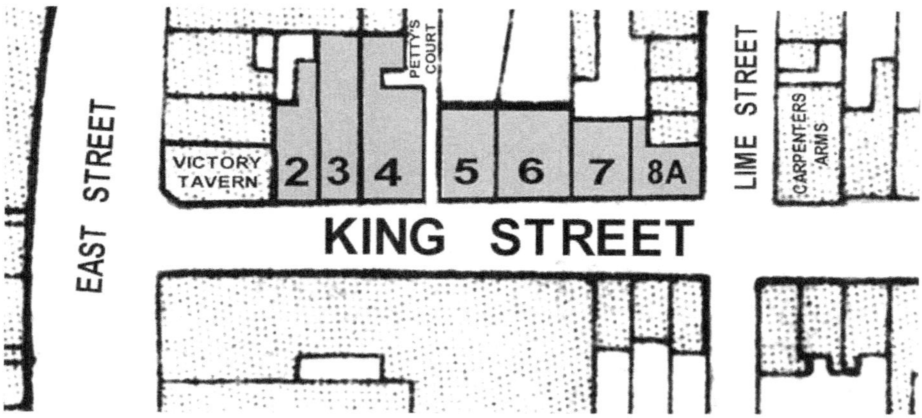

The north-east section of King Street ran down from East Street to Lime Street. The Victory Tavern on the corner of East Street was once No. 1 King Street, while No. 3 was a Mission Hall and No. 5 was at one time a pub under several names. A covered passage between Nos. 4 and 5 led to Petty's Court

The buildings in this section of King Street, between East Street and Lime Street were renumbered several times with the *Victory Tavern* sometimes being included but the latter-day numbering was 2 to 8A (No. 8 was south of Lime Street next to the *Carpenters Arms*).

Dealer George Grant appears in the 1834 directory and is shown running a shop at No. 2 in the 1840s. From around 1853 it had become the home of boot and shoemaker Cornelius Lewis who died in 1867 aged 50 but his wife Louisa, a needlewoman, remained there until she also passed on at the age of 70 in 1890. By the early 1900s, like so many in the street, No. 2 had become a lodging house and remained as such until the street came down. Hotel porter James Burness was an early name at No. 3 in 1851 but nothing more of not is seen at that address until 1901 when the census shows it as lodging house with some 17 dock labourers in residence. By the outbreak of World War One the site was occupied by the King Street Mission Hall, which has survived in various guises through to modern times. No. 4 was home to sawyer Aaron Whitmarsh back in 1851 and he was followed by rag and bone merchant James Clark and bill poster Thomas Davies. Chimney sweep George Riley had lived there from 1865 and stayed for a decade before the arrival of mariner Charles Smith who, after running a shop there, had turned it into a lodging house by 1881, which accommodated 15 poor souls at that time.

The entrance to Petty's Court was a covered passage between Nos. 4 and 5 where the latter had been a lodging house in the 1850s run by sawyer George Davis who also ran a beer house named the *New Inn* from that address. By 1855 it had become the *Sawyers Arms* with Thomas Gosling in charge, and a further change to the *True Briton* came in 1869. It was afterwards the home of a boiler maker, costermonger and a pensioner, with the final tenants from the early 1960s being the ice cream-vending Fella family who came from Italy. Fellow Italian Clement Rossi was an organ grinder who lived next door at No. 6 during the same period as the Fellas. The building had once been the home of pauper Mary Ann Barnes back in 1851 before it became a lodging house run by James Brown in the 1860s. Other occupiers through the 1880s and 1890s were corn store labourer James Archer, labourer Henry Humphries and charwoman Joanna Crimmons.

At No. 7, after an early entry of labourer James Jones in the 1841 and 1851 census returns, there's not much else until pensioner William Brown appears in 1859 and is there through the 1860s. In 1871, William Noyce is listed there as a mechanical chimney sweep but I assume that refers to his brushes rather than the man himself! We then have various labourers and wood dealer Mrs Holloway through the 1880s and 1890s before the early 1900s saw various branches of the Crimmins family at Nos. 7 and 8A with John at No. 7 and Thomas at No. 8A until the early 1930s. They were the final tenants before Nos. 5 to 8A were replaced by buildings named utility flats and then included in Lime Street.

Nos. 2 to 6 King Street where No. 3 was a Mission Hall and No. 5 was once a pub named the Sawyers Arms. The Victory Tavern can be seen at the far end on the corner of East Street

KING STREET
East Side, Nos. 8–21

South of Lime Street, the numbers ran from 8 to 21 to the corner of Russell Court. Once again there was some juggling of numbers with the *Carpenters Arms* pub on the corner of Lime Street sometimes being included (see Lime Street for details). On the 1870 map there was a building blocking King Street from Russell Street (see Russell Street) and, when this was removed, Little Russell Street became part of King Street. This section of King Street was demolished in the 1930s to make way for the Corporation Tenements but two houses formerly at Little Russell Street survived until the 1950s.

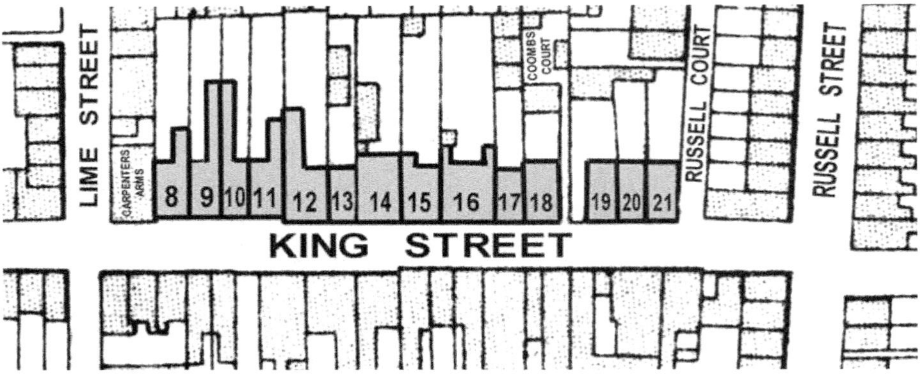

Nos. 8 to 21 King Street where several were lodging houses. The Carpenter's Arms on the corner of Lime Street was often listed as being in King Street

No. 8 stood next door to the *Carpenters Arms* and was originally the home of horse dealer Charles McDonald back in 1847. After he had moved on it became the abode of sawyer John Palmer through the late 1850s. Bill poster Thomas Davis (previously at No. 4) spent time there from 1863 until 1869 saw hairdresser William Carmichael snipping away. Labourer Timothy Donovan had arrived by 1871 but, although he was still there a decade later, by that time he had become an invalid. His seaman son Timothy was still at that address until Frederick Hayter moved in around 1900. By 1911 it had become a common lodging house run by Walter Brown who also took in boarders at Nos. 9, 10, 11 and 12 until Mrs Morgan took them all over in 1925. William Harding lived there in the early 1930s until demolition came in the mid-1930s.

Cordwainer Isaac Thomas worked his skills at No. 9 in 1851 and the later 1850s saw Thomas Doling, mariner John Scott and farm bailiff Thomas Harding as key holders. Harding stayed on until labourer Henry Coombes had moved there in 1867 while other residents included boiler maker Walter Hollins and shoe maker George Finch through the 1880s and 1890s. Walter Brown had added to his lodging house empire there by 1911 and that lasted until Mrs Morgan was landlady from 1925 before Arthur Roberts and Charles Cunningham saw out the 1930s there. No. 10 had been a bakery from at least 1841 when it was run by

John Batt and his wife Mary. Their daughter Elizabeth had taken over by 1851 and the business was family run until around 1870 when William H. Saunders took over the oven. The bakery ceased around 1880 and several tenants passed through its door until Walter Brown took in boarders from 1907 before handing over to Mrs Morgan. Arthur Witcher was the final tenant in the 1930s.

The Wheeler family were early occupiers of No. 11 in 1851. William was a carter and carrier while his son Charles was a town porter who was resident there until around 1870. The Sullivan family appear several times in this neighbourhood. Joanna and her husband John were previously at Cross Street but by 1871 she was a widow and a pauper living at No. 11 King Street and by 1881 she had moved on to Spring Court. A steady flow of labourers filtered through No. 11 until it became another of Walter Brown's lodging houses in 1907. When that closed around 1931 Ernest Thomas Ede was the final tenant. No. 12 looks to have been occupied only from 1865 when labourer and sometime dairyman William Littlecott was there until 1871. His son George, by then a Great Western Railway porter, was resident in 1881. Boiler maker John Horner was occupant in 1901 before William Brown snapped up the property as another of his lodging houses in 1907. Mrs Morgan ran the place until George Herbert Crabtree was the final name in 1935.

Nos. 8 to 12 King Street. The window of the former Carpenters Arms, which was on the corner of Lime Street, can be seen on the left and the other buildings were lodging houses from the early 1900s

Labourer Thomas Keeping and his wife Hannah spent many years at No. 13 where Hannah supplemented the family income by charring and taking in laundry until she died a widow there in 1889. Gentleman Walter Edmunds was another long-term tenant from 1907 until 1925 with Mrs Taylor the final name when demolition came in the 1930s. A No. 13A appeared briefly in the registers of 1931 and 1935 with Mark Slade and his wife listed. Barrow man and porter Richard Mitchell and his laundress wife Rebecca were at No. 14 in the mid-to-late 1850s. A widow by 1861, Rebecca worked on as a laundress. Coal dealer William Adams was next at that address in 1871 and set up as a general dealer and shopkeeper with his wife Eliza. He had died by 1901 and his widow ran the shop with their daughter Mary until 1935.

Boot makers George Lane and George Joy were the occupants at No. 15 in the early 1860s before Thomas Bulpitt was a general dealer there until 1871. After a spell away, he was back in 1891 but was gone again by

1901 when fish dealer Thomas Channell arrived with his ice machine and remained there until the early 1930s that saw Mrs Higham as the final tenant before demolition. Another boot maker, John Barnes, inhabited No. 16 from 1841 until 1851 while labourer Samuel Bundy was there from 1861 until 1871. Labourer, general dealer and shopkeeper Henry Maunder was also long term from then until his death in 1816 when his daughter-in-law Ellen took over the shop and continued until the 1930s.

No. 17 was home to sawyer John Palmer in 1851. Pavier and stone mason George Coombes arrived in 1861 and chiselled away until 1881 when there followed a high turnover of tenants including dealer Thomas Sherry around 1890, then coal Porter John Spreadbury through the early 1900s, before Henry Bridges and his wife from 1912, with Ernest Stanley Hibberd seeing out the street's time from 1925. Waterworks turncock operator Benjamin Coombes lived at No. 18 from 1851 until the mid-1860s but few others spent much time under its roof before widow Ellen Gilkes set up her boarding house there in 1907 and ran it until the 1920s. Thomas Lucas saw out the remaining years through to the 1930s. Between Nos. 18 and 19 was the entrance to Coombes Court, which we shall visit later. Seamstress Elizabeth Attwood was sewing away at No. 19 in the latter 1840s and labourer John Veal spent the early 1860s there before stonemason William Coombes arrived in 1867. He was succeeded in 1871 by porter Samuel Sawyer. Coal meter George Bartlett spent a decade there from 1881, as did furniture remover Walter Lott from 1891. By 1912 it was yet another common lodging house, this time run by Alfred Poulter who also took in boarders at Nos. 20 and 21. George Watkins was resident from 1914 until the mid-1930s with Henry Burton present in 1935.

Agricultural labourer John Veal was at No. 20 in 1851 and by 1855 its occupant was porter George Veal but I cannot find any family connection. They both had moved to No. 19 by 1861 when ships fireman John Clark took their place. A few others came and departed before waiter John Ford took residence in 1871 there and was engaged as a pewter cleaner before leaving around 1900. Ice cream maker and musician Antonio Paglia was briefly there until Alfred Poulter turned it into a lodging house in 1912. John Bushnell was a then regular boarder from 1914 until the building came down. Dairyman Edward Elsey was dwelling at No. 21, at the entrance to Russell Court, in 1847 and fellow milkman William Hayes had taken his place by 1851. Carrier, and later town porter, James Olive was a permanent feature from 1855 until 1884. Ice cream dealer Peter Paglia (a probable relative of Antonio at No. 20) was there in 1911. He and his wife Lilian set up a shop there, which lasted until 1935.

A gathering for the photographer outside No. 12 King Street looking down to No. 21 in the distance

Nos. 18 to 21 King Street with the entrance to Coombs Court between 18 and 19. The low building in the distance stands at the entrance to Russell Court. This was No. 8 Russell Street which was once a stables and a smithy

LITTLE RUSSELL STREET
Nos. 1 and 2

These were two houses that stood between Chandos Street and Russell Street. This was known as Little Russell Street before being regarded as part of King Street from around 1912 (see map for Russell Street south side). They were demolished along with others in the neighbourhood in the mid-1950s.

I have not come across any residents there before 1884 when No. 1 was the home of hammer man Samuel Williams, then army pensioner Christopher Jago lived there in 1891, as did general labourer John Brackman in 1901. Frank Kirby had moved in by 1912 and stayed until 1935, while Mrs Noonan was present in the postwar years. Labourer Henry Matthews, Mrs O'Connor and seaman William Simonds all lived at No. 2 through the 1880s before coal porter Alfred Mason and railway labourer Joseph Cullinan (or Cunningham) spent the early 1900s there. Edward Charles Crocker was in the rent book from 1920 to 1939 with James Francis McDonald in occupation from then until the final days.

KING STREET

West Side, Nos. 22–40

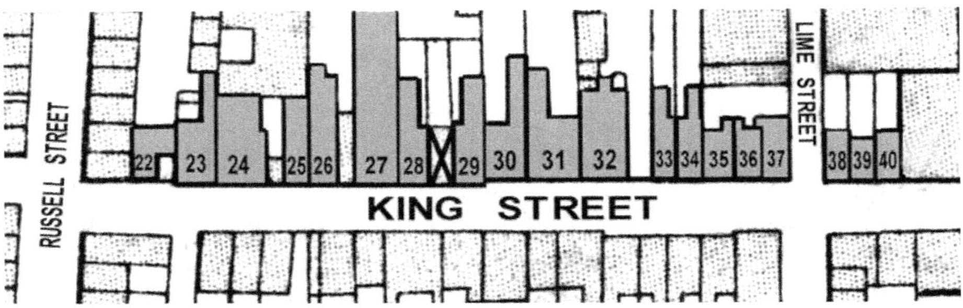

The west side of King Street showing Nos. 22 to 40. Several of these buildings were once pubs. They were Nos. 24, 28, 29, 31, 36 and 37

Most of this section of the street from Russell Street to Lime Street was demolished in the mid-1930s. No. 22 was a small premises that didn't feature much in the directories with Michael O'Callaghan shown there in 1907 and it was vacant in 1911. No. 23 was the home of dock labourer Thomas Stoneham in the 1860s and 1870s. Carter George Evans had a spell there through the 1880s and the building later became one of many lodging houses run by Walter Brown from around 1912. Mrs Matthews was the final tenant from 1920 until 1935.

There were several pubs, at least by name, towards the bottom of King Street but in some cases the records are unclear about their exact locations. At No. 24 was the *Phoenix Tap*, being the tap bar for the *Phoenix Inn* in Orchard Lane. William Mitchell was dispensing pints there in 1861 and George Mitchell for the remainder of the 1860s. Thomas Smart was then behind the bar until 1871. By 1881 the pub had a new name. This was the *Blacksmiths Arms* with Charles Yaldren as host. Yaldren had previously served at the *George and Henry Tap* at No. 29. Another change of name came about around 1901 when it became the *King and Queen* with dock labourer Maurice Haynes in charge. Others came and left until Ernest Pearsey arrived in 1914 and remained until the pub closed in 1921. Alfred Edward Gawn was the last to live there through the early 1930s. The late 1850s saw George Willis and carpenter James Errwood at No. 25. Brewer Henry Nutley lived there from 1869 until around 1881 when Charles Yaldren extended his beer sales from the *Blacksmiths Arms* next door but by 1884 his daughter Ann had changed it to a greengrocers shop. By 1907 it had become Crowley and Co.'s Brewery Stores and remained as such until iron merchants William James Axton took over the premises in 1931. James Down ran his grocers shop at No. 26 back in 1869 which lasted until 1876. It was home to unemployed labourer Maurice L. Vanner in 1881 and was Colliers Salt Store by 1884 before it became a shop again under Charles William Vanner in 1887. William Albert Plomer and his wife Mary Ann had moved behind the counter in 1901 and remained in business until 1931 when Alfred J. Slaymaker took charge for the final years.

For much of its time, No. 27 seems to have a workshop with an attached cottage. Carpenter John Norman lived there from the mid-1860s until the early 1880s but by 1891 the address had become a lodging house with some 23 inhabitants. Iron merchants William James Axton and Co. occupied part of the premises but had taken over completely by the early 1980s and extended through to No. 16 Orchard Lane. Remaining until the 1930s they were joined by furniture remover Thomas Smith from 1912 to 1920.

Nos. 28 and 29 were both pubs from the early days consisting of a single building with a central covered entrance leading to a yard with other premises. William Brown was a brewer at No. 28 in 1834 and was still there in 1851 by which time it had become the *Falcon Inn.* His son Edward had taken over by 1851 but after a couple more landlords it seems to have vanished after 1859 when wood turner Charles Brookman had arrived and remained until 1881. John and Alfred Clark were coal porters living there in the 1880s and labourer Ernest Sainsbury had a long spell from 1911 until the mid-1930s with fruiterer William Roberts resident from 1939 through to 1954. Blacksmith John Melsom was at No. 29 in 1845 and his wife ran a lodging house there in the latter 1840s until Charles McDonald opened up his beer house there in 1851. Horse dealer McDonald (previously at No. 8) named his house the *White Horse* which he ran until around 1857 when it became the *George and Henry Tap* which was the tap bar for the nearby George Brewery and was run by Ben Coombs senior in the 1850s, then by Charles Yaldren in the 1860s and a few others until it closed around 1887. By 1891 fish hawker Robert Rose was living there and by 1911 it was the home of Thomas and Ann Elizabeth McDonald who stayed on until 1940 and James Francis McDonald was the final tenant in 1954.

Porter John Drudge was living at No. 30 in 1863 but had moved out by 1859 when boiler maker John Wilcocks had arrived. Coal porter Charles Turl had turned up by 1881 and his family had an extended stay until 1912 when his son Charles James Turl was head of the household. By 1916 Mrs Ford had moved in and was still there in 1940 when the house was a victim of wartime bombs. Boiler maker John Jones was at No. 31 in the 1860s before George Butt took over in 1869 and decided to turn it into a pub named the *Rifleman's Arms*. It was a short-lived venture as he was gone by 1871 when John Wilcocks (or Wilcox) came from No. 30 next door and decided to stay there with his laundress wife Elizabeth until about 1890. Bricklayer Timothy Murphy and needlewoman Amelia Wood were next in the rent book before unemployed widower William Wright appeared in 1911. Occupation was sporadic after him with George F. Payne being the last tenant in the mid-1930s.

Labourer Stephen Stacey, previously of Cross Street, was an early fixture at No. 32 in 1865 until 1869. Seaman John Portlock and his wife Elizabeth were there from 1876 until 1881 (when they moved next door to No. 33). Labourer James Archer, and corn porter James Orchard were next throughout the 1880s and into the new century we see dock labourer Henry Cresswell there in 1911. By 1912, Walter Brown had added it to his growing number of lodging houses but the Cresswell family remained as tenants until 1931, with William Henry Tuck, being last of all in 1935. Wheelwright William Miller was noted at No. 33 from 1855 until 1881 when the Portlocks came from No. 32 next door. By 1891 John Portlock was a navy pensioner and after his death in 1908, his seamstress daughter Eliza and labourer son John Junior stayed on until 1916. Mrs Eyers (or Aires) then saw out the 1930s there. The Gookey family lived in No. 34 for quite some years, beginning with butcher Josiah back in 1841, then Thomas, who made soda water in 1851, who was joined by porter Joseph and both remained at that address until 1865 when Thomas and his wife Mary Ann moved next door to No. 35. Back at No. 34, labourer John Lott appeared briefly in 1871, as did drayman William Hebb in 1878 before seaman Charles Collins spent the early 1900s there. Boiler cleaner Henry Bishop was the final householder from 1911 until the mid-1930s.

Pauper Thomas Reed endured his bleak time at No. 35 in 1851 and at the close of that decade, coal meter Peter Lott called in. Bricklayer Amos Evans came along in 1863 before Thomas Gookey and his wife moved from next door at No. 34. Thomas died in 1874 and his widow Mary Ann stayed on until her own death in 1887. The rent book saw several more names added before that of Mrs Richmond in 1916 who stayed until the mid-1930s. Bricklayer Amos Evans lived at No. 36 from 1851 until he moved to No. 35 in 1863. Contractor Peter Lott then set himself up there and later had taken over No. 37, combining the two premises as a pub called *The Rose*. His wife Mary Ann ran it from 1884 until it closed in 1906, after which the family remained and her son-in-law William Lamont took over the tenancy from 1912 until 1935. No. 37 had an early association with the brewery trade as William Williams was a beer retailer there in 1834. It had been the home of labourer Stephen Jones in 1851 and dustman John Jones from 1885 until 1861. Fellow dustman James Long was there in 1865 before Peter Lott extended his house from

No. 36 in 1871.

Labourer William Willis was living at No. 38 in 1841 and was still there until chimney sweep George Riley made it his home in 1851. Riley was the tenant until around 1867 when James Long moved in from No. 37 next door. Costermonger Samuel Long had assumed the tenancy by 1871 and was a licensed hawker in 1881 before he died there in 1891 with his widow Eliza staying on for another ten years. Carman George Chalk, Arthur Churchill, Walter Pollard and finally, Charles Adams in 1940 came later.

No. 39 was yet another lodging house. It was run by Henry Harding and his family from 1851 when there were 16 boarders including a smith, baker, ships fireman, a gardener, several labourers, two tramps and a pauper. The Hardings had gone by 1861 when boot maker William Lewis was registered there, as was general dealer William Slimm in 1863. Costermonger Henry Maunder, later at No. 16, appeared in 1869 followed by Julia (or Jane) Murphy (the census and directory differ) in 1871. Jane Hatcher, Thomas Wood and George Neill took turns there through to the 1880s when chimney sweep William Noyce moved in around 1884. In fact, Noyce rented No. 40 at the same time and eventually stayed on there. Next at No. 39 came labourer John Cox and boiler maker William Lunt before several short-stay renters ended with John Metcalf in 1940.

No. 40, like its immediate neighbour, was a lodging house run by the Hardings in the 1850s and there is no further entry in the directories until 1869 when charwoman Mrs Hannah White was there until William Noyce arrived in 1878 and stayed until at least 1884 when he moved to No. 39. Then into the 1900s it became the corn warehouse of A. and F. Ray until the 1920s. Biscuit makers Carr and Co. were in occupation in the mid-1930s and finally, druggists Sutton and Co. prior to the outbreak of war.

King Street's west side with Nos 31 to 37 where Nos. 36 and 37 on the right was once a pub called The Rose

KING STREET COURTS
East Side

PETTY'S COURT
Nos. 1–4

Petty's Court underwent several changes of name in its time. Back in the 1851 census it was listed as Whitmarsh Court, then by 1861 it had become Petty's Passage. Petty's Court is mentioned in the 1871 census but no names are listed. It appears in the 1881 census as King's Court and the directories in 1884 and 1887 also refer to it as King's Court. Petty's Court returns in the 1891 and 1901 census and in 1907 it finds its way back into the directories and remains as such until 1940.

Its name as Whitmarsh Court in 1851 was no doubt due to the presence of sawyer Aaron Whitmarsh living at its entrance (see King Street). Set in a small blind court with access from a covered passage adjacent to No. 4 King Street, the four houses were said to be in fair condition according to the 1893 slum report, although none had through ventilation and all conveniences were out in the yard. (see Cozen's Court, Lime Street for map).

In the 1851 census (as Whitmarsh Court) pauper William Hack was at No. 1, cordwainer Isaac Brown at No. 2, and labourers Isaac Bull and James Brown at Nos. 3 and 4 respectively. By 1861 (as Petty's Passage) those living there were something of a family affair with gardener Charles Barnes and Mary Ann Barnes at Nos. 1 and 2, Charles Thomas Barnes at No. 3 and Jessie Philpot at No. 4. In 1881 (as King's Court) we find cycle maker John Baggs, charwoman Annie Travers, corporation labourer James Martin and gardener Samuel Chalk. Then in 1884, No. 1 is listed as a workshop, with Mrs Travers at No. 2, James Martin still at No. 3 and Mrs Harman at No. 4. In 1887 the line up was John Beggs, David Sanders, Mrs Martin and Mrs Beggs. In the 1891 census (now Petty's Court again) there were just two occupants with James Martin still at No. 3 and Henry Archer at No. 4. Moving on to 1901, No.1 was still unoccupied, corn porter Tom Grist was at No. 2, widow Sarah Bath at No. 3 and ships fireman William Passmore at No. 4.

Blacksmith John Smith was resident at No. 1 in 1911 with labourer Harry Everson at No. 2, charwoman Emma Bath (daughter of Sarah) in No. 3 and dock labourer Charles Toop at No. 4. The court is not listed again until the 1925 directory finds John Smith still at No. 1 where he remained until 1935 when Mrs Maloney arrived and stayed through to 1940. Joseph Panton was at No. 2 until 1939 when Mrs Jenkins was resident in the pre-war years, and Mrs Gatford was at No. 3 until 1939. No.4 did not appear in the years 1925 to 1940.

COOMBS COURT
Nos. 1–3

Three small houses occupied Coombs Court, which was entered by a narrow covered passage next to No. 18 King Street. Generally, the houses were in a fair condition compared to others nearby, although one was described as dirty, and another damp. None had through ventilation and all relied on facilities being out in the yard. (for map see Russell Court).

The three houses appear in the 1851 census when the occupants were pavier George William Coombs at No. 1 (probably from whom the court took its name), mariner Joseph Watkins at No. 2 and Chelsea Pensioner Richard Canson at No. 3. The next entry is not until 1881 where we find George W. Coombs still at No. 1 but now a coal porter. The court made it into the 1884 directory with cooper Augustus Weigel in No. 1, labourer William Jones at No. 2 and Mrs Madden at No.3. By 1891 George William Coombs was back at No. 1, this time as a labourer, with William Jones still at No. 2 and David Gordon at No.3. From that date onward at No. 1 were dock labourers John Wadmore and John Busnell who appeared in 1901 and 1911 respectively with John Hall, Charles Blake and George Henry Longman listed during the final years from 1925 until 1935. Labourer William Jones was still at No. 2 in 1881 and 1891 before Julia Chalk arrived in 1901, while dock labourer George Frederick Hamilton spent time there around 1911 with Albert E. Plomer being the last name in 1931. Dressmaker Mrs Jane Maddon was at No. 3 in the early 1880s with Mark Ford and David Gordon taking us up to 1901 when dock carpenter Barry Harty moved in. He was replaced by hotel servant Emma Brydges in 1911 and she was the last recorded at that address.

Dereliction at Coombs Court showing Nos. 2 and 3 shortly before demolition

RUSSELL COURT
Nos. 1–5

Otherwise known as Russell Place, running east from the south end of King Street, and north of Russell Street, this group of five houses also had access via a covered passage in Russell Street. Before the preparation of the 1893 report, the court had undergone several improvements, which placed four of the houses in fair condition, except No. 5, which remained unhealthy. Each house had its own yard and the court was demolished in the mid-1930s to make way for the Corporation Tenements.

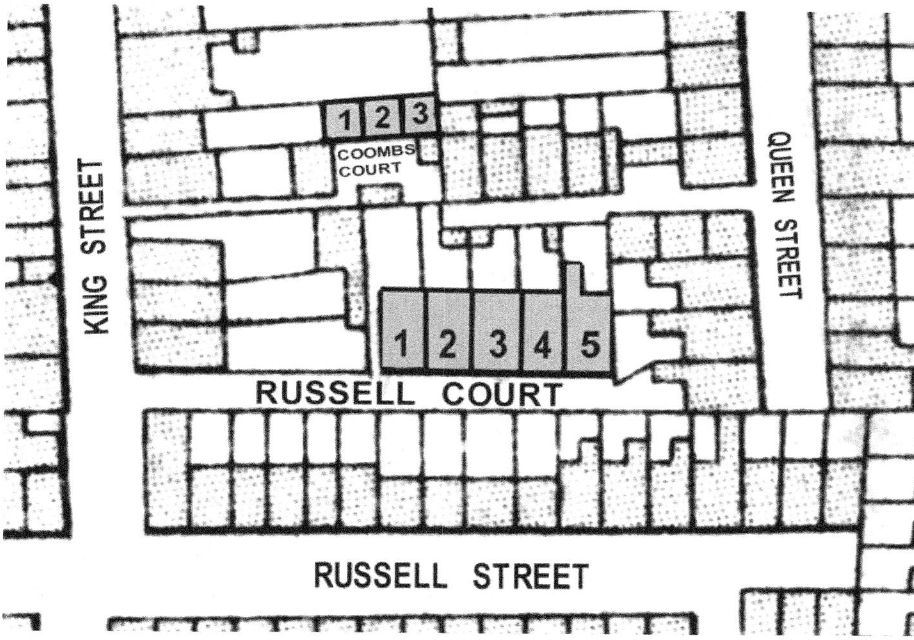

The three small houses of Coombs Court tucked away off King Street and the five in Russell Court

The first listings appeared in the 1851 census when No. 1 was the home of labourer Stephen Buckel. Elizabeth Portlock was there in 1861 but there was nobody further until Sarah Harper in 1881. Labourer Frederick Webb was next in 1884 before washerwoman and charwoman Margaret Burge, who was in occupation from 1891. Bernard Martin had moved there in 1914 and stayed until 1935. No. 2 was the domain of labourers William Nation and Henry Ward between 1850 and 1861.

Boatman George Kerley had arrived by 1871 followed by dock labourer Sivanas Maloney in the 1880s. Labourer Edward Smith and his wife Annie took shelter there in 1891 but Annie was a widow by 1901 and worked as a laundress while seeing out the remaining years at Russell Court until 1935. Elizabeth Wyatt and her five children were living at No. 3 in 1851. She was a 36-year-old widow and a pauper who ended her days living with her daughter's family in James Street where she died aged 78. Laundress Ann Curtis had taken her place at No. 3 in 1861 and mariner's wife Harriet Macey was there in 1871, before coal porter Thomas Sheath in the 1880s. Charles Yaldren and his wife arrived in 1901. Charles was the son of Charles Yaldren senior who ran a couple of pubs in King Street. He died in 1926 and his widow stayed on until 1935.

Fish dealer Ann Brown was the tenant at No. 4 in 1851. She was still there a decade later but in 1871 the house was vacant. Coal porter Charles W. Coombs and his wife Henrietta were in occupation in the 1880s before moving to Rotherhithe, then the 1890s saw labourers James Paul and Henry J. Potts until the Kelly family began their stay from 1911 until 1935. Lastly, at No. 5, laundress Jane Viney was scrubbing away in 1851 and then, in 1861, John Taylor arrived and lived there with his wife Jane until 1891. During his long tenure he was recorded as waterman, labourer, pauper, mariner and finally boatman at the age of 80. Dock labourer Frederick Littlefield saw in the new century until ships fireman Albert Horner and his 'wife' arrived in 1911. Albert was a widower and Annie Batchelor was his housekeeper, but when he died in the late 1920s, she remained as the tenant under the name of 'Mrs A. Horner' until 1935.

The five houses of Russell Court looking east from King Street

Looking back along Russell Court with King Street in the distance

MILLER'S COURT
King Street, West Side

Miller's Court appears in the 1851 census with seven occupants who are listed between Nos. 24 and 27 King Street. I have found no records of this court in the various directories but there is a group of dwellings shown on the 1846 map, which appear just north of Challis Court and to the rear Nos. 24 and 25 King Street. This area had been built over by the Phoenix Brewery by 1857. The seven people listed there were as follows.

Labourer John Thomas at No. 1, carpenter Charles Watts at No. 2, Charwoman Mary Anthoney was in No. 3, cabinet maker William Deadman lived in No. 4, labourer Charles Cummings was at No. 5, cordwainer Thomas Dowling in No. 6 and stone mason John Corbin at No. 7.

QUEEN STREET
Wheeler's Court, Bell's Court and Rose's Court
(see Threefield Lane for Sawmill Court)

Queen Street ran south from Lime Street to a dead end at the rear of the houses in Russell Street and had several courts leading off on both sides which we will look at separately. Sawmill Court (or Cut) ran through from Threefield Lane and is listed under that chapter. The street was demolished in the mid-1930s to make way for the Corporation Tenements.

QUEEN STREET
East Side, Nos. 2–17

The east side numbers ran from 1 to 17 but, as with other streets, these varied in previous years. Originally, No. 1 was the *Nelson Inn* on the corner of Lime Street but that became included in Lime Street sometime around the 1880s. Likewise, No. 5 became No. 6 Sawmill Cut.

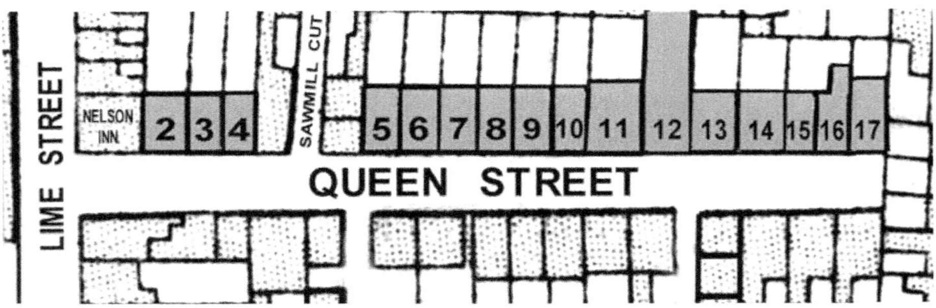

The east side of Queen Street with numbers 1 to 17 where the Nelson Inn was once No.1

Originally No. 1 Queen Street, the *Nelson Inn* became renumbered as 40 Lime Street and appears in that chapter. No.2 was home to whitesmith James Hicks in 1851. He and his wife lived there until hawker John Joliffe arrived in 1859 and he was followed by general dealer George Savage who lived there from 1861 until 1867. Fellow dealer John

Nicholas was next on the scene from 1867 until the mid-1870s when Frank Macey (or Mason) took up residence through to 1891, although laundress Mrs Mary Ann Maiden made occasional appearances in between. Dock labourer Charles Matthews and ships rigger George Henry Marsh were among later tenants that ended with Charles Slack in 1935. Labourer George Roe was biding his time at No. 3 back in 1851. He was still there in 1859 when working as an ostler. Mariner Richard Theasby (or Thesby) was a boatswain for the P&O line during his stay there from 1861 until 1869. He was followed by the usual assortment of labourers and coal porters until railway porter William T. Edgar arrived in 1911, and the final years through to 1935 were mostly taken up by John Newman and Alfred Mason.

In 1851 labourer John Curtis was occupying No. 4 until ships fireman, and sometime general labourer, William Harper held the keys from 1859 until 1865. Seaman George Wilton then had a spell there from 1867 through to 1881 when labourer Cornelius Donovan turned up. His son David was an errand boy before he put to sea and took up the tenancy in 1884. Others came and went before coal porter Ernest Bernard Martin made his home there in the early 1900s until Thomas Pagler (or Paglia) saw out the final years from 1916 until 1935. The entrance to Sawmill Court (otherwise Sawmill Cut) stood between Nos. 4 and 5, which we will visit later.

No. 5 was uninhabited at the time of the 1851 census but by 1859 the West family were in occupation with William, a shipwright, living there until 1874. Sailor George Wilton, with his laundress wife Charlotte and family had a long tenancy from 1881 until George Bagley arrived in 1925 and saw out the remaining decade there. Chelsea Pensioner Charles McDonald was an early occupant of No. 6 back in the 1850s. He was followed by labourer John Shea in the 1860s, then a succession of fellow labourers through the 1870s until the appearance of merchant seaman Francis Dragon in 1887 whose family stayed until the street came down almost a half century later. No. 7 was home to a variety of occupiers beginning with labourer William Knowlton in 1851, marine storekeeper Mickel Collins in 1861, coal heaver John Shay through the 1860s, and mariner John Williams in the 1870s. Labourer Charles Gilford appeared in 1881 and ran a general shop there from the early 1900s, handing over the business to ships fireman William George Harman in 1911. Harman and his wife Emily ran the shop until the 1920s when Charles Cairns and his wife became its final residents.

Musician George Mathews was serenading his neighbours from No. 8 in 1851. Nurse Catherine Hatch followed in the 1860s and a later occupant was baker William Card in the mid-1870s who was running the address as a sweet shop in 1884. After him, a succession of tenants reigned from 1911 until Lawrence George Smith was recorded there in 1935. Pauper William Macklin was under the roof of No. 9 in 1851 but by 1855 carpenter George Collins had moved and remained there until around 1865. His place was taken by a succession of short stay occupiers that included labourer Henry Thorn, mariner R.A. Baker, stewardess Salina Nicholas, fish hawker Mrs Margaret Cawte, and office cleaner Maria Green whose abode it became from 1911 until 1931.

Docks police officer Richard Major kept an eye on his neighbours from No. 10 between 1857 and 1891. Ships plate labourer George Godley and hawker John Newman were named in the rent book in the early 1900s, with Charles Lacey being key holder from 1916 until the 1930s. Mariner George Gilchrist was an early occupant of No. 11 in the 1850s before the family of carpenter George Noyce took residence in the 1860s. From then on, the usual assortment came and went, including turner Charles Brookman, hawker and general dealer John Hayes, and ships fireman Percy Taylor before the premises became the marine stores of Alfred George Axton, which it remained as until it became the fruiterers warehouse of A.G. Axton and Son in 1925.

No. 12 had an interesting history beginning in the 1850s as the home of carpenter Robert Rogers. By 1861 fly driver Francis Mason was there before boot maker William Eastman arrived in 1867 and stayed until 1871. The address next appeared as the St James Mission Hall in 1884 and remained so until taken over by insulating engineers Thomas Anderson Ltd in 1925. Carpenter James Biddlecombe and his laundress wife Harriet were the inhabitants of No. 13 through the 1860s. The house then changed hands many times before ships fireman George Smith and his family paid the rent from 1911 until the street came down. The principal tenants of No. 14 were labourer James Hall in the 1860s, bricklayer George Nineham through the 1870s and 1880s, and ships fireman George Martin and his family from 1891 until the very end. Mariner Silas Lawrence sailed in and out of No. 15 during the 1860s. Charles Cunningham and his wife Ann were there into the 1870s, followed by the usual short stay occupants before George Henry Cavill took up residence in 1916 and remained until 1925 when Mrs D.A.W. Warne became the last of the line in 1931.

Dressmaker Elizabeth Smith was the only name listed at No. 16 from 1851 until tailor Benjamin Clifford arrived in 1861. He was succeeded by smith John Lovell in 1865. Then from the 1870s there was the normal series of labourers and coal porters etc. before George Frederick Cooke moved in at the start of World War One. He was there until Walter Foote became the final resident in 1935. The final premises at the end of the street was No. 17 which was unoccupied in 1851 before bargeman and marine store dealer Thomas Mason appeared in 1861 and remained until 1867. The next residents of note were hawker George Channell and his laundress wife Ellen in 1907. Ellen's maiden name was Fowler and she appears as a washerwoman there in 1901 before her marriage to George and they remained there until the last days of the street.

The view southwards down Queen Street from Lime Street with the former Nelson Inn on the left of the photo

QUEEN STREET
West Side, Nos. 18–29

The west side of Queen Street ran north to Lime Street with Bell's Court entered between Nos. 20 and 21 and Wheeler's Court accessed between Nos. 27 and 28.

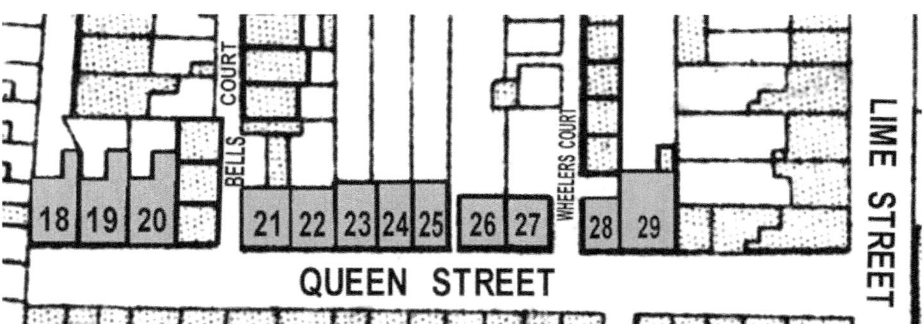

The west side of Queen Street showing Nos. 18 to 29 with the entrances to Bells and Wheelers Courts

Charwoman Sarah Blake toiled away at No. 18 in 1851 before tailoress Sarah King was stitching her garments there through the early 1860s but in 1871 the address was home to no fewer than 12 people, made up of three families and a lodger. The head of the house was hawker Michael Flinn but many others passed through its doorway before ships carpenter and joiner Edward Tyler stayed there from 1891 until 1916 and Edward Axton was the final key holder in the 1930s. Labourers and seamen made up the turnover of occupants of No. 19 from the 1860s until 1901 when storeman George Bichard (or Bushard) took up a long tenancy that lasted from 1901 until the demolition came in the 1930s. Carpenter Aaron Bick (or Beck) was living at No. 20 in the 1860s and others at that address included scavenger Charles Seale in 1867, charwoman Ann Rose in 1871 and labourer turned coal porter Henry Chalk who settled there in 1881. His widow Eliza was living there under her own means in 1901. Stevedore Thomas Bushard, father of George next door at No. 19, saw out the remainder of the street from 1911.

The entrance to Bells Court stood between Nos. 20 and 21, which we will visit shortly, and at No. 21 we discover the normal cross section of labourers and seamen until we come across George Tapper in 1874 who was then listed as a labourer but by 1881 had become a clicker (boot maker?) and in 1884 was working as a dock detective. He was gone by the 1890s that saw the resumption of seamen and labourers with William Sessions and his wife settling there from 1912 and seeing out the street's final years. Coal dealer George Gregory occupied No. 22 from 1851 and by 1861 he had become a dairyman, residing there until 1869 when Henry Glasspool moved in. Coal trimmer and labourer Henry appears there until 1891. Labourer John Wright, his wife Alice and their 12 children (so far) had squeezed into No. 22 by 1911 and were still there when demolition came.

Labourer William Richardson and his wife Phoebe were in No. 23 back in 1851, although she became a widow a decade later but stayed on until the late 1860s when coal porter Abner Barber and his wife Sarah showed up in 1869. Their son Robert, a coal trimmer, was head of the house from 1881 until 1925 with Alfred Lawler being the final tenant. James Peckham was a dock policeman living at No. 24 in 1861. However, he was unemployed by 1871 and gone in 1881 when costermonger and fish salesman Henry Cook was there. Coal trimmer John William Davis was head of the house in 1901 and in 1911 the house was occupied by John, his wife Georgina, daughter Nellie, adopted son Bertie Dyre and two boarders. The family remained until the 1930s and the final tenant there was William Edward Smith.

No. 25 was home to a couple of tailors, with Benjamin Biles and George Pennycott there in 1851 and 1861 respectively. In 1871 labourer James Fleming began a long tenancy that lasted until around 1890, during which time he tried his hand as a fish dealer. The next long-term resident was coal porter George Albert Billows from 1911 until around 1925 and Charles R. Adams was the final name in the rent book in 1935. Pauper Elizabeth Quick was sheltering at No. 26 in 1851 but plumber James Martin, along with wife Isabella and painter son Bernard, had replaced her by 1859. The Martins were there until 1876 but no others were recorded at that address until labourer George May in 1891. By 1901 widow Eliza Jackson, her five children and grandson were in occupation. Eliza remained until the 1920s when the final years saw James Sawyer as key holder. Cordwainer Benjamin Watts was the earliest tenant at No. 27 in the 1850s before the Gilby family arrived in 1859. Storekeeper William Gilby and his wife Louisa held fort until 1869 when labourer George Wheeler's family arrived and stayed on until the early 1880s. Fruit merchant John Godwin Hancock was there in 1901 and his widow gave up the tenancy in the 1930s when Alex Bavistock was the last in line.

Wheeler's Court had its entrance between Nos. 27 and 28 and we will return there presently but at No. 28 we find stonemason William Warren living in 1855 until 1861 when hawker Charlotte Edmonds and her laundress daughter Emma held court until 1871. Others of note who stayed under its roof were fishmonger John Brown in 1891, margarine factory worker Ernest F. Jackson in 1901 and charwoman Emily Jacobs in the early 1900s. Alfred Joyce had a spell from 1916 until Albert Moulsdale arrived in 1935.

The final roll call for Queen Street begins with Greenwich Pensioner George B. Page at No. 29 in 1845. He was there until at least 1851 but no others appear until 1863 when Hatrill Arnold is listed in 1863 with a Mrs Page in 1865. Next is gate keeper Robert Russell in 1871 but from then onwards there comes a parade of short stay labourers and seamen until the early 1900s sees the Cole family with Thomas and his wife Kate Martha. The Coles had moved on by 1914 and after Thomas Burton in 1916 came Harry Roberts through the 1930s.

Looking north up Queen Street towards Lime Street with Nos. 19 is on the left and the entrance to Bells Court where the couple are standing. The woman on the right is standing in the doorway of No. 13 with the former St James Mission Hall next door at No. 12, which by 1920 had become a marine store and finally Axton's fruit warehouse

QUEEN STREET COURTS
WHEELER'S COURT
Nos. 1–5

A problem arises regarding the early years of Wheeler's Court and Rose's Court. The census returns for 1851 to 1871 show just three households for Wheeler's Court, whereas Rose's Court is shown with five. The 1846 map shows five houses as Wheeler's Court and three at the rear (Rose's). The census returns list both courts together so it is likely the names were transposed. I believe that to be the case and have recorded the occupants accordingly. The 1893 slum report does not mention Rose's Court which it seems no longer existed after 1871 but describes Wheeler's Court as being a blind court measuring 68 feet long by 24 feet wide leading out of the Queen Street rookery with its entrance through a gap between Nos. 27 and 28 Queen Street. The court consisted of five houses, none of which had through ventilation. The court was demolished at the same time as Queen Street in the mid-1930s.

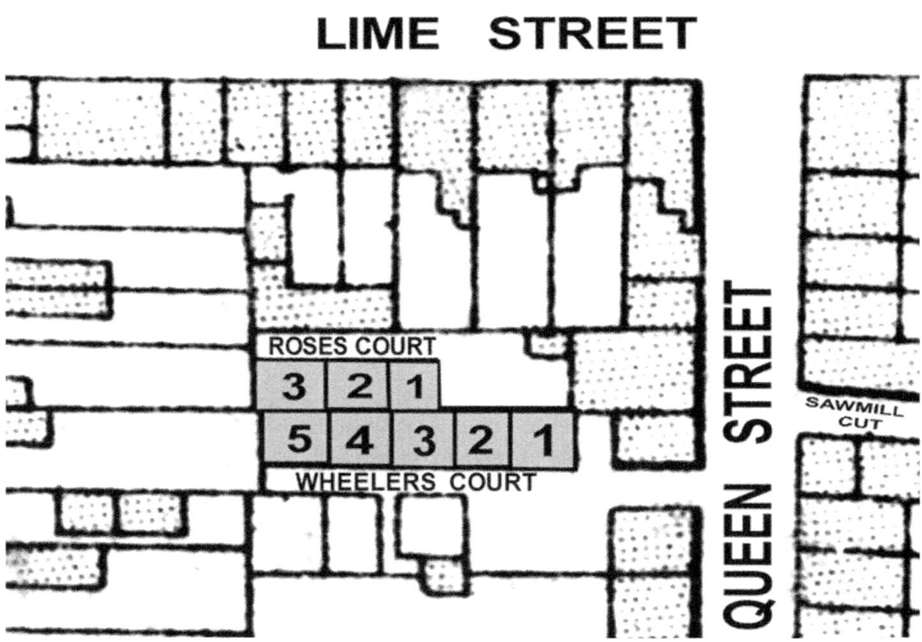

The five houses of Wheeler's Court leading off the west side of Queen Street. Also shown is the possible location of Rose's Court

Labourer James Collins was at No. 1 in 1851 and by 1861 stonemason William Warren was the occupant. By 1881 we find paint factory labourer George Seal as the tenant followed by painter George House just three years later. Charles Wheeler emerges in 1887 with ships fireman George E. Bailey in 1891. Carpenters labourer George West was resident through the 1900s and labourer William H. Cooper was key holder from 1911 until 1931. George Channell then appeared and George Baddams was the last name of all in 1935. Coal porter William Carter graced No. 2 in 1851 with labourer Roger Sullivan there a decade later, while ship keeper Christopher Young was there in 1881, and Walter Hollands in 1887, paper hanger Walter Barton had signed in by 1901 when Mary Newman and James Colverson saw in the early 1900s until Union Castle fireman Edward A. Purkiss spent 1911 until 1914 as tenant. The only other name to light was Henry Henbest through the last decade from 1925.

Butcher Charles Maunder wielded his cleaver at No. 3 in 1851 and labourer Charles Hoskins had taken his place in 1861. Labourer Charles Wheeler had moved in by 1871 and was ousted by charwoman Elizabeth Edmonds in 1881. Mrs A. Painter was present through the 1880s with charwoman Eliza Roper (1891), ships stoker John F. Auger (1901) and seaman Arthur John Nunn (1911) were next across threshold before Charles Twistan and Mrs Snellgrove lived through World War One there, with Henry A. Carter and Alfred Couper seeing out the final decade.

No. 4 did not feature until 1861 when blacksmith John Lovell was forging his future there. Moving on to the 1880s we find general labourer Daniel Crawley and ships fireman N. Shave, while needlewoman Emily Hilton was present in 1901. Maxwell Clements and his family had taken up residence by 1911 and remained until around 1930 when the final names were George Riggs and John Robert Skinner.

Needlewoman Ann Maynard was sewing away at No. 5 back in 1861 but we see no others until the Wheelers appear in 1881 beginning with general labourer George Wheeler (previously in Rose's Court) then in 1891 we see Emma Wheeler, described as a 'plain' needlewoman (not sure it that refers to her or her sewing), and later, 1901 finds labourer John Wheeler as head of the house. David Longman, George Roberts and John Jacobs entered the rent book through the early 1900s, while the final decades welcomed Edward Axton, George Lockyer and Arthur Terrell.

Looking into Wheeler's Court from Queen Street where its entrance was between Nos. 27 and 28 on the west side of the street

BELL'S COURT
Nos. 1–7

Bell's Court, leading off Queen Street (also referred to as a Rookery), consisted of seven houses in a blind court, three of which backed on to others and had no through ventilation. The luckier ones had water supplies and sanitary conveniences on the premises, but for the others, this was situated in the yard. All but one of the houses were described as internally fair but their outside conditions needed attention. As with many of these old courts, they were not included in the street directories until the late 1880s, prior to that we only have the census returns to guide us. As with Queen Street itself, demolition came in the mid-1930s.

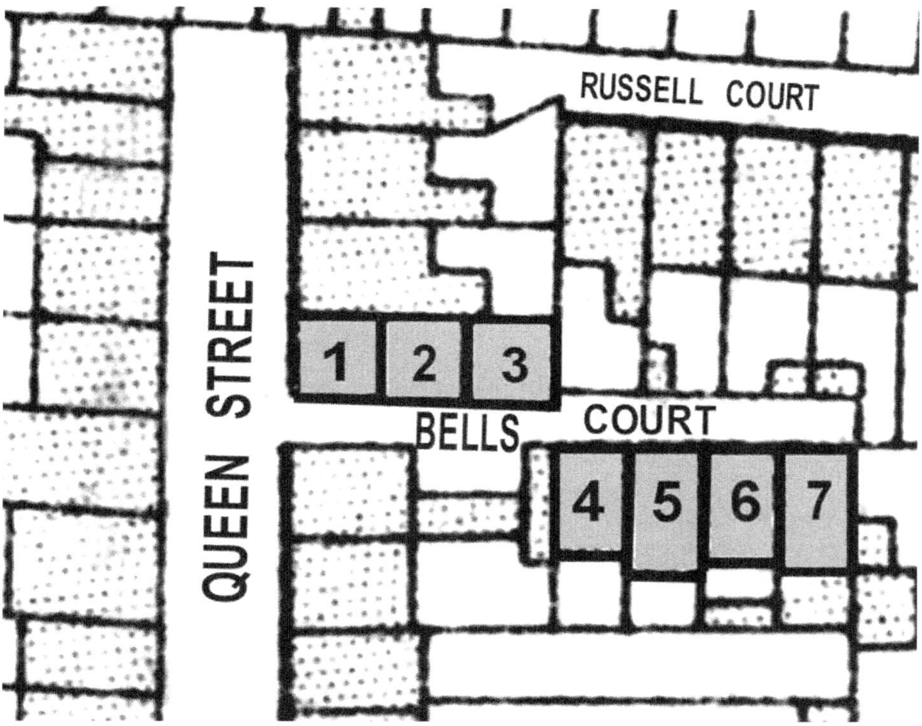

The seven houses of Bell's Court on the west side of Queen Street

The 1851 census gives our first glimpse as to the inhabitants of Bell's Court with carpenter Charles Giddens at No. 1. No. 2 was uninhabited and No. 3 housed labourer James Gatehouse (later in Wheeler's Court). In No. 4 was cork cutter Henry Pragnell with brewer's labourer James Peckham next door at No. 5. Butcher John Raymond resided at No. 6 and Fanny Harper was a pauper eking an existence at No. 7. Onwards to 1861 and we find labourer Charles West at No. 1 while No. 2 is still vacant. Labourers John Drake, John Glen and James Fleming are at Nos. 3 to 6 respectively and cooper Henry Brookman is in No. 7. All change again in 1871 with labourer Cornelius Donovan at No. 1 and No. 2 is again vacant. Labourers Michael Sleay, George Cooper and Thomas Channell are housed in Nos. 3 to 5 with dressmaker Mary Ann Dale stitching away at No. 6 and Patrick McCarthy is another labourer at No. 7.

With more information available from 1881 we discover labourer George Collins is in No. 1 but soon to make way for dealer George Channell (previously at No. 2). Grocer's storeman Robert Rose made a brief appearance in 1901 before coal porter William Smith made No. 1 his home from 1911 until 1931 with James Alexander Sessions there in 1935. George Channel had become what appears to be the first inhabitant of No. 2 in 1881 (it looks to have been vacant until then) but he soon moved next door to No. 1 when Mrs M. Instance arrived in 1884. She was the first of many females to live there, others being Mrs Cummings, widow Mary Ann Dawkins, charwoman Rosina A. Biggs and latterly Mrs Kathleen Judd in 1911. Silvester Hunt was next at No. 2, arriving in 1914 and his family seeing out the final couple of decades there before demolition came.

Labourer George Cooper (previously at No. 4) spent time at No. 3, in fact almost two decades until 1901 when scaffolder James Taylor arrived. George Bailey set up camp at No. 3 from 1912 until 1916 with Mrs Nellie Dyer, Arthur Whitcher and William John Wyatt filing through the doorway until the 1930s. Labourer Henry Horner dwelled briefly at No. 4 in 1881 before fishmonger W. Sherry spent an equally short spell in 1884. There then followed another succession of labourers ending with James White's tenancy from the early 1900s through to the final years. Mariner Francis Dragon was berthed at No. 5 from 1881 until 1887 and nobody else of note sailed through until dock labourer John Wyatt dropped anchor in 1911. He and his family remained until the mid-1920s, which saw the arrival of Frederick Richards who was the final occupant. Noah Callaway was a gas works stoker living at No. 6 in 1881 but his time there was short, as it was also for many others until James Alfred Joyce, his wife Amelia Louisa and their five children were there from 1911, then 1914 welcomed George Smith to become its long term occupant through to 1935.

Bricklayer James E. Martin, coal runner James Berry, coal porter William G. Harvey and bricklayers labourer John G. Knight were among the many to linger at No.7 from 1881 until the turn of the century. Then came Robert Aldridge prior to World War One, followed by George Taylor and his wife who became the final tenants of Bells Court before it was demolished.

Looking westward into Bells Court from Queen Street with Nos. 1 to 3 on the left and Nos. 4 to 7 on the right

Further into Bells Court with Nos. 4 to 7 on the right and the backs of Russell Court on the left

ROSE'S COURT

Rose's Court has little information, other than it was a court off Queen Street and was gone before the 1893 report. It appears in the 1851 and 1861 censuses where it is listed together with Wheeler's Court so the two seem to have been adjacent. The 1846 and 1870 maps show three buildings backing on to those in Wheeler's Court (see map) and I am certain that was Rose's Court. As indicated in the Wheeler's Court notes above, my feeling is that the two names were transposed in those early census returns. What we do know is that in 1851 there were three residents listed, these being labourer William Randle at No. 1, lodging house keeper Virtue Petty at No. 2 and stone sawyer Edward Dommit at No. 3. The Randles were still evident in 1861 where Elizabeth Randle was a laundress at No. 1 with labourer Andrew Rentowl next door and porter James Gatehouse in No. 3. It would appear that 1871 witnessed the final inhabitants of Rose's Court where No. 1 was the domain of bricklayer James Brodge, whose immediate neighbour was the unemployed Naurah Guan, with labourer Charles Wheeler at No. 3, soon to move to Wheelers Court.

RUSSELL STREET
Eldon Square

Russell Street ran between King Street and Eldon Street, just north of, and parallel to Chandos Street. It was closed off at either end by buildings in Orchard Lane and Threefield Lane. The eastern end was opened into Threefield Lane when properties there were demolished in the 1930s to make way for the Corporation Tenements. By 1936 the population along the north side of the street between King Street and Eldon Street (Nos. 8 to 24) were being moved away in preparation for the building of the new tenements that were planned along Lime Street and Threefield Lane, and demolition came soon after.

The numbers on the north side of Russell Street ran Nos. 1 to 7 from its western end as far as King Street, then, at that point, there were buildings that blocked off the bottom of King Street, although they had a narrow passage running through to Russell Street. Those buildings disappeared around 1865 and the site on the corner of King Street became a yard with stables for carrier James Olive who lived next door at No. 21 King Street. By the turn of the century the corner plot had become a smithy run by William and James Hartnell and by 1939 the street directory listed it as No. 8, a house occupied by Philip Miller. The remainder of the north side was then numbered 8 to 24, with the south side as 25 to 47. Nos. 22 to 27 were originally Nos. 1 to 6 Eldon Square. After Nos. 8 to 24 were demolished. With the exception of No.1, the remainder of the north side east of King Street survived until the 1950s, as did the majority of the south side.

RUSSELL STREET
North Side, Nos. 1–7

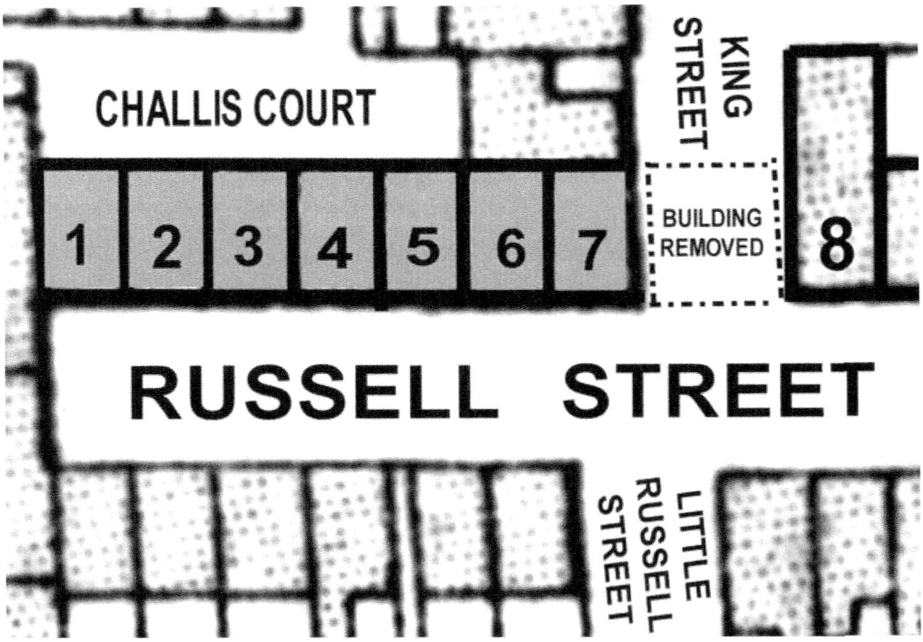

Nos. 1 to 7 on the north side of Russell Street, where Nos. 6 and 7 were, was the Russell Tavern, formerly the Ship Inn. Between Nos. 7 and 8 stood a building that once blocked off King Street

As ever, the early directories are unclear as to who lived in which house along this terrace but among those listed in the 1841 census were shoe maker Thomas Simpson, bricklayer Robert Perry, and Ursula Medus, a woman of independent means. A decade later, No. 1 was the home of Maurice Merrick, a marine store dealer. He was followed in later years by John Pim who also had a number of such outlets in the neighbourhood. 1881 witnessed the arrival of charwoman Mrs Sarah Holmes then a succession of labourers came and went until the final occupant was Peter Deering who had arrived there around there around 1930 but both he and his house disappeared after 1940. Fisherman Ambrose Parker was at No. 2 in 1851. He had moved into No. 4 a decade later but other occupants at the second house were an assortment of labourers, carmen, charwomen and seaman until Ernest Dragon arrived in 1920 and remained until 1940 with James Burrows resident in the postwar years.

Cabinet maker Thomas Strong was an early resident in No. 3 back in 1851. Selina Chiverton was running the address as a lodging house by 1881 but the longest spell there was by engine room labourer John Coakley whose family were there from the very early 1900s until the street was demolished in the 1950s.

No. 4's residents included mariner Robert Saunders and his wife Mary Jane, a tailoress, during the 1860s and 1870s. My maternal great grandfather William Cotton lived there in 1881 while employed as a dock labourer, before crane driver Thomas Bateman stayed briefly around 1901. Barrow man Herbert Houghton followed from 1911 until the 1930s with Mrs Summers seeing out the postwar years until the end of the street came about. Pauper Joseph Hutchins, a former carpenter, was living at No. 5 back in 1851. Boot maker William Dancy cobbled there in 1859, succeeded by a long line of mariners, ships firemen and porters. Dock labourer Frederick Wills had moved in by 1901 and remained until 1931, after which that house no longer appeared in the registers, although the building was still standing in the 1950s and may have been absorbed by the pub next door (see photo of the *Russell Tavern*).

Nos. 6 and 7 were taken up by a pub as far back as 1850 when William Kent was in charge. In those days it was the *Ship Inn*, a name it carried until the late 1800s when it was changed to the *Russell Tavern*. As with so many of these establishments there was a high turnover of landlords throughout its history, most notably George Bulpitt (1859–1863) George Henry Johnson (1876–1874) and Charles Yaldren in the 1890s. At one time owned by the Winchester Brewery it ended as a Marston's house run by Albert Edward Norman in 1956 when the street came down.

The final days of the Russell Tavern at Nos. 6 and 7 Russell Street on the corner of King Street in 1956. No. 5 next door had not been included in the street directories after 1931 and may have become taken over by the pub (Late David Goddard collection)

RUSSELL STREET
North Side, Nos. 8–24

The north side of Russell Street, east of King Street, saw many changes over the years. Nos. 22 to 24, along with Nos. 25 to 27 opposite, were once numbered 1 to 6 Eldon Square from the 1850s until around 1865 when they were renumbered as part of Russell Street. Most of the north side was demolished in the 1930s and replaced by the new Corporation Tenements.

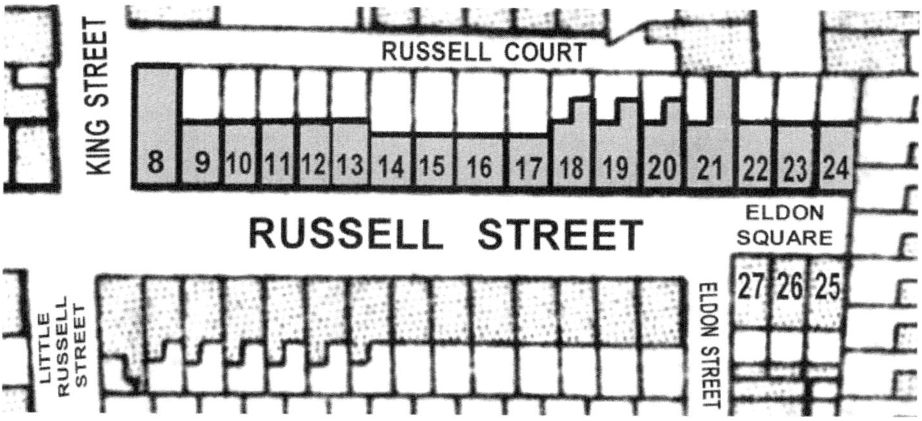

The north side of Russell Street showing Nos. 8 to 24. The site of No. 8 was once part of a building that blocked off King Street, while Nos. 22 to 27 formed an area known as Eldon Square

No. 8, on the corner of King Street, stood between Russell Court and Russell Street. It was once part of a building that blocked off the southern end of King Street from Russell Street. It was often regarded as being part of King Street from around 1865 when its occupant was mariner Charles Barter; from then on it was mostly a store or workshop. In the 1860s it was the premises of butcher John Osman. Later it became stores and then a stables run by James Olive. By 1907 it had become a smithy run by William J. Hartnell, whose brother James had taken over the business prior to World War One but the building disappeared from the directories after that.

Coal dealer William Smith appears in the 1841 census and also in 1851. He is listed at No. 9 but by 1853 customs officer John Toby was in residence until 1861. Among those that followed, we find general dealer Henry Jones, bricklayer John Richard Cozens (also Cosens) in the 1870s and boiler maker David Gordon in the 1880s. Into the 1900s we see coal porter George Summers resident 1911 to 1916, with Henry Giffard from the 1920s. Mariner John Hancock was at No. 10 throughout the 1850s until making way for poulterer Richard Allen in 1861 but from then onwards came a regular turnover of dwellers. Through the 1860s there were ships fireman Charles Nicholas and the Moxley family of brewers labourers. The 1870s and 1880s welcomed more ships firemen and labourers and then in 1891, customs officer John Shields joined the locals. Foreman stevedore William Turner and his family opted to stay from the early 1900s until 1925, giving way to William Barnes in the 1930s.

In 1851 No. 11 saw the arrival of scene painter and artist Alexander Frazer who created his masterpieces there for a decade. Some might have considered the tone lowered when his place was taken by laundress Mrs Jane Morse in the 1870s, then the 1880s heralded the arrivals of plumber Charles Cleak, labourer Henry Hicks and coal porter Walter Brown. On to the 1900s that saw the Summers family move in during 1911. Julia, her three sons and her sister were joined by husband George who had previously been at No. 9. Nathaniel Brown followed them in 1916 and obviously felt at home there as he stayed until 1935. At No. 12 Painter William Kendle tried his hand as a fly proprietor during his time there in 1859 to 1861 then ships fireman George Ashford and his wife Mary enjoyed a long stay from 1863 until 1876. Stoker Alfred Maiden and wife Ellen lived there through the 1880s before another substantial tenure saw labourer Alfred Ernest Gadd set foot in 1907 and stay until the end.

A mixed bag of mariners frequented No. 13 from the 1850s until the 1870s welcomed sail maker John Shergold in 1869 but his stay was brief, as he left in 1871, making way for butcher Walter Leggat who put his feet up there until 1884. Others of note included Royal Mail greaser Arthur Henry Sims in 1911 and Thomas Gothridge from 1916 until 1925 when George Lewis Colyer was the final tenant. No. 14 was apparently empty in 1851 and remained so until ships fireman Alexander Cunningham arrived in 1859 and settled for a couple of years. The house then seemed to attract several railway porters with Morris Jones in 1865, John Jones in 1867 and George W. Saunders in 1881. Plumber Charles Cleak transferred from No. 11 in 1884 before another host of seamen sailed in and out, ending with William Small in

1911 until 1914. The remaining years were taken up by James Shore until 1920, and finally John Smith in the 1930s.

Labourer George Meaden occupied No. 15 from 1859 until 1861, when ships fireman Robert Cunningham held the keys through the 1860s. Laundress Mary Bailey was scrubbing away from 1869 until 1876, then Frank and Mary Guiricin (also Eugine) were occupants from 1911 though to 1925 when Thomas Henry Jenkins, William Pragnell and James Bellows saw out the final years. The Snook family ran several greengrocery businesses over many years and John Snook set up his shop at No. 16 in the late 1850s, afterwards it reverted to a residence with labourer William Scott there in the early 1860s and fellow labourer James Gamble from 1865 until 1871. In 1884 it was a sweetshop run by Mrs J. Morse, then in 1891 butcher Henry Yaldraw was there. Early in the new century, labourer Sidney Peckham arrived in 1907 and remained there until 1935.

Journeyman shipwright James Green was one of the first occupants of No. 17 back in the 1850s and his tenure was followed by the usual host of seafarers, a procession of which lasted through to 1884 when blacksmith Benjamin Buckett arrived. After him, were labourers and coal porters and indeed more mariners well into the 20th century. Thomas Channell was the key holder from 1916 until Thomas Metcalf was a latecomer prior to demolition. Carpenter John Clench and his family spent an incredible quarter century at No. 18 from 1851 until 1876. Then seaman Allen Leggett dwelled through the 1880s and laundress Eliza J. Donovan followed in the 1890s. There was then another long-term tenancy with ships fireman Arthur Boyd and his family arriving in 1907 and staying on until the end.

As will be observed, there were a great many laundresses in the locality and Caroline Elcock at No. 19 was yet another back in 1851. London and South Western Railway worker Thomas Burt was stationed there in 1857 and tailor George Farmer followed him into the 1860s. The 1870s and 1880s saw the usual cavalcade of ships firemen until corn merchants assistant George Lee arrived in 1881. After him, grocers porter Thomas Ward enjoyed a long stay from 1901 through to the final days.

Waterman Isaac Blandford made No. 20 his home in the 1850s before cabinet maker John Bezant replaced him in 1859. There next came an assortment of short-stay occupants including railway fireman Patrick Boulger, blacksmith Robert Robinson, and laundress Mrs Green in 1869. Charles Stonadge was employed as a painter, labourer and carter during his time there in the 1870s before more labourers passed through its door. Then blacksmith William Maynard spent a decade there from 1901. Charles Davage dwelled there from 1916 until 1931 with Thomas Channell being the last of all.

Furniture japanner and polisher John Poor was lacquering woodwork at No. 21 from 1847 until 1851. Painter and plumber David Rogers was next in 1885 and lingered until 1861 when fellow painter Samuel Wilson featured briefly before Mrs Prudence Searle set up the premises as a lodging house which she ran from the early 1860s until 1871. It had returned to a normal abode by the time seaman John Henry Major and his wife Ellen carried their chattels through the front door in 1881. Railway porter and widower Alfred Higham and his three sons were on the 1901 census before fireman George Bagley took residence from 1907 until 1914. Ben Harty, Harry Richards and Mrs Callaway were the remaining tenants until the house was no more.

Nos. 22 to 27 were originally Nos.1 to 6 Eldon Square until the 1860s and at No. 22 from 1851 until 1861 were John Cook and his wife Martha. In fact, Cook was a cook for the P&O Shipping Company. Through the 1860s, this was home to mariner William Horne and needle worker Mrs Ann Hurst. Blacksmith Peter Brown was there in the early 1880s and after some brief lettings, marine fireman John Ireland and his wife set up home there, which lasted until 1935. William Butler was a porter for the London and South Western Railway while living at No. 23

with his laundress wife Mary Ann in 1851 but Mary was soon widowed and she and her daughter Jane continued there as washerwomen until around 1871. Of those who followed them, most notable were sail maker Tom Moxney in 1884, brewers drayman Percival Blake in 1901 and Edward Louis Warren, a dock labourer who lived there with his family from 1907 until the end. The final building on the north side of Russell Street was No. 24, which from 1859 until the mid-1870s was the home of widower Michael Cunningham and his son John, both of whom worked for the Ordnance Survey. In 1881 it was the house of widow Mary Ann May and her two tailoress daughters. The next incomer of interest was blacksmith David Longman and his family who arrived in 1911. Sadly David died in 1916 and his wife Mary Ann ran the house until she passed on in 1928 and, from then on, their seaman son Alfred was tenant until 1935 when the house was demolished.

The backs of houses in Russell Street viewed from Russell Court looking west towards King Street

RUSSELL STREET
South Side

On the south side, Nos. 28 to 41 were originally Nos. 20 to 33 running from Eldon Street to King Street (previously Little Russell Street) and finally Nos. 42 to 47 (earlier Nos. 34 to 39).

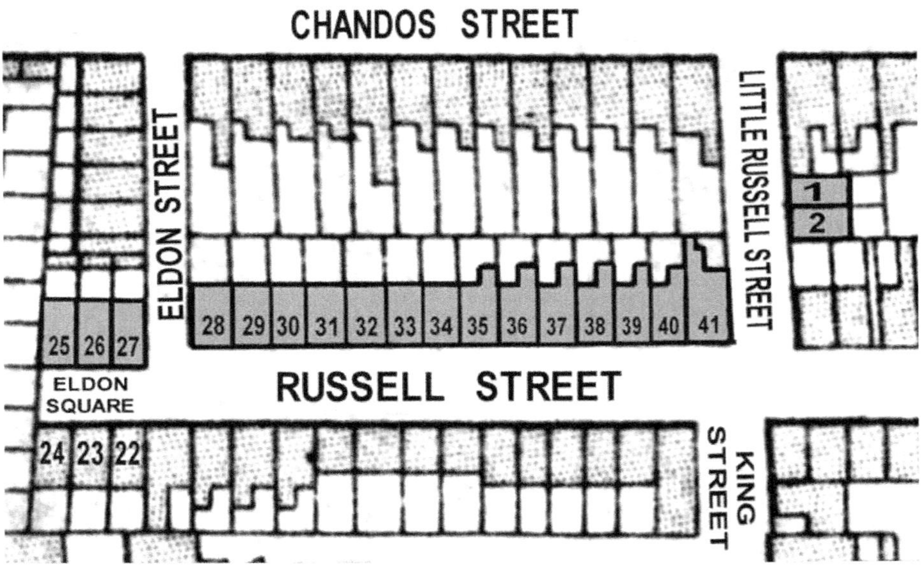

The south side of Russell Street showing Nos. 25 to 41. Nos. 22 to 27 were previously Nos. 1 to 6 Eldon Square and No. 41 was always a corner shop. The two houses in Little Russell Street were incorporated into King Street in the 1870s

RUSSELL STREET, SOUTH SIDE
LITTLE RUSSELL STREET
Nos. 1 and 2

Little Russell Street connected its bigger namesake with Chandos Street and became part of King Street in the 1870s when the buildings at the bottom of King Street were removed. There were only two houses, which retained their numbers through to demolition. (See King Street for residents)

RUSSELL STREET
South Side, Nos. 25 to 41

As previously stated, Nos. 25 to 27 were once part of Eldon Square until the 1860s. No. 25 was occupied by journeyman baker John Edmonds in 1851 but no others are recorded until labourer Henry Saunders in 1859. He was still there until 1861 when it would appear Ellen Barnes was running the address as a lodging house. Storekeeper Charles House was its last tenant in 1863 before it became part of Russell Street. Some of the principal dwellers then included ships fireman James Slade and carpenter Joseph Whittington in the late 1860s, then labourer Thomas Burns, dock labourer Ebenezer Axton through the 1870s, carman John Cutler and another ships fireman James Fox in the 1880s. Into the new century we find brewer's carman Henry Blake and bricklayers labourer Ernest Geary from 1912 until William Potter arrived in 1920 and stayed put through until the 1930s when Raymond J. Furber saw out the postwar and final years.

Journeyman blacksmith Richard Sutton occupied No. 26 in the 1850s until 1857 when Joseph Jannaway moved in. Joseph was a barrow man and dock porter during his time there, which lasted until 1869 when labourer Thomas Burns transferred from No. 25. Burns was resident around 1880. Others before the turn of the century included house painter John Fairchild and labourer Albert Lee. Coal porter Barry Thomas Harty had arrived by 1907 but was gone by 1914 when Frank Waters appeared and spent some 17 years there. Victor Morgan and finally a Miss Wiggers were the last names following the war. The last of the old Eldon Square houses, No. 27 was home to plumber's labourer Charles Stacey in 1851. P&O line fireman Peter Gallagher (or Gallaker) settled there between 1857 and 1863 when boiler maker James Anderson dallied briefly. London and South Western Railway porter Edwin Knowlton was in occupation from 1865 until 1874 when dock labourer Samuel Bundy held the keys for a decade. In 1901 we find fish hawker George Short – but not for long – as widow Mrs E. Bartlett had arrived by 1907 for a tenure that lasted until World War One broke out and from then George Robert Rainsley was its long-term occupant through to the very end.

Although most of the street survived until demolition in the 1950s, Nos. 28 to 34 were last recorded in 1948. Yet another journeyman, this time painter Richard Ryder, found himself at No. 28 in 1851. Ships fireman William Langtree found shelter there from 1859 until 1881 when widow Jane Morse made it her home. Plumber Charles Cleak (at other times in Nos. 11 and 14) dallied in the late 1880s and early 1890s before laundress Charlotte Brown brought her mangle there in 1901. Ships fireman Francis James Young was listed from 1911 before 1920 ushered in the Draper (or Diaper) family where Edward and then James were head of the house until 1946, when the postwar years welcomed Frederick Callaway as the final name in 1948.

Charles Reed was recorded as a labourer at No. 29 in 1851, then in 1857 we find Charles Read as a blacksmith (possibly the same person?) while Mrs Mary Read was there in 1859. In 1861, boiler makers William and Finley Moody were followed by mariner Hugh Duncan who was berthed there throughout the rest of the 1860s. Fellow mariner Ned Barter dallied from 1869 to 1871 and then came railway porter Edwin Knowlton, previously at No. 27, who at the age of 43 was promoted to railway guard. Edwin died aged 50 in 1891, leaving his widow Frances and their four children who finally moved away around 1900. Their place was taken by labourer John Young Jones until 1914 when William Thomas Mason became key holder through to 1935. Richard Stokes and John Chalk were the final names before 1948.

Cabinet maker and joiner Charles Hicks enjoyed a long occupancy of No. 30 from 1851 until 1871 before railway porter Henry Bousefield became a neighbour of fellow railwayman Edwin Knowlton. However, Henry was gone by 1887 when coal porter Walter Leggett arrived on the scene and remained until the turn of the century ushered in boiler maker Michael McNamara who rested his body there until the 1930s. Bertie Bray, Frederick Greenhow and Andrew Bellows appeared as the final names in the rent book. Former coachman and then pauper Charles Compton was evident at No. 31 in 1851. He was followed by labourers Edward Axton and John Hatchard who both appeared at various times between 1859 and 1865. The seafaring Barter family, Ned Frank and Charles, were there from 1867 until the mid-1870s and a few labourers, stokers and coal porters were evident over the next few years until the arrival of the Leggett family in 1911 when steamship foreman Bert Leggett, wife Nellie and family were part of the local scene all the way through until demolition in 1948.

Journeyman painter John Hensford was one of the street's early and longest inhabitants at No. 32 where he and his family lived from 1851 until 1884, while dock labourer Thomas Holloway and his brood enjoyed an even longer span from 1901 through to 1940, and John Burns was the final tenant postwar. Yet another long-serving renter was cordwainer John Mason who hammered his boots at No. 33 from 1847 and through the years until 1861. Bricklayer John Fairwell was yet another stalwart resident from 1869 until 1891. Obviously, there was something about No. 33, as dock labourer Henry James Maynard and his family filled the rent book from 1911 until 1939 before James Taylor and William M. Malan were the last entries. Railway porter John Bullan carried his bags into No. 34 through the 1850s, while boot maker Thomas Dancy cobbled away from 1861 until 1869. Others in later years included joiner James Beale from 1871 to 1881, and ships painter George Curtis and his baker son of the same name in the 1880s. In 1901 another long-serving tenant then arrived in the shape of seaman Charles Henry Edmonds, whose family were docked there until 1948 when the street disappeared.

Labourer George Willis held the keys to No. 35 in the 1850s before painter George Coombs with his laundress wife Hannah and family nestled there through the 1860s. Mariner Thomas Fall sailed in from 1869 until 1874 before the familiar turnover of ships fireman and labourers ensued; Benjamin Radbone gained entry in 1916 and stayed put through to 1940. He was the last tenant at No. 35 in 1940, possibly due to bomb damage sustained in World War Two. Labourer Charles Cull was noted at No. 36 in 1851 but a decade later Charles Dimmick was described as a 'common labourer'! Perhaps he had lowered the tone of the neighbourhood? He was gone by 1863 when laundress Mrs Mary Merrett arrived with her scrubbing brush and proceeded to clean the street's garments until 1891. She was yet another who found this section of the street to be worth staying in for many years. Having said that, the remaining years saw many others come and go from No. 36 before Peter Henry and his family entered in 1916 and were there until 1946 when Robert H. Ramsay saw out the postwar years.

Brick maker Charles Paddock (or Paddick) was at No. 37 for an unusually long spell in the early years of the street. He was occupant from 1851 until 1869 when labourer Thomas Crouch and his charwoman wife Ann moved in. They stayed only a couple of years before the house welcomed the usual parade of ships fireman, coal porters and mariners. The next settled tenant was a Mrs Smith who was landlady from 1912 until 1925 when Thomas Bellows and his family were in occupation until 1954. Then William Charles Britten was a brief resident. David Rogers was a journeyman painter and gilder at No. 38 in the 1850s but the house saw a string of paying guests through the 1860s, which included travelling draper John Spreadborough, barrowman James Wilton, tailor John Smith, laundress Mary Ann Bailey (later at No. 15) and engine drivers assistant George Tolman. The following decades welcomed boiler maker David Gordon, former laundress Mary Bright, coal porter Thomas Bridle, and retired charwoman Jane Hicks. Then, into the new century we find coal porter John Dugdale and labourer Frank Kimber before James Colman decided to stay from 1916 until 1939. Three ladies made up the final order, being

Mrs Dennison, Mrs Callaway and Mrs Shew.

House painter William Miller donned his brushes from No. 39 throughout the 1850s. He was followed through the 1860s by a throng of seamen including William Gover, John Ireland, Angelo Patch and William Parker. The 1870s and 1880s introduced laundress Lucy Smith, cooper Henry Knox, carter Thomas Olive and coal porter George Bellows (or Billows). Moving on into the 20th century, we see dock foreman James F. Colman (later at No. 38), before Alfred Maskell and John Morely who was the final tenant from 1935. No. 40 was reported as being empty in 1851 but by 1861 it was home to seamstress wife Mary Ann Rolfe and her engine driver son James. Mary continued living there until 1871 by which time she was working as a charwoman. After she left, there followed an incredible 15 occupancies ending with Thomas Appleton and his wife through the postwar years.

For most of its existence, standing on the corner of Little Russell Street, No. 41 was a shop, although in the early 1850s it was the abode of journeyman carpenter Samuel Day and horse dealer John Saunderson but by 1855 it had become a greengrocers, alternatively run by William Lywood and Jacob Travers until 1865 when Walter Williams had a brief spell as a fruiterer before general dealer Charles Bartlett arrived in 1867. He had moved on by 1871 when Thomas Gannaway was running it as a general shop. By 1874 dock labourer and coal dealer John Smith and his wife Emma were behind the counter and the business remained in the family with Richard Smith running it from 1939 before changing it to a marine store in 1940, the last year it was recorded.

RUSSELL STREET
South Side, Nos. 42–47

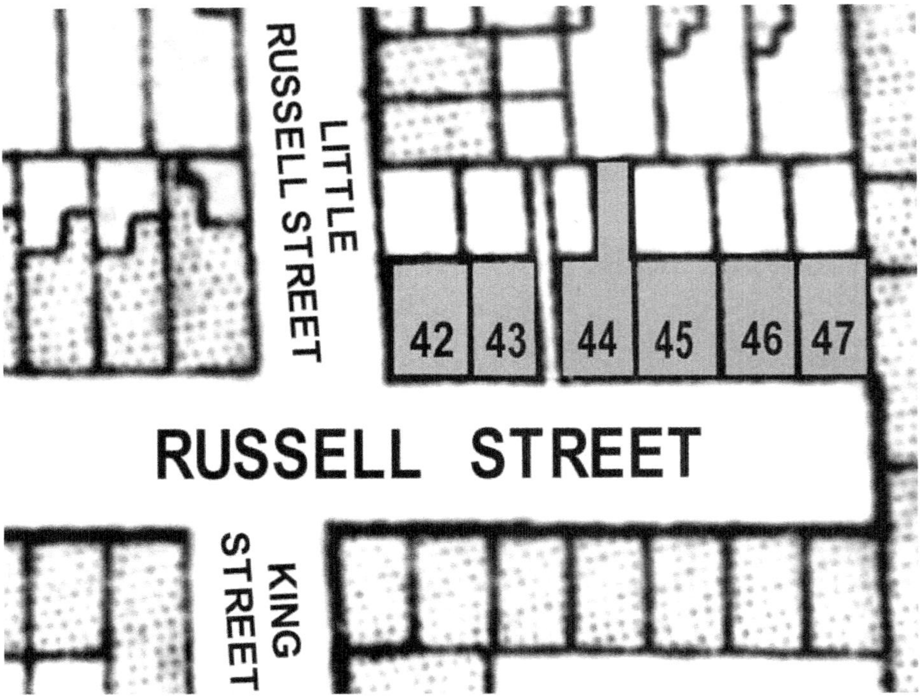

Nos. 42 to 47 at the western end of Russell Street. An alleyway ran between Nos. 43 and 44

The short cul-de-sac of Nos. 42 to 47 disappeared after 1940, possibly due to wartime bombing. Nobody was recorded at No. 42 until 1859 when steward George Evans appeared. This was another premises with a high turnover of residents, none of whom stayed very long. In fact, 15 came and departed before the arrival of crane driver Thomas William Bateman in 1907. He rested his jib there until 1916 saw George Summers as occupant until Alfred Maynard sat out the final years in 1939 and 1940. Yet another journeyman carpenter, this time Newell Ediss, was evident at No. 43 in 1851. However, Newell decided against travelling on and remained there until 1874 when fellow carpenter Alfred Wellman arrived. From 1881 the front door opened to seaman William Green, labourer Thomas Cokely and fish hawker William

Brookman before recently widowed Mrs Julia Chalk and her seven children held the keys from 1907, with Julia remaining there until 1940.

Engine driver James Rolfe, later at No. 40 was simmering in No. 44 through the 1850s until dock labourer John Farwell succeeded him in 1861. Mariner William Gover and his wife Fanny were next in from 1869 until 1874, which saw the start of the frequent tenancy changes that lasted until the early 1900s. John Bernard Nash, Thomas Harris, and Leonard A. Ferguson were among the final list of names from 1914 ending with Charles Anderson in 1940, when the houses in this terrace disappeared. Then, for some reason, this one dwelling had a short reoccupation in 1948 by Christopher J. House before it was demolished.

George Moxam lived at No. 45 for 30 years, beginning in the 1850s when he was a coal trimmer. During the ensuing years he was listed as ships fireman, seaman trimmer and labourer before his tenure was up in 1881. Next in line were dock labourer George Amey, ships fireman Thomas Redman, and sail maker James Sanger before 1907 saw dock labourer William Allen begin a long innings through to the mid-1930s and George Snook was last of all in 1939 and 1940. William Abree (otherwise Obree or Avery) was a painter and glazier who, with his wife Sarah and family, were living at No. 46 from 1851. By 1871 Sarah was a widow, dependent on her children for income, and from 1874 she was working as a laundress until her death in 1887. Others who moved into No. 46 included dock labourer Ernest Sainsbury, labourer George Covell and Walter Tyler William Dobson before William England and his wife held the tenancy from 1916 until 1939 with Harry A. White seeing out the final year or so.

The final house in this section of the street was No. 47, home to the Jupe family from 1851 until 1871. Charles Jupe was a druggists porter but by 1859 his wife Mary was a widow and became a monthly nurse until her death in 1869 aged 50. Painter Edward Callan was next in the rent book, being there until labourer John Kettle had a brief stay in 1881. Coal porter Richard Batchelor and his family arrived around 1900 and spent almost 40 years there before his wife Ellen took over the tenancy following Richard's death in 1922. Ellen then passed away in 1937 with Walter Butt moving in for the final couple of years.

ELDON STREET

Eldon Street was an inconspicuous row of five houses between Russell Street and Chandos Street, backing on to Threefield Lane. It is not to be confused with Eldon Place, which was part of Russell Street, or Eldon Terrace, which formed a section of Threefield Lane. Sometime around 1900 No. 1, the *Firemans Arms*, became No. 20 Chandos street and No.2 Eldon Street was taken over by the pub. Then the remaining four houses (3, 4 and 5) were renumbered as 2, 3 and 4, remaining so until the street was demolished in the mid-1950s.

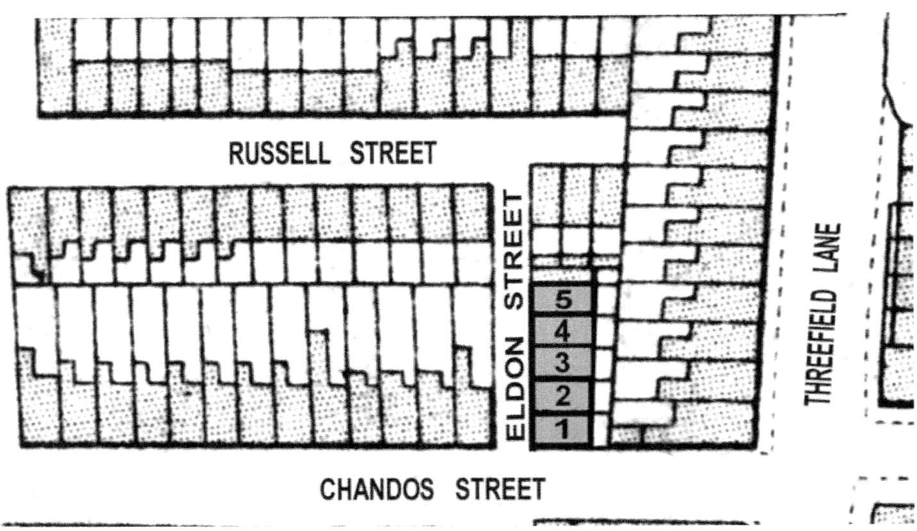

Nos. 1-5 Eldon Street where No.1 was once the Firemans Arms, often listed as No.20 Chandos Street.

No. 1 stood on the corner of Eldon Street and Chandos Street and, as it had an entrance in each street, was often listed in both. The early years saw laundress Mary Blandford washing away in 1851 and, a decade later, marine engineer Joseph Watkins was under its roof. He was followed by cook William Chapman and butcher Samuel S. Rose before John Maddon had turned it into a pub named the *Freemasons Arms* by 1867. William Grose was in charge in 1871 but by 1874 Ruben Groves had changed its name to the *Firemans Arms*. The 1881 census shows James H. Cox as a beer house keeper there and Tom Roe was landlord in 1891 but by 1901 the pub was renumbered as No. 20 Chandos Street and the licence was taken over by John Rainsley who presided until around 1925. Rainsley was a mariner by trade and fell foul of the law in 1903 when he was fined ten shillings for allowing after hours drinking. The pub changed hands several times between 1925 and 1935 when Albert E. Norman was behind the bar until he gave way to Alfred F. Cheeseman whose was the final name over the door from 1940 until 1954. At one time owned by Welsh's Hyde Abbey Brewery, it was later taken over by Cooper's Brewery before ending its days as a Watney pub when demolished in 1956.

The Firemans Arms on the corner of Eldon Street and Chandos Street in its final days as a Watney pub (Late David Goddard collection)

Journeyman blacksmith John Cox lived in No. 2 during the 1850s with charwoman Sophia Ealy there in 1861. Several others passed through its doorway, including mariner George C. Monckton in 1871, and fireman Thomas Elgar from 1874 until 1887. The house then seems to have been taken over by the *Firemans Arms* around 1900 and the remaining three were renumbered.

Dock storekeeper William Dalrymple was the tenant of No. 3 in 1851 before seaman Thomas Crouch had arrived by 1861. Crouch was key holder until the late 1860s when a host of mariners, ships firemen and labourers filed through until the turn of the century. In 1901 (now renumbered as No. 2) railway engine driver Charles Haythorpe had steamed in, while Union Castle seafarer Frederick Norris was there from 1907 until the Furber family arrived in 1920 and Joseph J. Furbur was the final inhabitant in 1954.

Mariner John Riddett was in No. 4 from 1851 until 1865 and later in that decade we find coppersmith George Handell, and labourers Alfred Surman and James Fox. Unemployed carman William Sisman bided his time there in 1871. The usual assortment of itinerants ended with charwoman Rachel Cook in 1901 (by then renumbered as No. 3). Confusion now reigns as Charles Wilton is shown there in 1907 but his spouse Rosina appears as widow Rosina Channell with her five children in 1911. Oddly, she appears on the census as having been married for 27 years – but not to Charles Wilton – who is not mentioned on the census – but he *is* listed in the directories from 1907 until 1920, after which Rosina becomes a widow once more and lives on there until her death in 1946. Her son, Albert Edward Channell, was then householder until 1954.

Labourer James Cozens was in No. 5 back in 1851 and seaman's wife Sarah Russell resided there in 1861, before bricklayer John Lock in 1863. Sawyer William Charlton materialised in 1867, followed by Mrs Walter in 1869. 1871 saw Caroline Bagley living on parish relief before labourer William Coombes arrived in 1874. Labourer Richard Kent in 1881, seaman J. Hackett and George Jeffrey in 1887 are the last names recorded at No. 5 before it became No. 4 with ships boilerman Michael MacNamara in 1901, and Ernest Bartlett, with his wife Alice Kate being resident from 1907 until 1925 when Alfred Scammell turned up and stayed on until the end.

CHANDOS STREET

Chandos Street ran west to east from Orchard Lane to Threefield Lane with Nos. 1 to 20 along its north side and Nos. 21 to 43 on its south side, going back to Orchard Lane. The street is in the 1834 directory and several names are listed there but most have no indication of street numbers, while one or two proved to be in nearby College Street. Aaron Whitmarsh is named as a broker in 1843 but appears as a sawyer in 1843. Robert Musselwhite is mentioned but with no other information. Then we have Miss Martin who was a straw hat and bonnet maker, along with John Bance who was a cooper. In its time, Chandos Street had three pubs and, like much of the neighbourhood, was demolished in the 1950s. A block of flats, Chandos House, now recalls its name. Sadly, I have not come across any general photos of Chandos Street other than one shown below.

CHANDOS STREET
North Side, Nos. 1–6

The first section on the north side of Chandos Street, between Orchard Lane and Little Russell Street (which was later part of King Street), contained five houses and a pub.

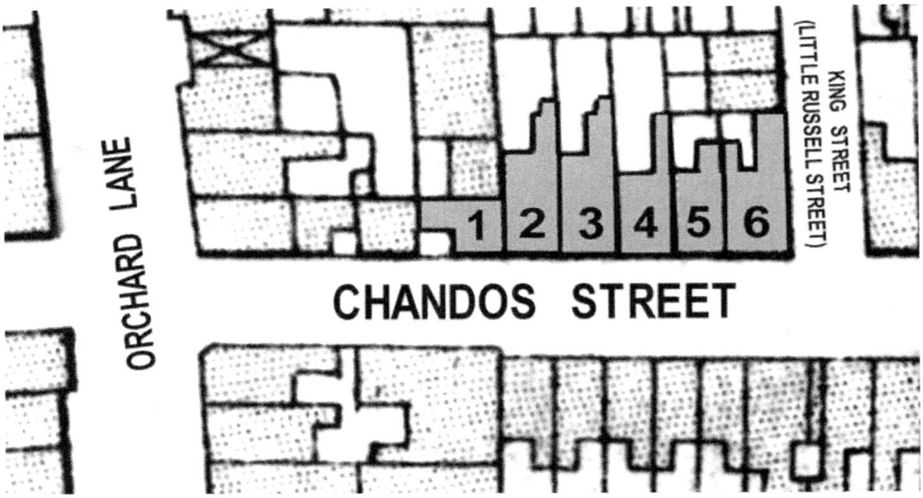

The north side of Chandos Street showing Nos. 1 to 6 between Orchard Lane and King Street (this section formerly known as Little Russell Street). No. 6 was the Chandos Inn

Alice Hughes and Maria Pack are named at No. 1 in 1851 and from 1857 Mrs Jane McVey ran a day school there. It did not last long as by 1859 ships fireman Timothy McCarthy had arrived with his wife Jemima Agnes who was a dressmaker and tailoress. The family were gone by 1884, which saw foreman Henry William Charlton as the key holder. Later occupants included policeman William Hudson and clerk George Clift before ships fireman George William Roe was there from 1911 until at least 1931. Miss Spencer Smith was the occupant in 1935 and the final name at that address was Alex Macintosh in 1939.

Journeyman joiner John Serridge lived at No. 2 in 1851 but no others are listed until tailor William Sewell set up shop in 1861 and stayed on until the 1870s when seaman James Wyatt and his wife Eliza dropped anchor. By 1887 Eliza was a widow living with her two sons and last seen there in 1901. Sail maker Harry Foot and his wife Elizabeth had moved in by 1911 and remained until Alfred B. Walter took residence in 1925 and stayed on until the street came down in the mid-1950s.

Journeyman coppersmith William A. Pollard was an early name at No.

3 in 1851 but was soon replaced by tailor Robert Knights by 1853. His tenure lasted into the 1870s when mariner Leonard Morton Hawkins and his family sailed in and were berthed there until 1907 when widow Mrs Keziah Jane Foot was next across the threshold before moving to No. 2 around 1914 where she joined Harry Foot and his wife. Julian Clare was then the occupant from 1914 until the 1920s when Charles Frederick Grubb and family settled in for the remaining years. Mariner Isaac Smith and his family were early settlers in No. 4 in the 1850s. They were followed by shipwright George Woodnutt and smithy Philip Stote (later at No. 23) and by 1861 seaman William Knight and his wife Eliza had arrived. The seafaring theme continued with mariner Edward Hibbard from 1865 and shipwright Thomas Scott in 1871. Marine stoker Thomas Foot and his laundress wife Jane had sailed in by 1876 but Jane was a widow by 1901 and in 1907 the Kearley (or Curley) clan had moved in. Ships fireman James Henry Kearley and his wife Daisy Ellen were securely moored there until at least 1939 when Ronald Tyler saw out the remaining years of the street.

Some of the street's earliest inhabitants appeared in the 1840s when printer James George Bunday and boot closer Samuel Carey were at No. 5. Samuel was a local man born in 1816 and plied his trade in Chandos Street (mostly at No. 41) before moving away to Northam around 1865. Boilermaker William Syms was at No. 5 in 1851 followed in that decade by painter William Bartlett (see also No. 42) and ships steward Thomas Redman. Butcher Robert Jewell and ships fireman George Wyatt saw out the 1860s there until drayman George Medhurst turned up in 1871. Coal porter William Smith rested his bones there for a decade beginning in 1876 with seaman William Hudson docking there in 1887. In the early 1900s, stationary engine man Joseph Ryder and his family were tenants until Harty West resided from 1920 until the outbreak of World War Two which saw the arrival of John George Mabey who remained until Alfred Charles Stanbrook was the occupant in 1954.

French polisher John Major was adding a shine to No. 6 back in 1843.

The premises, on the corner of Little Russell Street was for, much of its existence, a shop and a pub. Unmarried mother Mary Perren (always listed as Mrs) ran her grocery store there from 1851 until fruiterer William Travers took over in 1863. Arthur Cozens returned it to a grocers shop through the latter 1860s until around 1870 when it became a beer house named the *Chandos Inn*, run by William Marston who was landlord until about 1880 when Elizabeth French was licensee. Her stewardship ended in 1884, which saw William Alfred Mansell pulling the pints until 1891 when John Mason became its final host. Time was called in 1912 and the building became a private residence with a steady turnover of tenants until Frank Hinton dwelled there from 1940 until demolition came.

CHANDOS STREET
North Side, Nos. 7–20

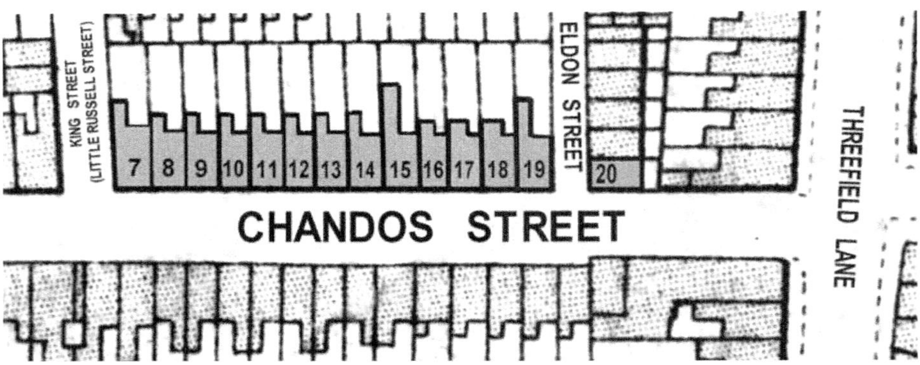

The north side of Chandos Street with Nos. 7 to 19 between King Street and Eldon Street. No. 20 was the Fireman's Arms pub which was often listed as No. 1 Eldon Street

On the other corner of Little Russell Street stood No. 7 which, for a while, was William Back's grocers shop in the 1850s and was later a greengrocers run by John Pelham Cooke. In 1861 it was the premises of hide and skin dealer George Smith before returning as a fruiterers belonging to William Travers. By the 1870s house and ship painter

Samuel Bond was in occupation then the 1880s welcomed the familiar turnover of seamen and labourers until the 1901 arrival of ships fireman William Taylor whose family decided to remain there until the final days.

Pauper Phoebe Ruddock was living in No. 8 from the 1850s and in 1857 was running it as a lodging house. Tailor William Gibbs was stitching away there from 1859 until 1863 and ships officer Henry Skaines with his wife Rebecca were moored there from 1869 to 1887. Next up from 1891 were letter sorter Walter Taylor, stonemason James Ford and railway porter George Holloway who parked his bags there from 1907 until 1925. Albert Doncom was the final name in the rent book from the 1930s onwards.

P&O Company steward Charles Dawkins was evident at No. 9 from 1851 through to 1871, while painter John Warren and storekeeper William Hyde took up the early 1870s. Boot maker Joseph Meadus (previously at No. 27) took residence there from 1876 until 1901 and the 20th century welcomed new faces Daniel Golding, William Hawkis and Harry Mullins through to the 1920s, while Patrick Bernard Hopper, and John B. Martin were the main tenants from 1935, with Mrs LeFeuvre (previously at No. 10) being last of all in 1954. Carpenter and joiner George Morse was sawing away at No. 10 in 1851 before harness maker Charles Kyte moved in during the latter half of the decade. Porter James Tanner and his wife Frances held the keys through the 1860s. Widow Mary Allen spent the early 1870s there before seafarers David Kennard (or Kinnard) and Henry Curtis, and labourer John Light had spells through to 1911 when dock labourer John L. Woodford dwelled through to 1920. William Dalton and Edwin Cyril Dyer were occupiers until 1940 when Mrs LeFeuvre spent the 1940s there before moving next door to No. 9 and making way for Mrs Bellows. Former carpenter James Jerram fell on hard times and was a pauper at No. 11 in the early 1850s. He was gone by 1855 when sail maker William Newman breezed in until around 1860. He was followed by painter Thomas Hearn, ships carpenter George Jacobs and butcher Benjamin Lukey. Mariner Henry Curtis (later at No. 10) arrived in 1865 and had departed by 1874 when labourer John Rawlings (or Rollings) and his wife Ann stayed on until 1887. Into the early 1900s we find ships fireman William Gooding and his family embark on a long tenure that saw them through until 1954.

One of the earliest residents at No. 12 was master mariner Peter Bunday back in 1843 but his place was taken by Thomas Taylor who was an engineer and one-time railway engine driver through the 1850s until tailoress Mrs Maria Coombes arrived with her needles in 1861 and sewed her garments there until 1876 when sailor George Hembery and his laundress wife Ann entered the front door. George died in 1891 and Ann continued her mangling there until around 1920. Mrs Winter took her place until Arthur Reginald Parker became its last occupant from the mid-1930s until the final days of the street. In 1851 labourer William Willis junior was the inhabitant of No. 13, which obviously proved lucky for him as he stayed there until 1881 during which time he became a porter and then a foreman. Seaman John Lonnen and his wife Mary then spent a decade there until dock labourer George Henry Lane arrived in 1901 but was gone by 1911 when railway carter George Thomas Tiller held the keys and hitched his wagon there all the way through until 1954.

Journeyman tallow chandler Edward Jones was briefly in No. 14 in 1851 but by the mid-1850s mariner Roger Widger and his wife Louisa appeared and spent several years there before deciding to move next door to No. 15 in 1869. Their place was taken by sailor John Lonnen who later moved to No. 13 in 1881. Charwoman and laundress Mrs Ann Crouch was the new name in the rent book, scrubbing and cleaning until around 1890. There next followed a succession of short term tenants including dock labourer George Page and divers attendant John William Short until Percy Doncom turned up in 1916 and stayed on until 1939, after which George Barnes and his wife saw out the final years.

Henry Thomas was making boots and shoes at No. 15 in 1847 where he continued cobbling until William Thomas (no relation) continued the business until 1869 when George Widger and family moved in from No. 14, staying on until 1881 when labourer Albert Charles Biles and his wife Elizabeth came along. Albert died in 1900 and widow Elizabeth lived on there until her death in 1930. Alfred Harris then took up the tenancy through to the final years when Arthur T. Parkhurst was the last name recorded there. Porter Henry Willis was living in No. 16 in 1851 but by 1855 his place had been taken by timber carrier William Willis senior (his son lived at No. 13) who died soon afterwards and his wife Martha was surviving on parish relief by 1861. Martha had gone by 1871 when her married daughter seamstress Sarah Collins became head of the house. Sarah's husband George, a navy winch man, was away from home most of the time and Sarah was last recorded there in 1884. After several short-term tenancies through the remaining 1800s, boiler maker Robert Borland was the occupier by 1907 before Michael Hennacher was resident from 1916 until the 1930s. The final name at that abode was John Fripp from 1939 until 1954.

Seafarer William Pedler and journeyman bricklayer William Fry shared No. 17 in the 1850s before harness maker Charles Kite (later at No. 10) made a brief appearance in 1853. He was followed by baker John Cook and paper bag maker John Savage, before tinplate worker and whitesmith George Gordon set up his brazier there which continued burning until 1876. At least seven others took his place until 1914 heralded the arrival of John Cooke who marked time there, with Ernest Edward Hayes being handed the keys in 1931 and holding on to them until 1954.

Boot closer Henry Mussell was stitching his leather at No. 18 in 1851 and those who followed in the 1850s included Mrs Ann Lane and P&O steward William Bance (also at Nos. 29 and 33), Carpenter James Barrett from 1859 until 1867, and then came bricklayer John Lock and painter and decorator Arthur Martin. Into the 1870s we find seamen

John Carter, George Langford and Edward Powell. In 1887 painter Joseph Stevens dipped his brushes there until 1911 when milk carrier James Edward King rattled his pail for a year or two and, finally, Arthur Smith spent a large chunk of his life there from 1920 until demolition came in the 1950s.

Yet another journeyman boot maker was Henry Wattridge who did his cobbling at No. 19, on the corner of Eldon Street, in 1851. His son John (Joseph) followed the family trade there in the later 1850s but by 1859 had become a schoolmaster. In 1867 the multi-talented John Wattridge was still teaching but also making paper bags and in 1869 he had taken up printing. By 1871 he was employing two others before moving his printing works to Sholing. Customs officer George Martell was the next occupant of note in the 1870s before porter Thomas Mason, labourer Arthur Clothier and boiler maker William McMahon had seen out the 1800s. McMahon held on until 1911 when mariner Daniel Abrahams sailed in but soon gave up his berth to Samuel Rowett. Railway porter John Edward Sparks and his son Edward James Sparks were the next names in the rent book from 1920 until 1940, when Walter Thomas Marlow saw out the final years of the street.

No. 20 Chandos Street was officially No.1 Eldon Street (see that chapter for its history) but, as previously mentioned, the building had two entrances, one in each street, so was often listed in either or both.

Celebrations by families in the Chandos Street to mark the 1953 coronation. The view is east towards Threefield Lane and the Fireman's Arms can be seen in the background on the corner of Eldon Street (Dave Marden collection)

CHANDOS STREET
South Side, Nos. 21–35

In the early directories and census returns, the *Anchor and Hope* pub (see Threefield Lane) was included in Chandos Street and the street was renumbered around 1860, which saw the first appearance of what became No.21, a building at the rear of the *Anchor and Hope*. Next door to it was Eldon Cottage, which appears through the 1850s and is then non-existent from when the street was again renumbered. It would seem that Eldon Cottage then became No. 22 as Edward Banks was the common tenant in both.

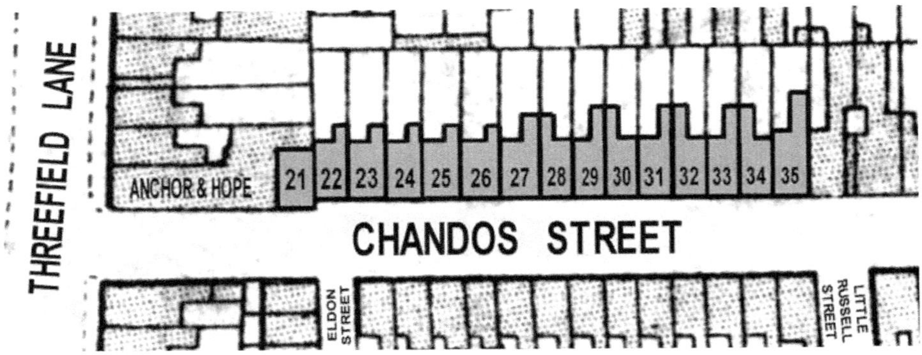

The south side of Chandos Street showing Nos. 21 to 35. The Anchor and Hope pub on the corner of Threefield Lane was often included in Chandos Street for the earlier directories. No. 22 was formerly Eldon Cottage until around 1860

Steward George Marshall is the first name that appears at No. 21 in 1863, evident there until he gave way to seaman Augustus Lervey in 1869. In the 1870s it had become a lodging house run by Mrs Betsey Woolstenholme from 1871 until 1881 when hotel porter's wife Mary Jane Mason had moved in. She was gone by 1884 when a high turnover of residents began until boiler maker William Christopher Wren appeared in 1907 and remained until William C. Self became the final name there in 1954. No. 22 was at one time named Eldon Cottage and its early occupant was journeyman carpenter Benjamin Cage in 1851. HM Customs officer Richard Taylor was next in line through the middle 1850s until replaced by mariner Thomas Hockley in 1857. Fellow mariner Edward Banks had moved in by 1859 and remained the tenant there through to 1863, by which time the street had been renumbered to include Eldon Cottage as No. 22. Carpenter William Meaton (or Maton) and his family then began a long occupation, which lasted from 1863 until 1925. William's laundress wife Martha had become a widow by 1861 and her French polisher son Edward had assumed the tenancy in 1907. Frank Richard Waters was next through the front door, remaining until Arthur Philpott arrived in 1940 and sat tight until the street was no more.

Pig butcher George Rose was in No. 23 in 1851 when Mrs Monk was his landlady. The next few years saw a number of short-stay mariners before Philip Stote and his family took residency in 1859, which lasted until 1887. Stote was previously a smith living at No. 4 back in 1854 but over time his occupation at No. 23 is described as engine driver, in 1861 being on a railway engine and latterly in a factory. Army pensioner John Moore and his wife Elizabeth were next to grace its living room until William Thomas Rea began a long stay in 1912 that lasted until 1940 when John Clark saw out the street's final years. Mariner George Elliot was a ships fireman when he entered No. 24 in 1851. His seafaring journey took him to the Isle of Wight Steam Packet Company and then on to the South Western Railway vessels before being promoted to engineer by 1863. His stay lasted until 1867 when fellow engineer John Bamborough was in charge before ships fireman Edward Stainer and his machinist wife Annie were tenants from 1871. Seaman Thomas Elgar and his wife Mary were next through the front door in 1887, a tenure that lasted into the 1900s. Several others came and went before Alfred J. Smith set up camp there in 1931 and stayed on until the end.

Boot maker Charles Cummins was an early occupant of No. 25 in 1851 before Mrs Charlotte Payne set up her day school there in 1857. The school lasted only until 1861 when whitesmith and bell hanger John Gordon arrived with his brazier. Laundress Mrs Ann Curtis was turning her mangle there from 1867 until fellow laundress Mrs Jane Cousins took over in 1901; by 1911 she was running the address as a boarding house and remained there until 1935. Harry Frank Bradley was the final name in the rent book from 1940 until 1954. Boot making was a flourishing business in Chandos Street and yet another of the trade was cobbling at No. 26 in 1851. This was John Haysom who lasted only until tallow chandler Edward Jones moved in around 1853 and stayed on until 1869 when mariner Samuel Algar sailed in around 1869. He soon hoisted anchor and was followed by an assortment of other seafarers until labourer James Pitford and his wife Adelaide Sophia were in occupation from 1891 until 1914 when Thompson McCarter embarked on a long stay that ended only when Harry Roberts spent the final year there.

Yet another boot and shoemaker was Joseph Meadus, working at No. 27 from 1851 until 1874 when he moved to No. 9. Coal porter and carter Stephen Lock was living there in the 1880s before the Vanner family arrived in 1891 and were evident there in 1901. Austin Vanner was a telephone lineman while Maurice L. Vanner was a casual labourer. Boiler smiths helper Charles Walton had moved in by 1911 but had moved on by 1914 when Thomas Clitheroe appeared through World War One years. Henry Hardicker had a spell there through the 1930s with Samuel William Oakley resident from 1939 until the end. Gunsmith Henry Goodfellow had a long association with No. 28 from 1851 where he spent at least 30 years and was last recorded there as unemployed in 1881 at the age of 71. Then steward William Crabb, porter Samuel Noyes and ships foreman William Godwin saw out the remainder of the 1800s. No one else stayed very long until Mrs C. Robinson arrived in 1916 and departed when Edward C. Tyler-Carstairs entered the rent book in 1931 and remained until 1940 when Henry James Gregory's tenure spanned the final years of the street.

Mariner Thomas Whitmarsh and his family were key holders at No. 29 in 1851 but their time there was short-lived as fellow mariner Charles Hurst took over in 1853. He, in turn, made way for P&O steward William Bance in 1859. Bance, who had previously been at No. 33 in 1855 and No. 18 in 1857, decided this time to stay put and remained there until butcher Henry Hitchcock and family arrived in 1867 and stayed there until his death in 1895. Grocers porter Samuel C. Noyce then stopped over for a while before blacksmith William Windebank had forged his way in by 1907 and left in 1916. From then on, tenancies were fairly short term until James Henry Frampton and his family arrived in the early 1930s and stayed on for the remaining years.

Henry Bailey was a coach maker's labourer living with his family at No.

30 from 1851. Their son Charles, one-time sail maker and now a general dealer, was head of the house by 1867 but had moved on by 1869 when mariner Christopher Young came ashore and stayed put until around 1881. Coach painter Fred Courtney was the next tenant and he saw out the remainder of the century that began with wine porter Charles Albert Stonadge and ships plate riveter Robert Nelson arriving in the early 1900s. Angus Graham was then occupant from 1912 until 1925. A trio of ladies then saw out the remaining years of the street when Mrs F. Humphrey became landlady for a decade from 1931, followed by Mrs Wells in 1940, and finally Mrs Webb in 1854.

Elizabeth Oliver was a widow at 40 by the time she came to live at No. 31 with her son George in 1851. Working as an upholstress, she was there until around 1871 when coach wheelwright George Privett rolled in. George continued his tenancy until mariner James Young dropped anchor there in 1881 with his wife Ellen Elizabeth who was 20 years younger. After James died in 1910, widow Ellen was working as an office cleaner in 1911 but oddly, the tenant of No. 31 from 1912 was still listed as James Young, some two years after his death. Ellen had no son of that name among their seven children. Nevertheless, the remaining Youngs stayed on until 1925 when Ernest Fielder moved in and Ernest John Stafford was last of all from 1939 onwards.

Laundress Ann Monk was an early bird at No. 32 in 1851 but porter Thomas Weeks had replaced her by 1855 and made it his home until 1871 when blacksmith James Hayter came along. He was there until around 1890, which saw LSWR porter William J. Sparks park his bags until well into the 1900s. Others that followed included Sydney Silvet Mulcaster, Edward Patterson, a seaman with the Royal Mail Steam Packet Company, and Harry Smith, all before 1914 when George Toy and his family spent their next 40 years there.

Stay maker Mary Cawte was building her corsets at No. 33 back in 1851. Later, in the 1850s, fly driver and labourer James Thompson trotted in until 1861 welcomed porter Charles Hunt and his wife Mary Ann. Charles died in 1876 and Mary Ann ran the household with her five children, three of whom were working, until the mid-1880s when Mrs Donaldson arrived. Ships steward Alexander Thomas Mead served there with his wife Jessie until his death in 1908. Jessie stayed on until around 1912 when Thompson McCarter appeared briefly before Charles McNelly took over in 1914 and remained until around 1925. Joseph Weatherall adorned the rent book from then until 1940 saw Alfred Nellthorp and his wife appear and see out the remaining years.

Pauper Margaret Dominey was head of the house at No. 34 in the early 1850s but by 1855 cabinet maker George Elliot was living there – not to be confused with mariner George Elliot at No. 23. In fact, George at No. 34 appears to have changed his name to Ellyett in 1865 and kept it as such until the end of his tenure there in the mid-1870s. Railway inspector William Sparks had moved in by 1876 (see also his son William, a railway porter at No. 32). William senior remained until around 1901, after which several others filed through the front door including railway engine driver William Eneas Turner in 1911. Samuel Biles (from 1914) and then Robert Smith (from 1925) made up almost all the remaining years until Thomas Frederick William Bichard was last of the line in 1954.

No. 35 was recorded as having builder George Lanham under its roof back in 1843, with tea dealer Andrew Hyslop evident in 1849. Arthur Spencer is listed as the occupant in 1851 when the census lists him as a printer, but in the directory of that year he is a tailor. Blacksmith Charles Heden is there in 1855 but Arthur Spencer reappears as both tailor and printer at No. 36 in the later 1850s. Meanwhile, Charles Heden replaced him at No. 36 in 1859. Confused? Yes, but the mist begins to clear in 1861 when grocers shop man James Brown arrives at No. 35 and Heden is shown at No. 36. Back to No. 35 and we find James Brown settling into a long and successful stay that sees him rise from shop man to foreman and then to corn merchant manager by 1891, a position he held when departing in 1907. Henry and Constance Stevens were in No. 35 in 1911 but the census tells us nothing more than they had six children. Then Alfred Hurst is the tenant from 1914 and into the 1930s when George Strange and his wife were in occupation until Archibald Scammell is the final name in 1940, possibly due to wartime bombing.

CHANDOS STREET
South Side, Nos. 36–43

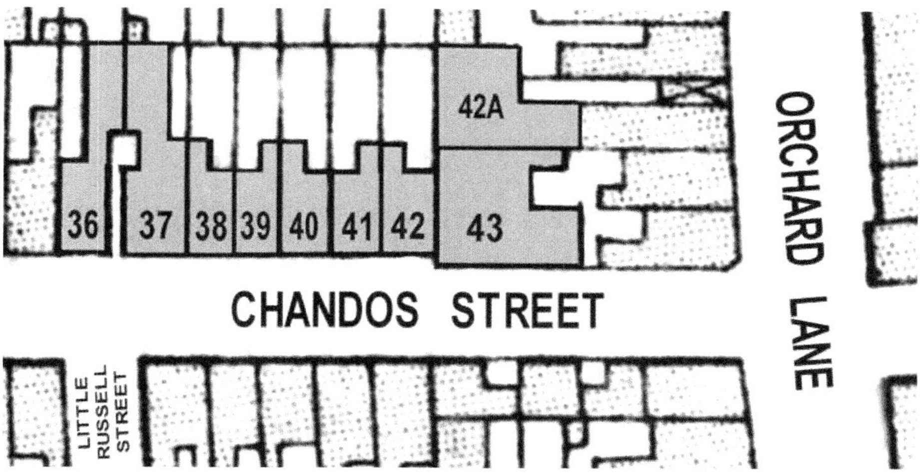

The western end of Chandos Street where it met Orchard Lane. No. 37 was the Medina Tavern pub with a covered passage running between it and No. 36. No. 42A was a workshop and No. 43 became a social club

Laundress Mary Ann Trim was a widow at No. 36 in 1851 before Arthur Spencer and Charles Heden began their shuffles from No. 35. All was settled by 1859 when coach smith Heden and his wife Mary settled in No. 36 through to Charles's death in 1890 and Mary's passing in 1894. Into the new century and Thomas Henry Clitheroe (previously at No. 27) is the tenant in 1914 followed by John Smith in 1935, and then Archibald Scammell, who had been next door at No. 35 until 1940, moved in and was still present in 1954.

What became No. 37 was originally home to baker Isaac Spencer in

1834. Nothing more comes to light until the premises is recorded as the *Fox and Grapes* beer house run by Romsey man Joseph Riouffe and his Jersey-born wife Jane. By 1857 the pub had been renamed the *Medina Tavern* under the ownership of Panton's Wareham Brewery and was in the hands of Joseph Wadham until 1863. The pub came into the hands of Scrase's Star Brewery in 1892 and the licensees then changed several times before Thomas and Mary Ann Lee were hosts from 1869 until 1876 when Mark Gordon had his name over the door. Then, after another long turnover of landlords, the Mason family were behind the bar from 1914, with George Mason being the last of the line when the pub was refused a licence in 1921 and then became a private residence with George remaining under its roof until, in the 1930s, the building became a store for St James Church in nearby Bernard Street, continuing as such until the street was demolished.

Ships steward Charles Humby and his laundress wife Eliza (not to be confused with the nearby Humbys of Sawmill Court) were resident at No. 38 from 1851. By 1871 Charles had died and Eliza was living on his annuitant along with her three working children but by 1876 they had moved to Union Street. Seaman Ephraim Clements and his wife Harriet were then occupants until 1907 and from then on the house welcomed a whole host of new names before Herbert John Wade and his wife settled there in 1935 and remained until the final days. Police sergeant William Foster and his wife Sarah had a long association with No. 39 from 1851. By 1871 Sarah was a widow and running the address as a lodging house until around 1881 when she moved away and seaman James George Smith and his wife Elizabeth took tenure. Sadly, Elizabeth was another widow by 1901 but stayed on until James Lewis arrived in 1931 but he was there only until the late 1930s when Gordon Grubb turned up to see out the remaining years.

Boot and shoe maker William Pratt hammered his way through the 1850s at No. 40 until ships steward Henry Bulbick (or Bulbeck) berthed there in 1859 and tied up for a decade before ships fireman William

Leybourne and wife Agnes arrived. They were in occupation until 1881, after which the name in the rent book belonged to coal merchant William Cotton. After William's death in 1898 his son David, a dock labourer, became head of the house through to 1940 when Ernest Frederick Sims became the final tenant. Postman John Walden's address was No. 41 back in 1843 but boot closer Samuel Carey had set up his business there by 1851 and remained until carver and gilder William Henry Sewell arrived in 1867. Sewell's tenure lasted until watch maker Henry Francis Russell became the tenant in 1884. Brewer Mark Ford spent time there before coach painter Fred Courtney arrived in 1901. Courtney, previously at No. 30, already had a store and workshop nearby (at No. 42½) from 1884 and had moved out of both premises by 1925. Samuel Keene and his wife Mary were next on the scene until Walter Rainlsey was evident from 1940 onwards.

The final house at No. 42 was shared by carpenter Lot Doller and coach smith William Russell back in 1834 and by 1851 mariner William Reeves had come ashore. He had sailed off by 1855, making way for customs messenger Benjamin Masters. Painter William Bartlett (previously at No. 5) perfected his brushwork there from 1859 until fly driver William Colmer galloped in around 1863. Colmer, variously described as a cab driver and coachman, died in 1892 aged 60 and his widow Sarah stayed on until 1907. Ships painter Edwin Gentry was soon in occupation until moving on in 1925 when Edward J. Doncom had a brief stopover before James William Jones spent the 1930s there. George Roberts and his wife were the final tenants from 1940.

Although the final house in this section was No. 42, there were further buildings at the western end of the street where No. 42½ was the address of marine store dealer John Kennedy in 1851 and by 1871 it became Porter Brothers tin plate works. It was subsequently occupied by coach painter Fred Courtney (see above) from around 1884 until the 1920s when Mrs Mary A. Keene ran her truck hire business there until 1925. From 1907, part of the site was developed as a workmans hall which was numbered 43 under secretary Robert Sergeant. It then became a social club and institute around 1916, which survived until the street was demolished in the mid-1950s.

THREEFIELD LANE
Humby's/Sawmill Court

The reference to three fields probably relates to the farming system when this area was still quite rural. Running south from Marsh Lane to Bernard Street, it was once known as Nightingale Lane, and the section north of Chandos Street was named Eldon Terrace in Victorian times. Threefield Lane has seen many changes in its time with sections and terraces being renamed and renumbered several times over. Nos. 2 to 32 were demolished around 1936 to make way for the Corporation Tenements but before then, Nos. 28, 30 and 32 had disappeared after 1914 while No. 24 lasted until 1920 and No. 26 remained until 1931. Over the years the lane has changed beyond recognition from being a fairly insignificant back street and having been straightened, widened and changed to one-way traffic while becoming a major part of the lower town road system. For the purposes of this book we will look only at the western side of the street, which forms the boundary of the historic area it covers.

THREEFIELD LANE
West Side, Nos. 2–32

This section was originally numbered 1 to 15 with Sawmill Cut being numbered separately, but after renumbering in the early 1880s the two premises at the entrance to the cut were included in Threefield Lane. No. 8 was a pub named the *Sailor's Welcome* and No. 9 later became a shop. Nos. 2 to 32 were demolished around 1936 but Nos. 28, 30 and 32 were already missing from the directories after 1914 and subsequent maps show they were knocked down by then.

The northern section of Threefield Lane showing Nos. 2 to 32. Nos. 8 and 9 were once part of Sawmill Cut

Beginning our journey down Threefield Lane we first arrive at No. 2, which was home to printer William Maiden in 1851. By 1859 painter Frederick Jones and his family were in residence that ended in 1871 with another Jones, mariner Paul, as head of the house. Dressmaker Frances Povey was next but like many others who followed, her occupation was short-lived as it seemed nobody liked to stay there for any length of time until coal porter William Grant moved in with his wife Minnie and their four children around 1907, a tenure that lasted until 1936. No. 4 was home to pauper Lucy Oakley in 1851 and around the same time, stonemason William Warren lived there until the 1850s saw labourer George Dawkins and his laundress wife Mary Ann move in. George's hobby was dealing with birds (the feathered type) and after his death around 1880, Mary Ann continued scrubbing there until 1887. Labourer James Tomkins then had his feet under the table until the early 1900s saw boot maker John Hill hammer his hobnails through to 1916. Thomas Burton was the new name in 1920 and he gave way to William Jones in 1935.

Following labourer George Payne's 1851 sojourn at No. 6 we find the Blake family, with porter William and his laundress wife Mary running the household until 1869 when mariner George Jones and his wife Elizabeth stayed until 1874. In the 1871 census Elizabeth is said to be a shopkeeper but she must have worked elsewhere as there is no evidence No. 6 was ever a shop. Mariner Robert Sevier and labourer George Wallis (later at No. 14) saw out the 1870s before cooper William Brookman rolled his barrels there from 1884 until 1907. Marine fireman George Hull and his wife Eleanor then began a long stint there, which lasted until the street came down.

Since at least 1851, No. 8 had been a pub named the *Sailors Return* run by Thomas Humby, although in those days it was listed as No. 7 Sawmill Cut until that was changed in the 1880s. After Thomas died in the late 1860s his wife Kezia took over and ran the place until at least 1887 when Henry Norris assumed control. He was a boiler maker by trade and under his stewardship the pub was renamed the *Sailors Welcome* around 1901. By 1911, his wife Martha was landlady and remained so until, owned by Barlow's Victoria Brewery, the pub was refused a licence in 1921. It then became a shop run by George Stride, then finally by William Donoghue. No. 9 on the opposite corner was originally Nos. 1 and 2 Sawmill Cut, which was renumbered into Threefield Lane in the early 1900s. By 1931 it had become a cycle shop under Henry Lawrence and Company and was latterly a motor car accessories store belonging to Frederick Henry Maunper (see Sawmill Cut for earlier history).

Baker William Hedges had his ovens in No. 10 in the 1850s but by the end of that decade he was running a general shop there until the mid-1860s. From then it became the berth of mariner John Burge until Thomas Bessant and his wife Constance arrived in 1874. Their stay ended in 1881 but Constance did make a brief return in 1884. Others came and went before ships rigger David Marsh took residence in 1901 and remained through to the very end. Confectioner James Fillmore (or Phillmore) inhabited No. 12 through the 1850s until carpenter John Fry arrived with his saw in 1859. The 1860s and 1870s welcomed labourers

George Wheeler and Harry Head, along with shoemaker Alfred Warren, butcher Charles Farling and cab driver Henry Vare. Dock labourer William Hayes dallied a while through the 1880s before the frequent turnover of tenants resumed with dock labourer Richard Nichollson, cooper and vat maker Henry Ninnim taking us into the 20th century. From then on the door was open to seaman Henry John Guyton and a host of others, the last of which was Walter Chalk.

Gardener James Painter planted himself at No. 14 through the 1850s before laundress Jane Brown and railway porter George Littlecott sampled its delights. Porter and labourer William Jannaway enjoyed his time there from 1867 until 1876 when there began a succession of labourers, coal carriers and a corn porter prior to Richard Battenbury (also Brackenbury and Rottenbury) appearing in 1907. He was a French polishers assistant by occupation and stayed put through to 1935. Cordwainer James Bridgwater worked his leather at No. 16 during the 1850s until dock labourer Thomas Gale began his occupation in 1859 which lasted until 1871 when painter George Medus briefly held the keys before they were handed to butcher Charles Bishop. From then it was almost an open door with frequent name changes until painter George Curtis cleaned his brushes there from 1907 until the 1930s when Henry Pollard and Francis Michael Connolly were the last in.

William G. Ubsdell was a cabinet maker who made his home at No. 18 throughout the 1850s. Then, as with No. 16, there followed another huge turnover of tenants until ships carpenter James Ferbranche parked his toolbox in 1871, an occupation that lasted for two decades, by which time he had graduated to become a joiner and ultimately a cabinet maker. In 1901 the house was vacant but no less than seven more occupiers emerged before George Llewellyn became the last. Blacksmith William Bowyer was at No. 20 in 1851 but no others are recorded until shoemaker Richard Cole arrived in 1861. The seagoing Taylor family were in occupation from William in 1865 and then his son Edward from 1871 were familiar faces until he and his wife Marie were last seen in 1881. As ever, there was another influx of names in the rent book through the 1880s, 1890s and early 1900s before the Roberts family settled there in 1920 and John William Roberts was the last recorded in 1931.

House painter William Hendle was in No. 22 according to the 1851 census but no later occupants are noted until laundress Mrs Mary Roberts is listed in 1859. Around that time, cooper John Brookman and his family moved in but Mary appears to have stayed on. The Brookmans were well established in No. 22 and son William, also a cooper, was head of the house in 1874, living with his two sisters until they moved to No. 6 around 1884. No. 22 then saw a host of new arrivals ending in 1911 when it became a store for fruit salesman Alfred George Axton, later A.G. Axton and Sons, who stayed on until the demolition.

Threefield Lane in the 1930s showing Nos. 14 (nearest) to 24. No. 22 was for many years Axton's fruit store

No. 24 did not appear in the directories until 1853 with mariner George May as occupant, remaining until bargeman Thomas Woods and his excavator son James arrived in 1861. Dairyman William Nineham and his family were resident from 1869 but after his death in 1880, his wife Frances Ann was selling sweets in 1881. The next tenant of note was the interestingly named Mackijaer Barnes (otherwise Mack or Matthew), a carpenters labourer and one-time iron moulder, who came along in 1887. He and his wife Miriam were present all the way through until 1920 after which the house was one of four that was demolished earlier than others in the street. Carpenter John Ireland was at home in No. 26 in the 1850s until 1859 welcomed George Sangster, a marine engineer with the South Western Railway, and his wife Susannah and their four children. The late 1860s saw Mrs Eliza Hickman turning her mangle there before William Brookman moved in from No. 22 in 1876. Next in from 1881 was John Hanson Barton, a house painter and plumber by trade, who remained until 1907 when mariner Patrick Corbett and his wife Mary arrived and were the last at that address in 1931.

The Dove family roosted at No. 28 from 1851. Whitesmith William, wife Maria and his carpenter father Josiah were resident there until 1863 when railway porter William W. Prowting arrived with his bags. Mariner Thomas Fielder was next in the rent book from 1869 until 1874 and from then on, several others passed over its threshold before the new century when West India Company fireman William G. Barnes was present in the house for its final years from 1901 until 1914, being one of a trio (28 to 32) that disappeared after that date. No. 30 saw little early habitation with only Samuel Jones in 1851 and blacksmith George Dove in 1859 being recorded until there was a flurry of inmates from 1861 that included brewer James Terry, barrow man Stephen Ponting, labourer Albert Hunt, Mrs Ledicott, and Mariner Thomas Palmer, all by 1871. Labourer Enoch Shelley arrived in 1874 and had worked his way up to foreman at a ships coaling firm by the time he died in 1887 at the age of 64. His widow Sarah had vacated by 1891 when Thomas and Ellen

Moody arrived with their family, a tenure that ended after the house was demolished after 1914.

The third of the vanishing trio from 1914 was No. 32 which seems to be one of the older properties as it was occupied by Samuel Winship in 1845. By trade, he was a washer and bleacher before he became a porter in 1851, remaining there until 1857 when pork butcher George H. Rose arrived with his cleaver. He was gone by 1865 when William Dove transferred briefly from No. 28. Then from 1867 we find engineer George Blake and tailor John Godley before 1874 when licensed barrowman Frederick Hatchard wheeled in until 1891. An assortment of labourers then followed before Thomas and Elizabeth Boyle became the final tenants from 1911 before the house was no more after 1914.

THREEFIELD LANE
West Side, Nos. 34–68

The collection of houses from No. 34 to 54 was originally numbered 1 to 11 and named Eldon Terrace dating back to the 1830s while the *Anchor and Hope* pub, officially in Chandos Street, was occasionally listed in Threefield Lane. No. 68, at the end of College Street, had its front door in Threefield Lane and was regarded as such. Nos. 34 to 40 were demolished in 1935 when Russell Street was extended through to Threefield Lane and everything north of Russell Street, was bulldozed around the same time to make way for the Corporation Tenements, otherwise known as the utility flats that replaced everything between Lime Street and Russell Street and from King Street to Threefield Lane. Those south of Chandos Street remained in place until the mid-1950s.

The southern end of Threefield Lane showing Nos. 34 to 68. Nos. 34 to 54 were originally known as Eldon Terrace and Nos. 62 and 63 was the Rose and Thistle pub. No. 56 was taken over by the Anchor and Hope in the 1930s. Nos. 34 to 40 were demolished in 1935 when Russell Street was extended through to Threefield Lane

Dyer Joseph Hiscock was the inhabitant of No. 34 in 1834 and carpenter William Weeks was recorded there in 1841 before mariners wife Mrs Mary A. Linney received an equally brief mention in 1851. One or two others are declared before painter William Long is tenant in 1859 then mariner William James and carman Charles Alder take us on to fish and fruit dealer George Savage who was trading there until the early 1870s. From then onwards came a comprehensive turnover of names that changed with each directory and census with none of them appearing more than once until boiler maker George Metcalf and his wife Harriet collected the keys in 1911 and held them until their home was demolished in 1935 when Russell Street was extended. This old part of the street was graced by the presence of cabinet maker Stephen Ward in 1834 when living at No. 36. Boot maker William Penton hammered away there from 1841 until railway porter John Webb moved in around 1874. His tenure lasted until dressmaker Sarah Kelley began stitching there in 1881. She was followed by labourer William Diaper in 1884, then dock foreman Henry Dungey in 1891. Dock labourer Benjamin Smith had settled there by 1907 before he made way for the Russell Street extension in 1935.

Another early resident was picture frame maker and carpenter Charles Pardy who carved away at No. 38 from 1834 until around 1851. Ships carpenter James Arcus made it his abode from 1857 until 1865 when barrow man Stephen Ponting parked up for a few years. By 1869 mariner Charles Bance was the tenant and, during his long stay, he came ashore and worked as a dock warehouseman. Upon his death in 1901 aged 73, his widow Jane became head of the house until 1907 saw plate layer Albert Wells as occupant through to the 1935 demolition. Thomas Bromfield was a serving man at No. 40 in 1836 but by 1841, carrier John Browning had moved in before making way for engineer John Paul in 1847. Pilot Edward Rowcliffe, previously at No. 54 through the 1840s, steered into No. 40 around 1849 and had moved on by 1853 when steward Thomas Redman settled there through the middle 1850s. Mariner John Eldridge then held the keys from 1859 until 1871 when fellow mariner Thomas Parker made a brief stopover until school mistress Maria Mielle ran her day school there from 1874 until 1887. Her departure saw another flurry of short stay renters that carried on into the 1900s and then welcomed dock labourer Horace Woodford and carpenter Bertram Selby among others before George Barnes, Mrs Wilson and finally Mrs C. Gibson were the final residents from the 1920s.

From 1935, the west side of Threefield Lane was demolished between Lime Street and Russell Street with the removal of Nos. 2 to 40 for the construction of the Corporation Tenements that were begun in 1936 and occupied by 1939. Although living standards of these new buildings were a great improvement upon what previously existed, they were life-expired by the mid-1970s and replaced by the present-day Challis Court.

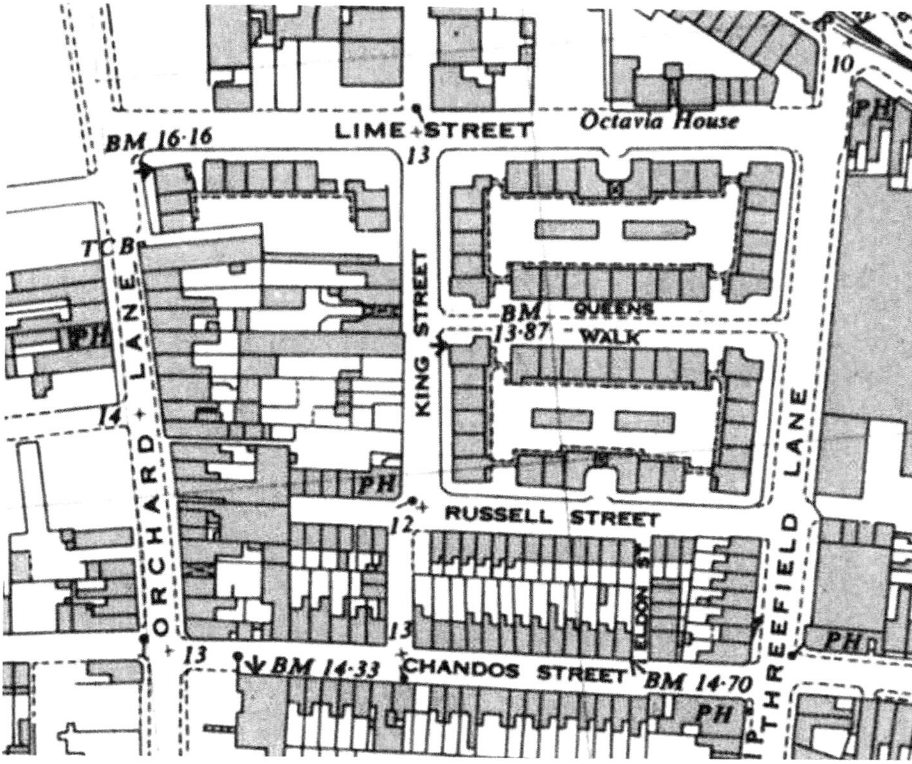

The new tenements bounded by Lime Street, Threefield Lane, Russell Street and King Street as they were in 1945

No. 42 was in the middle of a terrace until it found itself on the corner of Russell Street from 1935 after its neighbours were demolished. From 1841 until 1857 it was the home of Joseph Abraham Goldman who was a Jewish clergyman and synagogue reader. Laundress Sarah Stroud was its next inhabitant in 1857 who scrubbed the locals' shirts until 1876. Seaman Frederick Budden was to spend a decade there before fellow mariner John Hosmer and his wife Annie arrived in 1891 and had departed by 1912. Harry Harvey and his family were next under its roof from 1916 until 1940 with Mrs Davis and John Connis being its final inhabitants before demolition in 1954. Painter C.L. Darking was an early name at No. 44 in 1834 and by 1839 its occupant was jeweller Henry Bacharsat but no-one else was recorded there before boatman Henry Rowcliffe rowed in around 1851 and stayed afloat until 1867.

Commander George Wilcox, mariner William Knowlton and pilot George William Stubbs (see also No. 58) had passed through its doorway by 1876 when William Walters and his wife Sarah were tenants. William died in 1882 aged 56 and his widow became a charwoman there until her own demise in 1909. Mrs Love E. Noyce and her family were next in the rent book and remained so until 1935 saw Harry Jowett as the final occupant through to 1954. Thomas Higgins was a writing clerk living at No. 46 in 1839 and the next to appear there was cook Elizabeth Kelly in 1841. By 1851 Mrs Elizabeth Beale was running it as a lodging house while her husband James was at sea but by 1861 she was a widow supported by her three working children until they had gone their separate ways by 1869 when journeyman painter Henry Warren began a long tenancy that lasted until 1901. Stevedore Alexander White was the next named in the rent book before George Pinckney showed up in 1916 and was another long stayer, eventually giving way to William Potter in 1939. Aaron C. Wellington was the last of the line in 1954.

Dairyman William Bridle was the tenant of No. 48 in 1839 but he had moved to No. 58 by 1841 when widow Mary Lebourn had arrived but no others are shown there until 1851 saw plumber Martin Wilson living there before the Lovelocks family held the keys from 1857. Seaman William Lovelock and his wife Sarah had moved on by 1865 when boot maker James Tarrant set up shop there through to 1891 when labourer Henry Bellows turned up. Widow Mrs Jane Westerman was next at that address from 1901 and became a fixture there until 1939 when Walter Murrey was the inhabitant for the final years. Engineer Daniel Fensham was an early arrival at No. 50 in 1839 but no others are mentioned before smiths labourer Andrew Ford carried his irons there in 1851. After becoming a fully qualified smith by 1853 he had moved on by 1859 when mariner William Williams and his wife Charlotte dropped anchor for a decade before boatswain James Eve and his wife Emily took their place in 1869. The Eves remained until seaman Henry Long arrived in 1887. Henry had become a dock labourer by 1911 but died two years later at the age of 60. His widow Martha stayed on until her own passing in 1920. George Jones and William Du Maresq spent time there before Charles Lewis became key holder in 1935 and remained so until the end.

Jane Richmond graced No. 52 with her presence in 1841 but no more was heard of the address until smith William Crew, engineer Ralph Middleton, Mrs Jane Grant and William Rosen had all moved in and out before master tailor Charles Russell, and his tailoress wife Ann, bestowed their chattels there in 1859 but a decade later Charles had died at the age of 42 and Ann continued there until 1891. From then on No. 52 experienced a hefty turnover of souls with John Henry Gayton (1914 to 1920) and William Corringe (1920 to 1935) being the only ones to spend much time there. Cycle dealer Richard B. Parsons then extended his business from next door at No. 54 before handing over to George Rogers who pedalled on until 1954. For most of its existence, No. 54 on the corner of Chandos Street was a shop, with William Wickham being a wheelwright and grocer there in 1851 but by 1859 it was in the hands of Charles Billett, also a grocer but being a wire worker as a second occupation. Billett continued to run the shop until around 1881, during which time he remained a wire worker but doubled as grocer, fruiterer and greengrocer. The next proprietor was William Mansell, who in 1881 was an unemployed marine engine but decided to try his hand as a shopkeeper. His tenure ended around the turn of the century with George Henry Young running a general shop there in the early 1900s. The shop changed hands fairly regularly with John Thomas Sawyer and Mrs Pinckney in charge before cycle dealer Richard B. Parsons moved in around 1925 and eventually handed the business to George Rogers.

The cycle shop at No. 54 Threefield Lane on the corner of Chandos Street was run by George Rogers and Son in the postwar years. Nos. 52 and 50 are to the right and the Firemans Arms is seen on the left (Dave Marden collection)

The next section between Chandos Street and College Street had several identities over the years. In the earlier directories it was numbered 1 to 7 until regarded as an extension to Eldon Terrace as Nos. 12 to 17, before finally being listed as Threefield Lane Nos. 56 to 66. Over the years, the house numbers appear jumbled as the various transitions took place and I have had difficulty placing who was where at various times. Hopefully, I have solved the conundrum.

The *Anchor and Hope* pub stood on the corner of Threefield Lane and Chandos Street. Historically, it was always included in Chandos Street but that changed somewhat in the late 1930s when the pub was extended and took over No. 56 Threefield Lane. Brewer Henry Cave was fermenting his beer there in 1834, born locally in 1797, he and his wife Mary, ran the establishment until 1867 until his death around 1851 when Mary remained behind the bar until their son James, a coach painter by trade, became licensee and ran the pub with his wife Cecelia from the

1850s. James died in 1864 and Cecelia continued as landlady until Joseph Croome became innkeeper there around 1867. Apart from his bartending, Joseph was also a fly driver and, having combined the two until his death in 1897, looks to have become a wealthy man as he left £7,197 in his will. After such long tenancies, William Graham's reign from 1914 until 1935 seems rather brief, with Thomas Kearon from 1935 to 1946, even more so. Under his watch, in the late 1930s, the local redevelopment saw the pub expand and take over No. 56, an address it adopted from then onwards. After belonging to Eldridge Pope and Company from 1875 it was one of the few original buildings remaining in the area when it was demolished around 2006 to make way for a block of flats.

The Anchor and Hope pub and No. 56 Threefield Lane on the corner of Chandos Street as they appeared in 1925 (Dave Marden collection)

Threefield Lane in the 1960s with the Anchor and Hope pub on the left and the Corporation Tenements beyond (Dave Marden collection)

An early occupier of No. 56 was sawyer Henry Gifford in 1851 and his tenure lasted until 1869 when whitesmith/locksmith Alexander Parsons had the keys. Engineer George Timmis was there from 1871 until 1878 and then, into the 1880s, a new arrival was Mrs A. Symes who stayed until 1907, followed by engineer James Harbinson, Mrs Olive and then Mrs Lockwood with her son Frederick from 1916 who remained until the late 1930s when the house became an extension of the *Anchor and Hope* pub.

No. 58 was for many years the home of master mariner, and later pilot, George Henry Tubbs. Born in Millbrook in 1815 he was present in the house from 1847 until his death in 1880. His son George William Tubbs, also a pilot, had assumed head of the house by that time. The changing tenancies then became frequent with engineer William Cleol, George Moon and cab proprietor Henry Porter through the 1880s. General labourer Harry Pelham was resident from 1907 until 1931, which heralded the arrival of William Henry Cooper who stayed on until the end. No. 60 was the long-term abode of the Bridle family when

Yorkshire-born dairyman William Bridle settled in Southampton and married local girl Mary. Having previously lived at No. 48 in 1839 they moved to No. 60 around 1841. William died in 1866 when his son Thomas took over the business and, with his wife Ellen, remained there until his own death in 1873. The shared accommodation at No. 60 was also home to many others including mariner Richard Andrews and his family from 1851 until 1859 when Isle of Wight Company engineer George F. Blake arrived and dallied until ships cook James Wills became key holder in 1867 before sailing off in 1878. Mrs Mary A. Poulton was custodian in the late 1880s and early 1890s, while ironmongers warehouseman William Ernest Amey was in occupation through to 1931. Albert Joyce then saw out time there from the early 1930s until the street came down.

Nos. 62 and 63 appear to have been one large building with a central covered passageway giving access to a yard and the entire premises was home to a number of tenants and tradesmen. The *Rose and Thistle* pub took up much of the two buildings that dated back until at least 1845 when Nathaniel Skeets, (also Skates or Skeates) was landlord from then until at least 1867. William Smith, William Sevier and William Lewis were hosts through the late 1860s and mid-1870s before Alfred Aldridge held the licence in 1876. Others behind the bar included Richard Atkinson, William Graham and Charles Diaper. Under the ownership of brewers Mew Langton of Newport, the building was in such poor condition, it was closed in December 1920. The premises then saw a variety of traders with potato salesman David Thompson, ice cream makers T. Wall and Son, along with a trio of fishmongers plus a fried fish outlet run by the aptly named Mrs F. Fryer in 1939. Others present in the final years were printers A.R. Simmonds and Co, together with Globe Cars Motor Hire in 1954.

Blacksmith Thomas Roberts had set up his anvil at No. 64 in 1851 and by 1853 fellow smith William Crew had taken over but oddly, his final entry in the 1859 directory lists him as a carpenter. Boot maker Joseph

Barrow was next in line before joiner William Walters lived there in the late 1860s and from then on we find the usual regular turnover of tenants with general labourer William Amos Oakley living there from 1907 until 1939. We then witness the name of Harry Horner whose tenure lasted to 1946 when Harry Poland and his family arrived. Harry was a 'Turf and Football Agent' when the street came down in 1954. On the 1846 survey map, No. 66, on the corner of College Street is shown as *Vansittart Cottage* and appears to have been another multi-tenanted premises with the prime occupant being James Dible who, in 1841 was shown as a boatman, then a waterman, and by 1853 was a coal dealer before his death in 1869 aged 63. Earlier tenants at that address are listed as accountant Thomas William Spencer in the 1840s, then later we see ships fireman Duncan Connell in the 1850s and shipwright William Small through the 1860s. References to *Vansittart Cottage* disappeared after 1857 and by 1880 No. 66 had become a shop run by Richard Augustus O'Dell, at first a boot maker and then a grocer. By 1907 Mary Quick was behind its counter then, in 1912, along came Mrs Sarah P. Dyke who lasted until 1939 when Mrs Violet Blake ran it through the war years. Thomas Norris was the final name over the door in 1954 when the shop was a tobacconist and confectioners, then latterly a newsagents when it closed in 1957.

Thomas Norris's newsagents shop at No. 66 on the corner of Threefield Lane and College Street. The address was once known as Vansittart Cottage (courtesy of Ronald Norris)

The final house in this part of the street was No. 68 on the corner of College Street. It was an end of terrace but its front door was in Threefield Lane. Carpenter and joiner Lot Dollar was an early name there in 1851 until 1857. The next inhabitant shown is Robert Howell Symes who was an engineer with the USS Company while he was there from 1867 until 1878. No others are shown until Mrs Davies and John Emerson in the early 1900s. Then in 1914 John Henry Young is there under the banner of the National Union of Gasworkers, which seems to have been their headquarters under William Ambrose Flack and William James Cook who resided from 1920 until 1960. The house still stands along with what little remains of College Street (see photo in that chapter).

Blocks of utility flats replaced the crumbling houses between Threefield Lane and Russell Street in the 1930s. Most of these were further replaced by modern blocks in the 1970s (Dave Marden)

Dereliction off Threefield Lane as the old tenement flats were demolished in the 1970s (Dave Marden)

SAWMILL/HUMBY'S COURT

Sawmill Cut ran from Threefield Lane to Queen Street and took its name from the large sawmill that stood opposite its entrance. It was originally named Sawmill Court and reverted to that name in its latter years but back in the 1800s it was known as Humby's Court, after the Humby family who ran the *Sailors Return* pub there. The earliest record I can find is in the 1861 census, which lists the inhabitants in Sawmills Court, although it does appear on the 1846 map. The court contained a pub and six houses, with those at the Queen Street end being described as being exceedingly damp and unhealthy. All were without through ventilation with ground floors below pavement level. The upper portion of the houses was constructed of lath and plaster that was covered with wood.

Pinning down exactly where each house was has proved difficult but the sequences in the old directories and census returns suggest at one time there were seven premises beginning with Nos. 1 and 2 at the Threefield Lane end and Nos. 3 to 6 at Queen Street and No. 7 which was the *Sailors Return* pub and became No. 8 Threefield Lane. Eventually, Nos. 1 and 2 became No. 9 Threefield Lane, which became a bicycle shop in the latter years.

SAWMILL CUT
Nos. 1–7

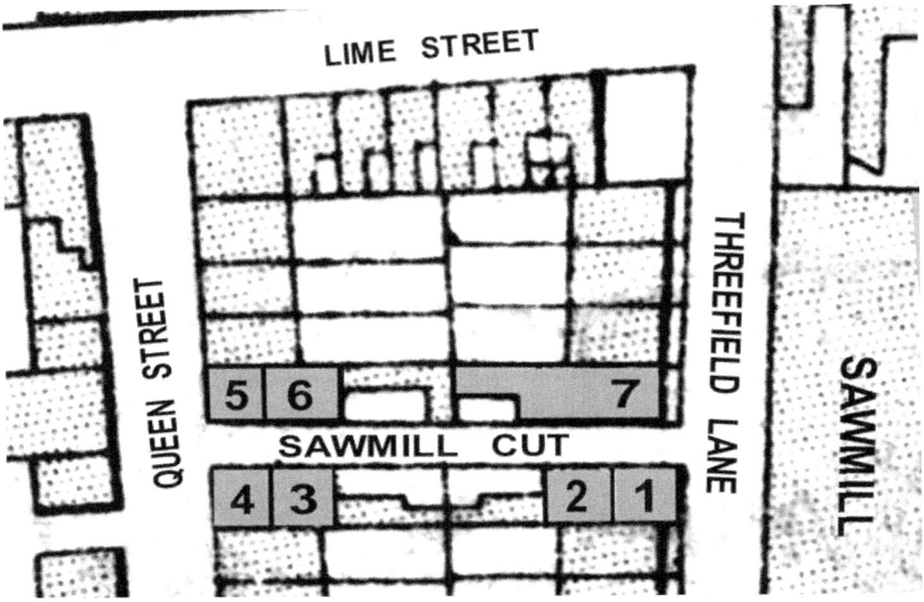

Sawmill Cut showing the seven buildings. No. 7 was once a pub named the Sailors Return and Nos. 1 and 2 became a cycle shop

In the 1861 census, fly man Charles Miller was at No. 1, then there is nothing more until sailor's wife Emily Rouse a decade later. Another ten-year leap finds general labourer Isaac Hapgood until the directories finally discover Sawmill Cut in 1884 when seaman Edward Roberts is noted, and then sweep Henry Edward Noyce in 1887. Now it's back to the census returns again with wine cooper Henry Nennim in 1891 and merchant seaman Charles Joyce in 1901. The directories then rediscover Sawmill Cut in 1907 when just two names appear at Nos. 5 and 6. By then, Nos. 3 and 4 had been condemned, while Nos. 1, 2 and 7 and been 'moved' to Threefield Lane as Nos. 8 and 9.

Back to the 1861 census which recorded labourer Abner Barber at No. 2. He was followed by mariner's wife Elizabeth Harvey in 1871 and seaman James Smith in 1881. 1884 saw cook Charles Collins there and he made way for Frederick Hallum (later at No. 3) in 1887 before two coal porters took up residence in the shape of John Campbell in 1891 and Daniel Kennedy in 1901. It seems nobody fancied living at No. 3 until 1881 when widow Mrs Mary Flarty (or Flaherty or Felorty) arrived and stayed on until 1891 when Frederick Hallam moved in from No. 2. Railway porter Joseph Kinsman was the last known inhabitant of that address in 1901.

Labourer George Payne was evident at No. 4 in 1861 but 20 years had passed before we find bricklayers labourer George Brown as the next occupant. He was still there in 1884 but by then was working as a chimney sweep. Daniel Donovan was next in the rent book in 1887. He succeeded labourer Alfred L Geer in 1891 and fish hawker William H. Cook in 1901. Widow Sarah Young was the tenant at No. 5 in 1861 before laundress Agnes Sherlock a decade later. Plain needlewoman Rebecca Chalk brought her sewing box there in 1881 before gardener James Woods held the keys in 1884. Next we have some continuity with ships fireman Robert Potter being present from 1887 until we come to labourer James Channell and his family arriving in 1907 and remaining through to 1935.

Ships fireman James Davis (1861) and shoe maker Charles Brown (1871) were the earlier names at No. 6 before the coming of labourer Henry Richards in 1881. Charles Bolt was in and out like lighting in 1887 before blacksmith Dave Longman was found in the 1901 census. The 1900s then hosted Mrs Colbourn, fitter Thomas Lewis, Jack Simmonds and Alfred Greenwood, all before 1920 when Mrs Brady almost saw out the remaining years before Mrs Powell was present in 1935. As indicated above, No. 7 was a pub named the *Sailors Return* and the earliest reference I have found is in both the 1851 directory and census where Thomas Humby is the proprietor, remaining so until his death in the mid-1860s when his wife Kerzia took over. It would appear she held the licence until around 1884 when the pub was renamed the *Sailors Welcome* and the address was changed to No. 8 Threefield Lane. (see Threefield Lane for further information).

Looking west along Sawmill Cut from Threefield Lane towards Queen Street. The cycle shop at No. 9 Threefield Lane was originally Nos. 1 and 2 Sawmill Cut

The western entrance to Sawmill Cut where No. 5 stood on the corner of Queen Street. Nos. 3 and 4 Queen Street can be seen on the left. Note the street sign once displayed the name as Sawmill Court, now with a couple of letters painted out

Printed in Dunstable, United Kingdom

84038003R00179